Preface

Approaches to the teaching of processor systems vary greatly as many topics are associated with the subject. Some selection of material is necessary to fit the limited time available for a single subject within most engineering courses. There are many valid, but differing, opinions regarding the selection of topics and the emphasis placed on each one chosen. This book is primarily concerned with hardware aspects of processor systems, as it is based on courses given to engineering students at the University of Liverpool. These students may also select a separate software engineering option. Some aspects of software are included here as software and hardware are strongly interdependent. Before studying this material some knowledge of logic circuit design is required. In addition a little experience of programming, at both high and low level, is probably necessary.

To describe hardware aspects of processor systems, several subjects have to be introduced. Difficulties may arise as the relevance of one topic is not always apparent until several others have been introduced. Further, processor systems, although simple in concept, are large and complex in scale. To attempt to reduce these difficulties this text is in several sections; the first is a brief overview and outline of simple processor systems. The sections which follow consider each major element in detail. The final short section examines one or two applications and considers some features and alternatives not examined in other sections.

A good understanding of processor systems requires practical experience; in particular, engineering students require practice in system design and application. Consequently, a significant part of any course must be spent learning details of one specific processor, however a student may never use the type chosen after qualifying. For reasons of cost and simplicity this processor will usually be an 8-bit microprocessor, even although these often have irregular features. The need to concentrate on a single processor type is unfortunate, an engineer's education should be general to allow application of techniques without restriction to particular examples. This applies particularly to the use of microelectronic devices; because developments of new devices are frequent, knowledge based on one or two current devices rapidly becomes out of date. Examples in this text concentrate on 8-bit microprocessors, for simplicity and to match the type of laboratory exercises most students will undertake. However, general methods and concepts are presented whenever possible. Techniques adopted in larger processor systems are described, provided that they are not too complex.

Just as there is no ideal processor system for all applications, there is no ideal approach to teaching the design and application of processor systems. I have attempted to compromise between a general treatment and one studying a few specific processors in depth. Emphasis is strongly towards hardware as software is now a sufficiently important subject to require separate treatment. The text is intended primarily for engineering students, it should also assist students of computer science and related disciplines requiring knowledge of hardware and its limitations.

Acknowledgements

Many items are reproduced with permission of the copyright owners. Often modifications have been made; any errors are entirely the fault of the present author. In particular permission to reproduce the following is gratefully acknowledged.

Heap and Partners Ltd: Figs 15.2 and 15.3.
Intel Corporation (UK) Ltd: Figs 2.7; 4.7; 5.2; 5.5; 5.9; 15.10; 15.11; 16.1; and the instruction sets for the 8080 and 8086 processor families.
Motorola Semiconductors Ltd: Figs 2.9; 11.9; and the instruction set for 6800 processors.
Rockwell International Ltd: Figs 2.8; 11.12; and the instruction set for the 6502 processor.
Rodime PLC: Figs 9.2 and 9.3.
Texas Instruments Ltd: Fig. 7.5.

So many people have helped in the preparation of this book that it is impossible to name them all. My thanks to all my colleagues who have answered many questions, provided information and in other ways helped in the preparation. Also thanks to past and present students whose comments have influenced the content and presentation of the text. Many individuals in several companies have answered queries, supplied information and arranged for the use of copyright material; their assistance is greatly appreciated. Finally, thanks to the staff of Edward Arnold Ltd, for encouragement and tolerance.

J.R. Gibson
October 1985

Electronic Processor Systems

J.R. Gibson
Department of Electrical Engineering and Electronics
University of Liverpool

Edward Arnold

© J.R. Gibson 1987

First published 1987 by
Edward Arnold (Publishers) Ltd
41 Bedford Square, London WC1B 3DQ

Edward Arnold
3 East Read Street, Baltimore, MD 21202, USA

Edward Arnold (Australia) Ltd
80 Waverley Road, Caulfield East,
Victoria 3145, Australia

British Library Cataloguing in Publication Data

Gibson, J.R. (John Raymond), *1943–*
   Electronic processor systems.
   1. Microprocessors
   I. Title
   004.16   QA76.5

   ISBN 0-7131-3571-9

Text set in 10/11 pt Times Compugraphic
by Colset Private Limited, Singapore
Printed in Great Britain
by J.W. Arrowsmith, Bristol.

Contents

Part 1
Introduction to Processor Elements and Systems

1 Evolution of processor systems

Digital computers and related machines are now widely used. At some time most electronic engineers will design, construct, or make connections to systems which incorporate either computers or devices which have a structure similar to that of a computer. Computers and related devices form a group of machines best classified as stored program controlled digital (or binary) processor systems; these are more conveniently called **processor systems** or just **processors**. Processors range from small *single-chip* devices having the complete system on an integrated circuit less than 10 mm square to large multiple computer systems housed in specially designed buildings.

Although all processor systems are basically similar they vary greatly in capability, speed of operation and physical size. Systems tend to be classed according to size; such class boundaries are arbitrary and indistinct. The term **mainframe** is usually applied to large computers requiring a controlled environment; these can perform complex calculations and manipulate large amounts of data. At the other end of the size range is the microprocessor; strictly this is the name of a single integrated circuit incorporating the control and calculator sections of a computer. A microprocessor and a small number of additional integrated circuits may be assembled to form a microcomputer; home computers and small business machines are typical examples. Very small systems with all sections on a single integrated circuit are often called **microcontrollers**. Processor systems with sizes between micro-computers and mainframes are **minicomputers**; these are available in a wide range of speed and size at relatively low cost. Most are capable of operating with few restrictions on their environment and provide computing facilities wherever required. For example they are incorporated in sophisticated products such as machine tools and aircraft flight simulators.

Despite the great range of size and capability, all processor systems have common features and their designs are based on a small number of fundamental ideas. The main purpose of this text is to describe the general features of common processor systems and to introduce their design and use. In many applications the processor may be regarded as a component of some larger system. This larger system is often controlled automatically with the processor undertaking many of the control functions.

1.1 Simple sequential control systems

The concept of automatic systems which perform one action after another in strict sequence is very old; it dates back to medieval times or earlier. Among common early examples are striking clocks; the minute hand makes one revolution every hour and each time a revolu-tion is completed a hammer automatically strikes a bell. The system has a fixed sequence of operations as the bell is struck once after the first revolution, twice after the second, and so on. After striking twelve times the complete sequence restarts with the next revolution being the same as the first.

As improved materials and engineering techniques were developed, more elaborate sequences of operations became possible. Most of the important developments in auto-mation originated in machines used for manufacturing processes such as weaving cloth and cutting metal. Today automatic machines perform complex sequences of operations; many are controlled by electronic units and often incorporate processor systems.

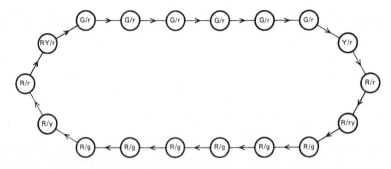

Fig. 1.1   State diagram: simple traffic signal control

A relatively simple approach to automatic control of a process with N steps is to design a sequential logic circuit with N states. Each different state corresponds to a particular step, and combinational logic circuits are connected to the sequential circuit outputs. These combinational circuits detect a particular state (or states) corresponding to a specific action and their outputs initiate the action. The most simple systems are similar to the striking clock, they repeatedly loop through a fixed sequence at constant speed. This is best illustrated by example; a greatly simplified road traffic signal control is chosen because the sequence of events is familiar and easily observed. (The UK sequence is adopted.)

Example

An outline design of a simple controller for traffic signals at the crossing point of two roads.

The controller is less complex than those used in modern signals. The chosen system allows traffic on each road to move in turn for a preset fixed time; there are no traffic actuated control features and no pedestrian crossing signals.

Table 1.1   State table for traffic signal control

State	Road A Lights ON	Road B Lights ON	Comment
S_1	Red	Red	All traffic halted
S_2	Red + yellow	Red	Changing to road A on
S_3	Green	Red	
S_4	Green	Red	
S_5	Green	Red	Traffic moving, road A
S_6	Green	Red	
S_7	Green	Red	
S_8	Green	Red	
S_9	Yellow	Red	Stopping traffic on A
S_{10}	Red	Red	All traffic halted
S_{11}	Red	Red + yellow	Changing to road B on
S_{12}	Red	Green	
S_{13}	Red	Green	
S_{14}	Red	Green	Traffic moving, road B
S_{15}	Red	Green	
S_{16}	Red	Green	
S_{17}	Red	Green	
S_{18}	Red	Yellow	Stopping traffic on B
$S_{19} = S_1$	Red	Red	All traffic halted

It is assumed that signals for both roads show red for two seconds before changing to
signal that traffic may move on one of the roads. Intermediate conditions (e.g. yellow lamp
on) also exist for two seconds, and the signals are green for twelve seconds. Figure 1.1 is the
state diagram for the sequential circuit with eighteen states, each state existing for two
seconds. Six states have been used each time a green light is turned on so that it remains on
for twelve seconds. The states are labelled S_1 to S_{18}; the signal lamps which are on when the
circuit is in a particular state are indicated by 'R' or 'r' for red, 'Y' or 'y' for yellow, and
'G' or 'g' for green. Upper case letters indicate the lamps for road A and lower case letters
those for road B. Table 1.1 is a state table for the circuit.

The control circuit consists of three main sections and is shown in block diagram form by
Fig. 1.2. A clock oscillator produces pulses at two second intervals; these are applied to the
clock input of a single direction divide-by-eighteen counter which moves through the
required states, remaining in each state for two seconds. The outputs of the counter indicate
its state and are themselves inputs to a combinational network which generates the control
signals to turn the signal lamps on or off. The design of the sequential and combinational
logic circuits requires simple techniques which should be familiar to anyone intending to
study the design of processor systems.

This control system is obviously more simple than any required in a real situation; for
example the times at green are shorter than those in common use. Longer times at green
could be obtained by designs having more states or by alternative techniques; features such
as traffic actuated control and the co-ordination of signals at several junctions could also be
added. While these circuit modifications are useful design exercises, the resulting circuits
are complex. A more significant disadvantage of this approach to traffic signal control (and
other controllers) is that every installation requires a unique design. Consequently each
controller is expensive to manufacture, or modify, or repair. Some form of standard
control unit is required into which a relatively small component is fitted. This component
converts the standard unit from a general purpose unit into one for a particular application.

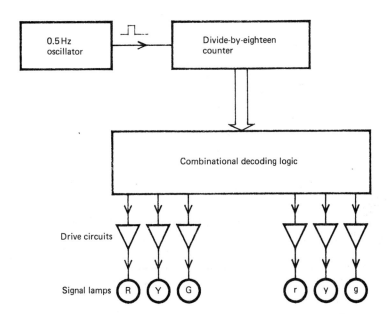

Fig. 1.2 Traffic signal control: circuit outline

One method of achieving this is by use of a stored program controlled sequential machine, more briefly a **programmed machine**.

1.2 Programmed machines

Examination of the columns *Road A Lights ON* and *Road B Lights ON* in Table 1.1 shows that these may be used as an exact sequence of instructions describing the required behaviour of the controller. This set of instructions is a **program**; that is it is a list of events which must occur in a specified order in time. A useful machine would be one which could *read* the program and perform the actions required. To construct such a machine the instructions must be converted into some form **(encoded)** which can be *understood* and **obeyed** by the machine. Additionally the encoded instructions must be held **(stored)** in some mechanism from which they may be retrieved when required; such a storage mechanism is a **memory**.

   If the requirements of encoding instructions and provision of a memory can be met, then a simple circuit which follows the sequence shown in Fig. 1.3 will perform any task for which a program can be devised. This is another very old concept; well known early examples are musical boxes in which the program is encoded by fitting pegs into a rotating drum. As the drum rotates the pegs strike tuning forks or gongs, this produces notes in a fixed sequence; the sequence of notes is a tune. Changing the drum for one with a different pattern of pegs changes the program, that is a different tune is played.

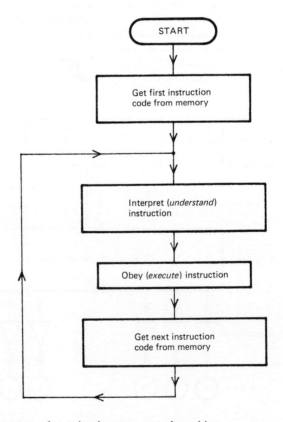

Fig. 1.3 Operation sequence for a simple programmed machine

A machine which is controlled by a program held in a memory is a stored program controlled machine and many simple programmed machines have been developed. Most early mechanical machines were limited by their speed of operation and by the range of instruction codes they could obey. The range of instructions is particularly important; for example to loop repeatedly through the traffic light control program, the instructions allowed must include one which results in the action *return to the first instruction.* (Simple programmed machines such as a musical box operate in a loop with the end of the memory joined to the start.) Programmed machines are usually designed with the instructions held in order in successive positions in the memory. Each memory position, called a memory **location**, is identified by a number called its **address**, and the usual *JUMP* or *GOTO* instruction is of the form *GOTO the instruction at address N* where the number of a valid address is substituted for *N*.

1.3 Calculators

Advances in science and engineering have often been assisted by increasing the speed of performing calculations. During the early 1940s, calculating machines incorporating some electronic circuits were developed for special research applications. Although slow by present standards these were much faster than the available mechanical calculators. A major limit to the speed of early calculating machines was the time required to enter numbers from the keyboard or other input mechanism. This was particularly true when the results from one stage of a calculation had to be re-entered to perform the next stage. The solution to this problem is obvious in retrospect, it is to fit the calculator with some form of automatic control. To allow a range of different calculations to be performed, stored program control was adopted.

A simple stored program calculator is not a processor system. Two additional features are required to produce a system with the capabilities of a processor. In any calculation intermediate results and working values must be stored; clearly some form of memory mechanism is required. If a single memory unit whose contents are easily changed by the machine itself is used for both programs and numeric values, then a very flexible machine is formed. This also offers the possibility that a running program can alter itself! This is a very important attribute of processor systems, however the reader is advised not to attempt to write programs which modify themselves by putting new instruction codes into their own instruction sequence. The usual way a processor modifies its own program while running is by making choices between different sections of an already complete program. The simple *GOTO* instruction is modified to one of the form *IF some specified condition exists GOTO address N*. The condition is usually very simple and consists of testing a logic signal for values of 0 or 1 leading to TRUE or FALSE conditions. It is understood that if the condition does not exist the *JUMP* is ignored and the next instruction in the normal sequence following the *CONDITIONAL JUMP* is obeyed. Implementation of **conditional branch** (jump) instructions is an essential feature of processor systems. They form the mechanism which gives processor systems the apparent ability to make decisions, and are the second feature which distinguishes processors from programmed calculators.

The fundamental ideas behind modern digital processor systems have been introduced; the concepts are similar to those described by von Neumann (1946). While the technology used and some design features have changed, allowing much larger and faster machines to be constructed, the basic concepts are little different. It should be noted that many other forms of processor system have been designed and built; many have features making them particularly useful for certain applications. However, nearly all systems in large scale production loosely fit the von Neumann machine structure (architecture).

1.4   Numbers

When a machine can perform arithmetic operations a method must be devised to represent numbers within the machine. Further the instructions of any programmed machine must be encoded for storage in the memory and a practical form of encoding is to represent each possible instruction by a different number, an **instruction code** or **operation code**.

Because electronic two state circuits (logic circuits) are cheap, fast, and easy to manufacture on a very large scale nearly all processor systems are constructed using them. The two states are used to represent the digits 0 and 1 and systems operate using binary numbers for both arithmetic operations and codes to represent instructions. Processors have been designed using other components and other bases, but all common systems are based on logic circuits and binary numbers so only these will be considered. A variation is to use groups of binary digits as codes representing digits in another base; base ten is a common choice. Many processors have features allowing operations with binary coded decimal (BCD) numbers to be performed. Bases of eight and sixteen giving octal and hexadecimal numbers are also used, because conversions to and from binary are trivial.

Most processor systems use binary numbers with a fixed number of digits. A binary digit is known as a **bit**, and the fixed size group of digits is called a **word**. Although the terms 'bit' and 'word' strictly refer to a binary digit and to a group of digits, these terms are used in other ways. It is inconvenient to refer to 'a memory location for a word', so the term 'word' is often used to refer to the group of devices which form a memory location as well as to the value stored in it. Similarly 'bit' may refer to the storage device for one bit as well as to the binary digit it holds. The terms bit and word may be used in other inexact ways, in such cases the meaning is usually obvious from the context. Groups of eight bits are so common that such a group is known as a **byte**; a group of four bits is called a **nibble** or **nybble**.

1.5   Elements of a processor system

It is convenient to consider processor systems in four parts, because the function of each is well defined. The parts may be considered separately provided that an overall concept of a complete processor system is retained. A processor system is shown schematically in Fig. 1.4; this does not show the actual structure or connections. The section often regarded as the processor is the **central processing unit (CPU)**. This contains the timing, instruction decoding, other control circuits and the **arithmetic and logic unit (ALU)**; the ALU is essentially the calculator section.

Any processor system requires a **memory** to hold programs, data and other values. Processor system memories range from a single integrated circuit to large complex systems, often, the memory is the most expensive physical component of the system.

The third necessary element of a processor system is some method of entering information and a method of obtaining the results (output). An input and output system **(I–O system)** is required and its form depends closely on the application. Many electronic engineers will never design CPUs or complex memory systems, but most will have to design and connect some input and output devices to processor systems.

The fourth part of any processor system performing a useful task is the **program**. Engineers often find it difficult to regard an essentially abstract entity, a program, as a major system component. The program is the element proposed in Section 1.1 which converts a general purpose machine, in this case a processor system, into a unit for a particular application.

While study of the various units of processor systems in detail requires their separate examination, they are interdependent, and an understanding of all of them and their interaction is essential when designing processor based systems. To meet the need for simultaneous descriptions of several complex components and their interrelation, a general

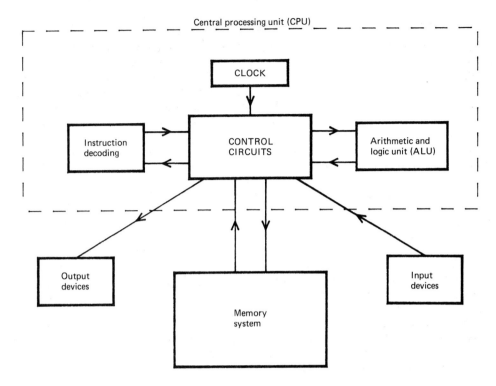

Fig. 1.4 Schematic outline of a processor system

introduction to processor systems follows in this part of the book. Brief descriptions of the elements of systems are also given. Separate parts then describe each major element and a final part describes some applications and alternative systems.

Whenever possible, a general approach is followed with examples which are as simple as possible; hence most illustrations involve microprocessors. These devices also allow students to attempt design and laboratory exercises using processor systems; this would be too difficult or too expensive with larger processors.

2 System components

A binary processor system is just a logic circuit; the main difficulties in understanding the circuit design and behaviour are problems of scale. Even a small microprocessor system will contain over 10^5 logic elements while a large mainframe computer may have over 10^{11} elements. However, the problems of understanding large scale systems are reduced because processor systems contain many identical components arranged in a very uniform and well organized manner.

2.1 Processor components

While there are a number of complex combinational and sequential logic circuits, mainly in the ALU and control unit, much of a processor system consists of registers, decoders and multiplexers. To some extent a processor may be regarded as an arrangement of a large number of registers with multiplexing, decoding and control circuits to copy the contents of one register to another.

2.1.1 Registers

A single bistable circuit may be used to store one bit. When several bistables are grouped together, with their clock inputs connected to a common clock source, they can store a word. The group of bistables is known as a **register** and several forms of register may be constructed. A parallel input register is one where all elements (stages, bistables, flip-flops) may be loaded simultaneously from multiple, parallel, data input connections with one input per stage. Shift registers usually have a single data input connection and each clock pulse causes the register contents to move along (shift) one stage with one new bit input for each clock pulse. Some parallel input registers have a shift feature, an extra control input is available so that the register may be selected to operate with either parallel or serial input. When all outputs from a register are available simultaneously it is a parallel output one; if the end bit is the only available output it is a serial output register.

Simple register designs include parallel in–parallel out (PIPO), serial in–serial out (SISO), and serial in–parallel out (SIPO) forms. By the addition of control inputs a wide range of features, such as selectable shift or parallel load, and shift in either direction, may be added to a register. Many different types of register are found within processor systems; PIPO types are the most common because a memory to hold many binary numbers contains a large number of equal size PIPO registers.

2.1.2 Decoders

Within processor systems a binary number is often used as a code to define which particular member of a group of similar items is to be used. That is, each item in the group is given a unique number, an **address**, by which it is identified. When an item is used, its address is generated as an m-bit binary number; consequently 2^m different items may be specified. A circuit used to select one particular item by having m inputs representing the binary number, and 2^m outputs, each of which selects a different item, is an m-line to 2^m-line decoder. Most

Table 2.1 Truth table for a 2-line to 4-line decoder

Inputs			Decode Outputs			
Enable E	Address B	A	S_3	S_2	S_1	S_0
0	0	0	1	1	1	0
0	0	1	1	1	0	1
0	1	0	1	0	1	1
0	1	1	0	1	1	1
1	0	0	1	1	1	1
1	0	1	1	1	1	1
1	1	0	1	1	1	1
1	1	1	1	1	1	1

decoders have enabling inputs to allow several to be used in more complex decode circuits. Table 2.1 is the truth table of a simple 2-line to 4-line decoder with a single active low enable input and active low outputs. **Active low** defines the condition that logic 0 is the input or output value corresponding to an operation taking place, i.e. an action, and in such cases logic 1 implies no action. The opposite case is **active high** with logic 1 corresponding to action and logic 0 to no action. Figure 2.1 shows five of the simple decoders connected to produce a 4-line to 16-line decoder.

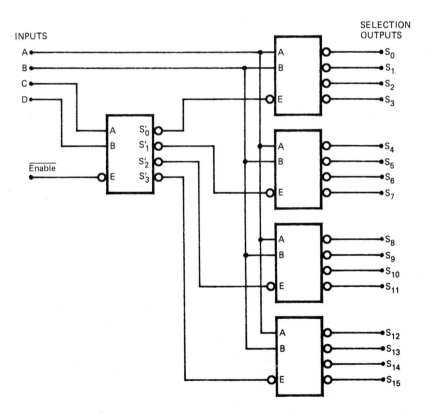

Fig. 2.1 4-line to 6-line decode by cascaded 2-line to 4-line decoders

Decoders are sometimes called **de-multiplexers** as they can be used in circuits which reverse the action of a multiplexer. That is they may be used to direct a signal from a common data path to a particular destination.

2.1.3   Multiplexers

Multiplexing is used in many signal transmission systems, not only for transmission of logic signals. It is a method by which signals from several sources are transmitted along a single transmission link, each going to its own, different, destination. In logic circuits the most simple form of multiplexing consists of switching one signal source to the transmission system. A reversal of the multiplexing process occurs at the destination end of the transmission system and the signal is correctly routed to its destination. Definitions of multiplexing vary, partly because different techniques are used for different types of signal. The simple form reserves the transmission system for a single source and destination while all the data in one message is transmitted.

Within logic circuits the term **multiplexer** is usually used for the circuit which selects and connects one source from several to the transmission system. The circuit which connects the signal to the required destination is known as a de-multiplexer. In cases of single direction connections the multiplexer is also known as a **data selector**. A data selector is a simple combinational logic circuit; a condensed form of truth table for a 1-from-4 selector controlled by a 2-bit code at its inputs is given in Table 2.2.

Table 2.2   Truth table for a 1-from-4 data selector

Data inputs				Selection inputs		
D_3	D_2	D_1	D_0	B	A	Output
X	X	X	0	0	0	0
X	X	X	1	0	0	1
X	X	0	X	0	1	0
X	X	1	X	0	1	1
X	0	X	X	1	0	0
X	1	X	X	1	0	1
0	X	X	X	1	1	0
1	X	X	X	1	1	1

(X = either 1 or 0; both input values give same output)

When signals may travel in either direction along some connection in a multiplexed system, the routing circuits have to pass signals in both directions; the bi-directional switching unit is another type of multiplexer. Essentially it consists of a data selector and a de-multiplexer combined with tri-state devices to control the direction of signals.

2.2   Memories

To a system designer a memory unit for a simple processor system is a large number, usually exactly 2^m with m integral, of equal word length PIPO registers in a well organized arrangement. The word length is often known as the **width** of the memory and the number of words is its **length**. The position of each register is identified by its own unique number, the **address**, which specifies that particular memory location (register). Addresses are contiguous, starting at zero for the first location and continuing through 1, 2, 3, . . ., up to $2^m - 1$ for a memory with 2^m words. The various decoders and data selection circuits are incorporated within the memory, and the complete memory unit appears to be constructed as shown in Fig. 2.2.

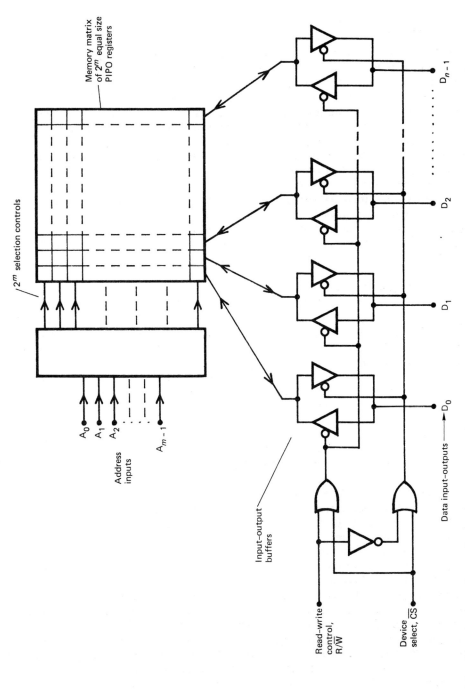

Fig. 2.2 Organisation of a random access memory unit

Values of *m* are usually so large that the symbol 'k' is used for a unit of $2^{10} = 1024 = 1k$ (i.e. in digital electronic systems k $= 1024$ rather than the more conventional k $=$ kilo $= 1000$). Increasingly, the larger memory systems being developed have led to the use of 'M' for $2^{20} = 1048576 = 1M$.

The action of storing a number in a memory location is a **write** operation, while retrieval of a number from a location is a **read** operation. Either operation using a memory location is termed an **access** to the memory and the minimum time necessary to perform the operation is the **access time**. Usually, but not always, the access time is the same for read and write. A memory of the form shown in Fig 2.2 is a **random access memory**; at any time any address may be used for a read or a write access. Locations do not have to be accessed in any particular order, therefore, the address used for one operation does not have any relation to that used for the operation immediately preceding or following. The locations may be accessed in a completely random order. An important consequence is that the access time is independent of the address of the location; other memories exist with access times that depend on the address of the word in the memory.

A memory for which read and write accesses are both possible with random access is called a **random access memory**, usually known as a **RAM**. This name is badly chosen but is so well established that it must be used. Alternative random access memories exist which have permanently fixed contents so only read operations are of any practical use. Such a random access read only memory is known simply as a **read only memory**, a **ROM**.

2.3   Interconnection

As indicated in Chapter 1, an elementary processor system consists of a CPU, memory, and I–O devices. The total assembly outlined in Fig. 1.4 was a haphazardly connected set of units, and does not show the actual organization of a processor system. To organize a system with large numbers of components, a well ordered connecting structure is desirable and most processor systems are assembled using a bus structure.

A **bus** is a group of connecting lines, all of which serve a similar purpose, and generally all lines of a bus are connected in parallel to all units of the system. The number of individual lines in a bus is the bus size or width. For processor and other logic systems the bus width is usually specified as a number of bits, as this is the maximum number of binary digits which may be simultaneously transmitted on the bus. Two broad classes of bus exist; single or uni-directional buses in which signals may only travel in one direction, and bi-directional buses on which signals may travel in either direction. Many processor systems use a three bus structure; these are the data bus, address bus and control bus and they implement the functions *WHAT, WHERE, WHEN* and *WHICH*.

The **data bus** is bi-directional and carries the actual binary values, data, to be used (*WHAT*) to or from the CPU. A memory location or an I–O device is used as the source or destination of the data value.

The **address bus** is uni-directional outward from the CPU. It carries binary numbers which define the address of the memory location or the I–O device to be used as the source or destination (*WHERE*) of data being transferred on the data bus.

The **control bus** is a little less consistent than the other two as some lines are outward from the CPU, some are inward, and others are bi-directional. However, in a simple processor system the essential lines in the control bus are a small number of connections outward from the CPU that provide information regarding the operation in progress (*WHICH* action) and the time (*WHEN*) this action occurs. This enables other sections of the complete system to be synchronized to operate at times defined by the control unit in the CPU, itself driven by the clock.

Diagrams of circuits which include bus systems rarely show the individual lines of a bus, because the result would be difficult to interpret. Instead, bus lines are combined into a

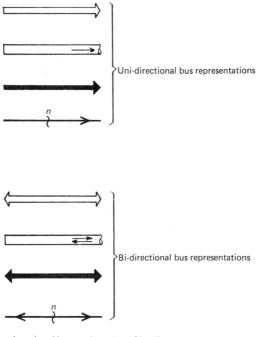

n is replaced by actual number of bus lines

Fig. 2.3   Common representations of bus lines

single symbolic form to represent connections between all corresponding points of all units connected to the bus. That is bus line number 0 is joined to connection point 0 on every unit connected to the bus, line number 1 connects to every connection 1, and so on. A wide range of representations are used for buses on circuit diagrams, and several are illustrated in Fig. 2.3. The outline of a broad arrow will normally be used here to represent a bus, but other methods are adopted when appropriate or to conform to a particular manufacturer's practice. Bus representations other than those illustrated in Fig. 2.3 are also used; most alternative methods are systematic and easily interpreted.

2.4   A simple processor system

Figure 2.4 outlines a simple processor system using four separate control lines; $\overline{\text{READ}}$, $\overline{\text{WRITE}}$, $\overline{\text{INPUT}}$ and $\overline{\text{OUTPUT}}$. The overlines indicate that these are active low controls; that is they are all normally high and only one may be low at any time. When a control line is low this is a signal that the particular operation associated with it must take place while the line is low. The four operations using this control bus are shown in Fig. 2.5. These are logic circuit timing diagrams; hatched areas indicate that the condition of the particular bus is undefined or unimportant at that point (it may be 0, 1, or tri-state) while a heavy central line indicates that each line of the particular bus must adopt the required logic state. Only one control line is shown for each operation; the other three must remain at 1 throughout the period shown in the diagrams.

   Using the write operation as an example; it is assumed that before starting the operation the previous operation is complete and all bus lines are undefined, except that the control lines must all be high. To perform the write operation the binary number equal to the address of the memory location is output on the address bus by the CPU. Next (or simul-

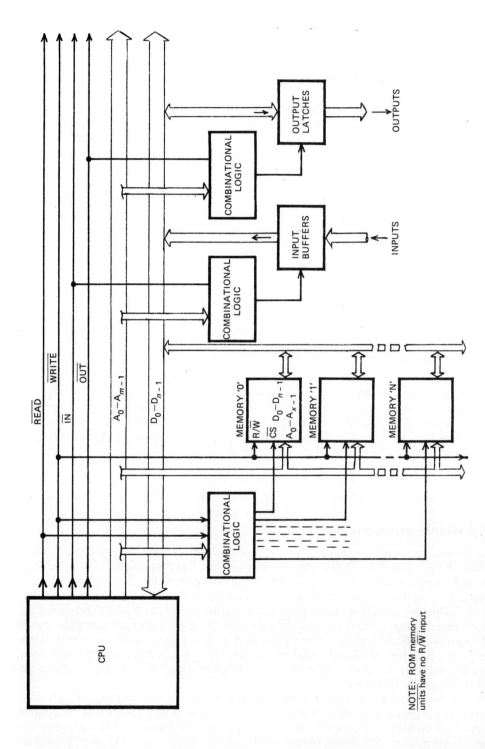

Fig. 2.4 Simple processor system structure

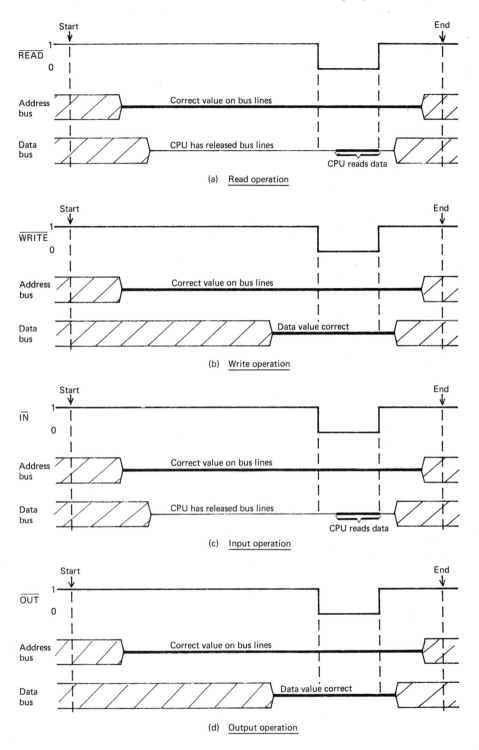

Fig. 2.5 Processor timing for data transfer operations

taneously) the data to be stored is output on the data bus. After the address and data buses have reached their correct levels, the control line $\overline{\text{WRITE}}$ goes low for sufficient time to allow the memory to copy the value from the data bus into the correct location. It is entirely a function of the memory unit to perform this copy operation at the time indicated by the CPU. After an adequate time at 0 the $\overline{\text{WRITE}}$ line is returned to logic 1, and only when it has been at 1 for sufficient time for the memory to end its copy action are the data and address buses returned to indeterminate conditions.

The other three operations are very similar; the main difference is that for the two input operations, read and input, the CPU sets the data bus lines inward instead of outward. The memory or input device selected must copy the data required by the CPU onto the data bus lines and the CPU takes this value at the time just as the $\overline{\text{READ}}$ or $\overline{\text{INPUT}}$ line returns to 1.

Using these four operations a processor system can perform a wide range of tasks if it is supplied with the necessary programs.

2.5   Basic operation

To follow the sequence set by some program, the control section of the processor must obtain instruction code numbers from the memory in the correct order, interpreting and then obeying each in turn. The usual method is to have a special counter (a register whose contents may be easily increased by one) in the CPU; this holds the address of the memory location which contains the code number for the next instruction. The name of this counter varies from one manufacturer to another: a frequently used name is **program counter (PC)**; another common name is **instruction address register (IAR)**. Using the contents of the program counter as an address, the control unit obtains an instruction code from memory. This is the **instruction fetch** which is a memory read operation. The code is usually copied to a register in the control unit called the **instruction register (IR)**; again this may have other names, for example **decode register (DR)**. The contents of the program counter are increased by one (incremented), and then the control unit determines the action represented by the contents of the instruction register, **instruction decode**. Finally the control unit performs, **executes**, the required operations to obey the instruction. Once the instruction has been executed, the control unit repeats the cycle of obtaining, decoding and obeying instructions as outlined in Fig. 2.6.

The complete system operation follows a very simple sequential loop which may be controlled by a small logic circuit. This sequential control circuit is driven at constant speed by pulses from the clock unit, normally a crystal controlled oscillator running at constant (within ± 0.001%) frequency. This simple description ignores the initial start up of the system. When power is turned on (or when a manual reset is performed) the program counter is forced to some specified value; usually all other registers will contain random values.

2.6   Some CPUs

There are several thousand different CPU designs in use; suitable ones for initial examination are the 8-bit microprocessors that appeared in the early 1970s and led to the incorporation of processors in a wide range of products. These are known as 8-bit processors because the data bus width, the size of number handled by the ALU, most internal registers, and the required memory word length are all 8-bits.

Although many different 8-bit microprocessors are available the market is dominated by three families. One group is based on the Intel 8080 architecture; mainly the 8080A, 8085, and Z80; a second group is the Rockwell 6502 family, while the third is the Motorola 6800

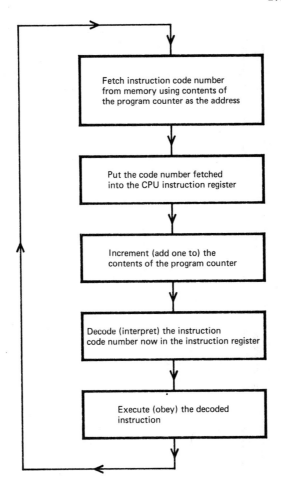

Fig. 2.6 Steps of a processor instruction cycle

family. These are totally different systems although all are of similar capability and were designed at about the same time, so there are common general features.

2.6.1 The 8080A

Although the 8085 is now selected for new applications (programs for the 8080A will run on the 8085 and Z80 although the reverse is not always true) the 8080A is the least complex of the group. A simplified outline of the CPU structure is shown in Fig. 2.7; systems are built using three integrated circuits to form a complete CPU. (When the 8080 was designed, all the circuits could not be built on one integrated circuit; this is one reason for development of the 8085, which has all functions on one device.)

The basic 8080 system has an 8-bit data bus, a 16-bit address bus, and four control lines (others are present but may be ignored initially). The controls are $\overline{RD}$, $\overline{WR}$, $\overline{IN}$, and $\overline{OUT}$; these are very similar to the four controls used in the simple processor described earlier.

The CPU has six simple 8-bit registers, B, C, D, E, H, and L; an accumulator, A, which is essentially an 8-bit register used mainly in conjunction with the ALU; two 16-bit registers, PC and SP; and five single bit registers or flags. The 16-bit address bus allows up to

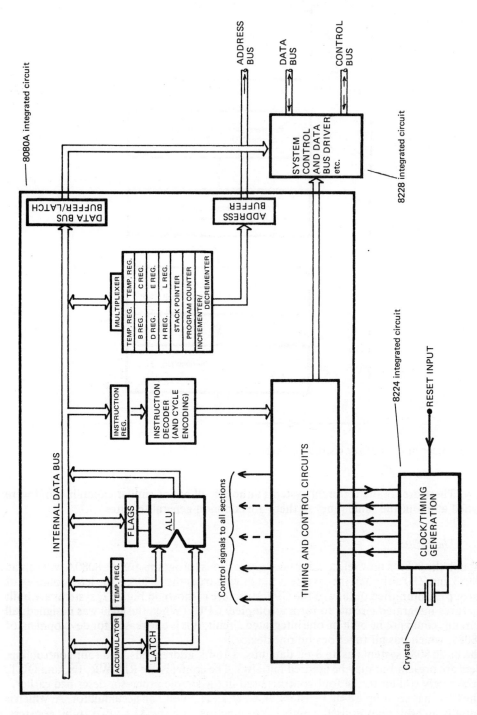

Fig. 2.7   Intel 8080A CPU system

$2^{16} = 65536 = 64k$ memory locations to be used with the CPU. Note that in many applications memory units are not fitted at all locations and the user must take care not to access a missing location.

2.6.2 The 6502

While initial applications of the 8080 and 6800 were in industrial control or to improve existing products, most early applications of the 6502 were in one type of product, the microcomputer. It is unusual that this product was totally new; although many other CPUs are now used in microcomputers the 6502 is still used in a large proportion. The early popular microcomputers appeared under the brand names 'PET' and 'APPLE'; both have the 6502 as their CPU and more recently the popular 'BBC computer' has been produced using the 6502.

The single integrated circuit CPU is illustrated in Fig. 2.8; it has an 8-bit data bus and a

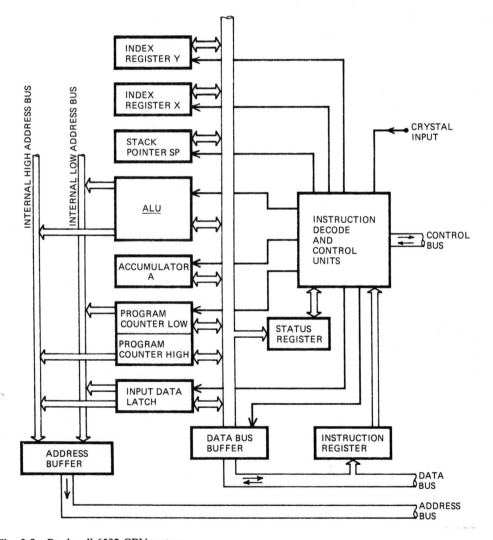

Fig. 2.8 Rockwell 6502 CPU system

16-bit address bus. Very few control bus lines are essential for simple operation; those necessary are the line R/$\overline{\text{W}}$ and phase ϕ_2 of the clock. Note the lack of inut and output control lines. I–O devices must be connected to a 6502 so that they appear to be memory devices; they are said to be **memory mapped** I–O devices. To output to a device, the data is sent to it by a memory write operation; similarly an input device is used by a memory read operation.

The CPU has fewer registers than the 8080 although an area of memory is reserved for special use and acts to some degree as a large number of registers. There are three 8-bit registers, X, Y and SP; an 8-bit accumulator, A; a 16-bit register, PC; and five single bit flags.

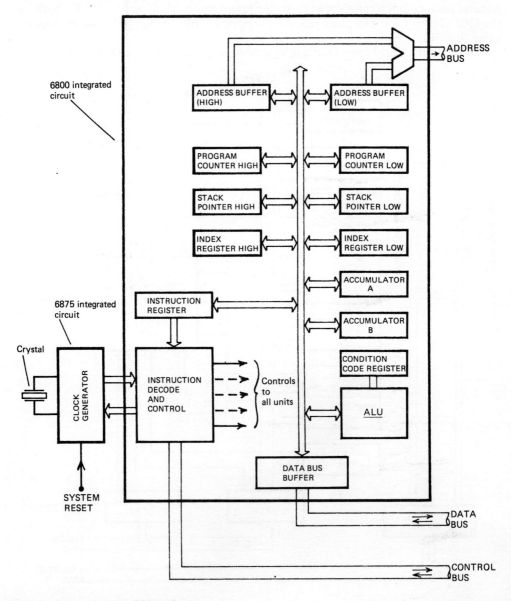

Fig. 2.9   Motorola 6800 CPU system

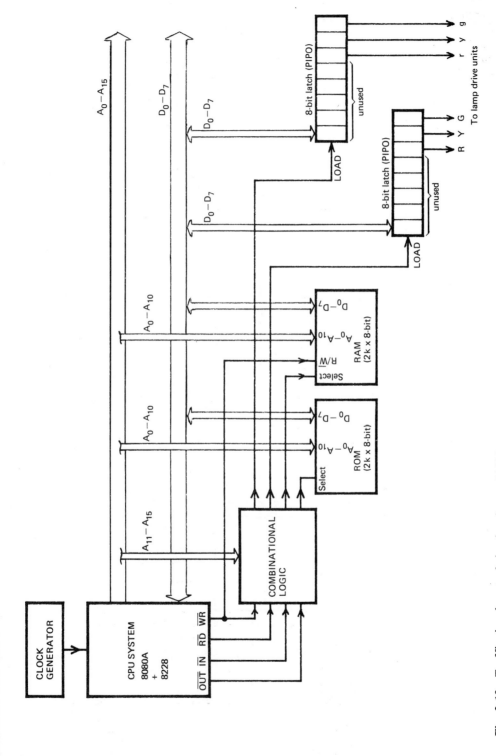

Fig. 2.10 Traffic signal control circuit using an 8080A processor

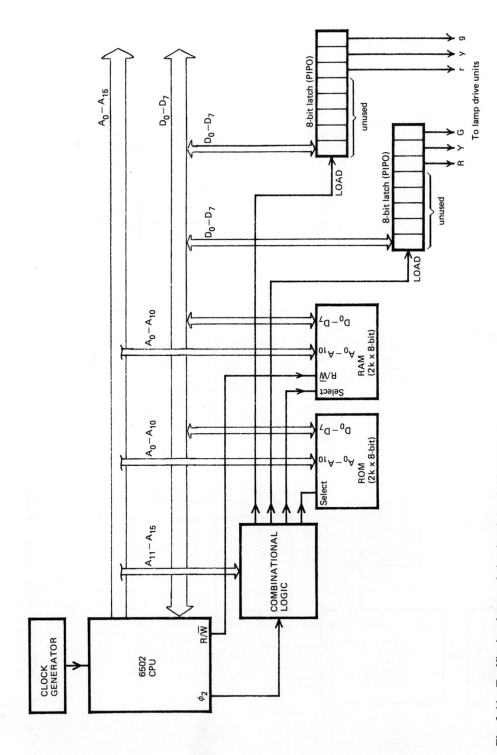

Fig. 2.11   Traffic signal control circuit using a 6502 processor

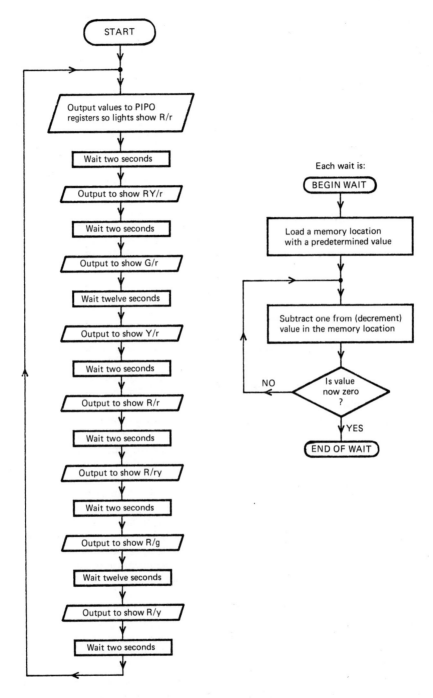

Fig. 2.12 Flow diagram for a program to control traffic signals

2.6.3   The 6800

The 6800 CPU is one of a family of related designs; an outline of the basic member, the 6800, is shown in Fig. 2.9. As with the 8080A, more than one integrated circuit is required to form a CPU; again a later replacement, the 6802, is a single device combining all functions. The CPU has an 8-bit data bus and a 16-bit address bus. The control bus for simple operation is similar to that of the 6502 and requires only two lines. One is the R/$\overline{\text{W}}$ line and the other is VMA-ϕ2 which is a logical combination of the clock phase ϕ_2 and the processor output VMA (valid memory access). As for the 6502 I–O devices are memory mapped.

The CPU differs from the other two described; it has two 8-bit accumulators, A and B. The only other registers available to the user are the three 16-bit registers, PC, SP and IX; there are six single bit flag registers.

2.7   Simple systems and use

An 8-bit CPU, one ROM device, one RAM device, and some simple I–O devices can be connected to produce a useful small processor system for many applications.

Example

Outline the design of simple processor systems to replace a logic circuit for the elementary traffic light controller described in Chapter 1. One circuit is to be based on the 8080A, the other on the 6502.

Figure 2.10 is the circuit for the 8080A system and Fig. 2.11 is that for the 6502 system; the blocks labelled 'combinational logic circuits' are designed for the particular application and set the actual addresses of the memory units fitted and the positions of the I–O devices. These selection circuits consist mainly of decoders and are designed as part of the total system interconnection.

Each circuit contains a ROM to hold the program which remains fixed and unalterable even if the power is removed. There is a RAM to hold temporary working values; also two simple PIPO registers are connected as output devices which supply the lamp control signals (shown as 8-bit registers but only 3-bits are used and only these would be built). The RAM and ROM have each been selected with 2k words (2048 words) of 8-bits.

All that is missing from the example systems to make them perform the traffic signal control is a program. Preparation of programs is a major part in the development of processor based systems. Total design of a processor system to perform any task depends upon both the processor system components, the **hardware**, and on the program, the **software**. Figure 2.12 is a simplified flow diagram, a specification, which describes the behaviour required when the program is run; the same notation is used as in Chapter 1 to denote which traffic signal lamps are on at any time.

Although the primary concern of this book is processor hardware, this cannot be examined without reference to software. In many cases it is possible to trade one for the other, that is a particular action may be achieved either by incorporating some circuit or by writing a program. For example, in the simple traffic light control time intervals are set by making the CPU waste time by looping many times through sequences which perform no useful action. An alternative is to use a timer circuit which is started by the CPU and indicates to the CPU when the required time is up. During the time interval the CPU could be used to perform some other task. The designer must have experience of both hardware and software in order to decide the best balance in any application.

Before considering the hardware of processor systems in detail it is necessary to examine the types of instruction that most CPUs can execute. It is also important to know how these instructions may be combined to form a program.

3 Instruction sets and programs

To perform a particular task a processor system requires a program, that is a list of instructions in the required order of execution. Each possible instruction is represented by a unique binary number and a program is a list of binary numbers placed in order in memory. The actual instructions that can be obeyed by any CPU depend upon its design and are unique to that CPU; all the possible instructions for a CPU form its **instruction set**.

Instruction sets vary greatly from one CPU to another, but there are many common features because the essential requirements are the same. Similar size CPU designs tend to have similar capabilities. Microprocessors have rather large and irregular instruction sets making it difficult to practise good programming techniques. Larger processors not limited by the restriction of fitting the whole system onto one integrated circuit tend to have smaller but more powerful instruction sets. In general small and well designed instruction sets are better than large instruction sets.

3.1 Instructions

Each instruction is a binary code number; for some processors all codes are of a fixed length and consist of a single word. Other processors have variable length instruction codes; these are usually restricted to small numbers of words placed in successive memory locations. As it is difficult to remember multiple digit binary numbers it is customary to give each funda-mentally different instruction for a processor a short name, its **mnemonic name**. This is usually a few letters chosen to indicate the action of the instruction. For example, both the 8080 and 6502 include instructions with the mnemonic name LDA, which means load the accumulator, A, with some value. (The two binary codes are different.) These instructions put a value into A by copying it from somewhere else; at present the source of the value has not been specified. It is possible to load A in several different ways, so there are several different binary codes corresponding to the manner in which the data is obtained for loading A.

When a mnemonic such as LDA is written it is followed by additional information, the **operands**; these specify sources and destinations of data required by the instruction when it is executed. Using the mnemonic and operands together the exact code for the required operation, the **OPCODE**, may be determined. This code determination consists of looking up a table of values; for many processors the codes are constructed from the basic instruction plus operands using several components, each being obtained from a different table.

Full instruction sets for several processors are given in Appendix C. Although these are complete they are brief, and the manufacturers' manuals should be consulted for complete explanations of the instruction sets.

3.2 Instruction types

All processor operations may be regarded as simply moving data around; this even applies to arithmetic and branch operations. It is convenient to divide the operations into classes, although a few instructions do not fit conveniently into rigid classifications. A reasonable division is into data transfer operations for which the transfer is the only purpose of the operation, arithmetic operations, logical operations, transfer of control, shifts, and processor control functions.

3.2.1   Data transfer

These operations move numeric values from one place to another. For example, in an 8080 system with a number of registers it is useful to be able to move (copy) values from one register to another. The 8080 instruction MOV performs this; its full form with operands is

$$\text{MOV r1,r2}$$

The operands, r1 and r2, must each be replaced when an actual instruction is required by a letter indicating any of the CPU registers A, B, C, D, E, H, or L. The instruction is move (i.e. copy) the contents of register r2 into register r1; for example MOV E,L means copy the contents of register L into register E. Note that the contents of L remain unchanged, while the original number in E is lost (overwritten) and an exact copy of the value in L appears in E. The binary code for MOV E,L is 01011101; it is a one word (byte) instruction as the 8080 has an 8-bit word length.

A written description of the action of an instruction is lengthy and it is often difficult to be precise. Several notations have been developed to describe these actions, and a simple one is to use parenthesis to indicate *contents of*. In this notation (A) means the contents of A; $(aaaa_H)$ means the contents of memory location with address $aaaa_H$, whereas $aaaa_H$ without brackets is the value $aaaa_H$ itself. Using $\leftarrow$ to represent *becomes equal to*, the action of MOV E,L is

$$(E) \leftarrow (L)$$

read as *the contents of E become equal to the contents of L*.

Writing or printing binary numbers is inconvenient, so instruction codes are commonly written as hexadecimal (base sixteen) or octal (base eight) numbers; binary to hexadecimal or octal conversions and reverse ones are trivial. The code for MOV E,L is $5D_H$ in hexadecimal form and 135_8 in octal form; suffixes H and 8 indicate hexadecimal and octal numbers respectively. When confusion is possible, binary numbers have a suffix 2 and decimal numbers a suffix D or subscript 10.

With few registers, there are only a small number of cases of register to register copying in the 6502 and 6800. Rather than a general register to register instruction, there are a small number of special instructions. For example the 6502 set includes TXA and TAX, transfer (copy or move) contents of X to A and A to X respectively. The corresponding codes are

Table 3.1   Some 8080A register load and store instructions

Instruction	Action
LDA $xxxx_H$	Load A with contents of memory location address $xxxx_H$
LDAX B	Load A with contents of memory location; address used is the contents of registers B and C
MOV r,M	Load r with contents of memory location; address used is the contents of registers H and L
STA $xxxx_H$	Store contents of A in memory location address $xxxx_H$
STAX B	Store contents of A in memory location; address used is the contents of registers B and C.
MOV M,r	Store contents of r in memory location; address used is the contents of registers H and L

Table 3.2 Some 6502 register load and store instructions

Instruction	Action
LDA $xxxx_H$	Load A with contents of memory location address $xxxx_H$
LDA dd_H	Load A with contents of memory location address $00dd_H$ (address restricted to 0000_H to $00FF_H$, page zero)
LDX $xxxx_H$,Y	Load X with contents of the memory location whose address is formed by adding contents of Y register to value $xxxx_H$
STA $xxxx_H$	Store contents of A in memory location address $xxxx_H$
STA (dd_H,X)	Form an address from 0000_H to $00FF_H$ by 8-bit addition of the contents of X to value dd_H (ignore carry). The contents of this location and the next are the address where the contents of A are stored
STY dd_H,X	Form an address from 0000_H to $00FF_H$ by 8-bit addition of the contents of X to value dd_H (ignore carry). The contents of Y are stored in this location

$10001010_2 = 8A_H = 212_8$ and $10101010_2 = AA_H = 252_8$. Similarly the 6800 has instructions to copy the contents of one accumulator into the other; TAB, transfer (copy) contents of A to B; and TBA, transfer contents of B to A. The codes are $00010110_2 = 16_H = 026_8$ and $00010111_2 = 17_H = 027_8$ respectively.

The copy register contents to another register are simple operations for data transfer; more important operations are those to copy the contents of any specified memory location to a register, or to store (copy) a register contents in some memory location. Examination of all processor instruction sets shows several different instructions for such transfers. Tables 3.1, 3.2 and 3.3 outline a few (but not all) of the instructions available for memory transfer operations using the 8080, 6502 and 6800 processors respectively. Many are two or three word (byte) instructions with the bytes placed in successive memory locations; the second and third bytes are numbers which are associated with the operands. Note that these 8-bit processors do not have instructions to copy the contents from one memory location to another. If this action is required in a program, two instructions must be used in succession to transfer via a register.

A final transfer required is loading a predetermined value into a register or memory location. This operation is called an **immediate** data transfer, and the number is an operand which becomes part of the instruction code. One immediate instruction for the 6502 is a version of the LDA instruction which is LDA #XX_H. This is LOAD A immediately with the value XX_H; it is a two byte instruction with $A9_H$ as the first byte and any 8-bit number XX_H as the second.

Table 3.3 Some 6800 register load and store instructions

Instruction	Action
LDAA $xxxx_H$	Load A with contents of memory location address $xxxx_H$
LDAB dd_H	Load B with contents of memory location address $00dd_H$ (address restricted to 0000_H to $00FF_H$)
LDS dd_H,X	Load S with contents of two successive memory locations; address of first is formed by adding contents of register X to 8-bit value dd_H
STAA $xxxx_H$	Store contents of A in memory location address $xxxx_H$
STAB dd_H,X	Store the contents of B in memory location whose address is formed by adding the contents of X to the 8-bit value dd_H
STX dd_H,X	Store contents of X in memory locations addresses $00dd_H$ and $00dd_H + 1$ (both in range 0000_H to $00FF_H$)

3.2.2 Arithmetic

The basic arithmetic operation is addition. This should require three operands; to add the contents of x to the contents of y and place the result in z, that is $(z) \leftarrow (x) + (y)$. However, most processors put the results of arithmetic actions into an accumulator; when there is only one accumulator the destination need not be specified. Further, one initial value is usually taken from the accumulator and addition becomes add the contents of a register (or memory location) to the accumulator contents, leaving the result in the accumulator. Thus the accumulator is a special purpose register which collects, *accumulates*, a total result as a sequence of calculations progresses; hence its name. If there is more than one accumulator, as in the 6800, the same accumulator is normally both the source of one number (one operand) and the destination for the result.

The 8080 instruction ADD r is add the contents of register r (again r is any one of A, B, C, D, E, H or L) to the contents of A and leave the result in A, that is

$$(A) \leftarrow (A) + (r)$$

For example the code for ADD H is $10000100_2 = 84_H = 204_8$. The addition is the simple binary addition of the two 8-bit numbers. In some cases the result will exceed 8-bits, giving an overflow or a carry-out from the **most significant bit, MSB**. After each arithmetic operation the **flag bits** indicate certain features of the result; one function of the **carry flag, CY**, is to show overflow after addition. The carry flag is cleared to 0 when the addition produces no overflow and is set to 1 when there is an overflow.

Example

Determine the contents of the accumulator and carry flag of an 8080 CPU after obeying the instruction ADD E when the initial contents of A and E are the following:

	Contents of A	Contents of E
a)	01011010	00101111
b)	01100111	01011110
c)	10101100	11011001

These are straightforward binary additions.

```
a)        01011010  (A)
          00101111  (E)
          _____

        0 10001001  (9-bit result)
          ========
```

The MSB of the 9-bit result is put into the carry flag and the other 8 bits go into A. Therefore after execution of the instruction, A contains 10001001_2 and the carry flag is 0.

```
b)        01100111  (A)
          01011110  (E)
          _____

        0 11000101  (9-bit result)
          ========
```

In this case the contents of A become 11000101_2 and the carry flag is again 0.

```
c)        10101100  (A)
          11011001  (E)
          _____

        1 10000101  (9-bit result)
          ========
```

Here the contents of A are left as 10000101 but the carry flag is set to 1.

Inspection of the 8080 instruction set shows another addition instruction ADC r; the 6502 only has this form of addition instruction. This is add with carry and is similar to the basic 8080 instruction ADD but the value of the carry flag before execution is added into the LSB position.

Example

Repeat the first case of the previous example for the instruction ADC E when the initial value of the carry is (a) 0, and (b) 1.

a)
```
    01011010  (A)
    00101111  (E)
           0  (initial carry)
  _____
  0 10001001  (9-bit result)
  ==========
```

In this case the result is unchanged.

b)
```
    01011010  (A)
    00101111  (E)
           1  (initial carry)
  _____
  0 10001010  (9-bit result)
  ==========
```

The extra 1 from the carry has increased the result by 1, carries from one bit to the next are formed in the usual way for addition of three numbers. The instruction is

$$(A) \leftarrow (A) + (E) + (CY)$$

This instruction is very useful for multiple word addition (see Chapter 6). The absence of a simple addition instruction for the 6502 requires use of the instruction clear carry, CLC, before any addition not requiring addition of the carry to the result.

Instructions for further arithmetic operations will be found in most processor instruction sets. The simple 8-bit processors only have addition and subtraction operations whereas larger processors can perform other operations, for example multiplication and division.

When writing programs it is frequently necessary to add one to or subtract one from the contents of a register (or memory location). Addition of one is called **incrementing** while subtraction of one is **decrementing**. These increment and decrement arithmetic operations are used so often that most processors have special instructions. In this case one operand of the instruction, the value 1, is implied by the instruction itself. The operation is so useful that it is an arithmetic operation which is not restricted to accumulators in most processors; there are increment and decrement operations for most registers, and often for memory locations, in a processor. Increment and decrement instructions are found in all the instruction sets in Appendix C. Although the actions are arithmetic ones their effects on the flags vary from one CPU design to another.

Earlier it was stated that even arithmetic instructions are executed as a sequence consisting only of data movements. The ALU is a combinational logic circuit with three registers connected so that their contents are the inputs to the ALU. Two registers hold the two initial operands and the third a pattern forming a set of control signals to determine which arithmetic operation is performed. To perform an arithmetic operation the sequence in Fig. 3.1. (or one similar) is executed; this sequence consists only of movement of data. Although correct this description is an over-simplification. To reduce circuit complexity, some arithmetic operations may be performed as a sequence of steps by a sequential arithmetic circuit; however sequential execution is not necessary in principle.

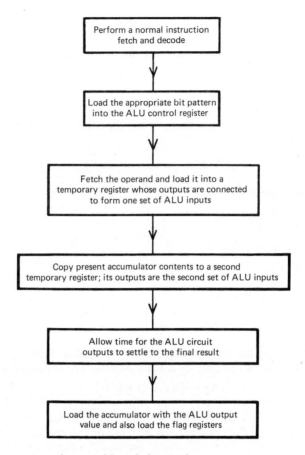

Fig. 3.1   Execution sequence for an arithmetic instruction

3.2.3   Logic

These instructions are so closely related to arithmetic ones that they are often regarded as arithmetic operations. The instruction sets of most processors include operations AND, OR and exclusive-OR (XOR); these have operands exactly as arithmetic instructions. The concept of the Boolean AND operation being applied between multiple bit words appears unusual; the operation is performed by separate logical AND operations between all corresponding bits of the accumulator and the source operand, and the results are placed in the appropriate bit positions of the accumulator.

Example

The 6502 instruction AND $xxyy_H$ ($xxyy_H$ represents a 16-bit address) has the three byte code $2D_H$ yy_H xx_H. This performs logical AND of the contents of memory address $xxyy_H$ with the contents of A, leaving the result in A. Determine the contents of A after execution of this instruction if, before execution, A contains 10110010_2 and the memory location $xxyy_H$ contains 11010111_2.

Taking the **least significant bits (LSBs)** first these are 0 and 1; as 0 AND 1 = 0 the LSB of the result is 0. The next bits are both 1; 1 AND 1 = 1 so this bit of the result is 1. Continuing gives

```
1 0 1 1 0 0 1 0    initial (A)
1 1 0 1 0 1 1 1    (memory)
```
```
1 0 0 1 0 0 1 0    final (A)
```

3.2.4   Transfer of control

When a programmed machine was introduced in Chapter 1, it was stated that instructions of the form *GOTO instruction at ADDRESS N* were a necessary feature. Also instructions of the form *IF condition exists THEN GOTO instruction at ADDRESS N* were required. These are jump, branch or transfer of control instructions, and are an essential feature of all processor instruction sets.

The simple form is the unconditional absolute jump found in many instruction sets. The new address is an operand and usually forms part of the instruction code; this is normally a multiple word code as address lengths usually exceed the word length. Some examples are illustrated in Fig. 3.2 for the 8080, 6502 and 6800; note the low then high order of the two bytes forming the 16-bit address in the cases of the 8080 and 6502. This order can have advantages in CPU design but requires careful use if codes are manipulated manually.

Conditional branches are implemented by testing the single bit flag registers, the **flags**. The structure is similar to that of the basic jump instruction, but instead of automatically performing the jump when the instruction is reached in a program, the CPU first examines the condition of the specified flag. If the flag state is that specified, the jump is made; if the flag has the opposite state, the jump is ignored and the instruction executed is the one immediately following the conditional jump in memory. For example the 8080 includes the conditional branch instructions *jump if carry* (JC) and *jump if not carry* (JNC). When the instruction JC is executed, the jump is performed if the carry flag at the time of execution is 1; otherwise the jump is ignored and the next instruction in the normal sequence is obeyed. The JNC instruction operates in the inverse sense.

Examination of the instruction sets for the 6502 and 6800 show that they adopt a different method to specify destinations for conditional branches. These use an operand with only 8 bits representing a signed integer in the decimal range -128 to $+127$; values 0, -1 and -2 are allowed but serve no useful purpose. The branch is known as a relative branch; if the condition is such that the jump is made, this signed value is added to the value in the program counter after all bytes of the instruction have been fetched. That is, if the signed value is K and the address of the first byte of the conditional branch instruction is N, then the destination address is $(N+2)+K$. These relative branches have advantages in developing advanced software; the short form of address also reduces program storage space without many problems as most branches in a program are to nearby locations. Many larger processors have several forms of branch instruction so that the most suitable may be used in any application. A more elaborate form of branch instruction is required for subroutines. Most CPU designs include special *CALL* and *RETURN* instructions; these allow a program to jump to a block of instructions and, after completion of the block, jump back to the instruction immediately after the initial calling point. Subroutines are described in detail later as their implementation affects the design of a CPU.

Implementation of branch instructions is one reason why the simple processor control loop, introduced in Chapter 2 (Fig. 2.6), indicated that the program counter is incremented before the instruction is obeyed. During branch execution the new address, the destination, is brought into internal CPU buffer registers and the final stage of execution transfers the buffer contents into the program counter. (Conditional instructions simply skip this transfer when the condition is not met.) If the program counter was incremented late in the instruction cycle, the new value would be incremented and the programmer would have to

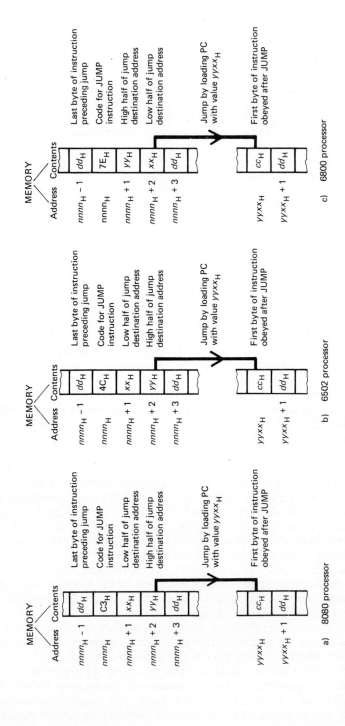

Fig. 3.2   Memory contents for 8-bit CPU jump instructions

take this into account when determining the destination address. Also the address stored for the return from a subroutine would require care in its interpretation.

3.2.5 Shifts

There are large variations in the methods available to move data within a single register. Possibilities include moving the data left or right by one or more places with a fixed value, usually 0, moved in and the value moved out lost. Alternatively the data may be rotated with the bit moved out returned as the new bit. Shift and rotate operations may operate on the bits of the register only or may include a flag, usually the carry, to form a longer register.

Some CPUs only allow shift or rotation of accumulators; others may allow these operations with any register or even with any memory location. Most 8-bit microprocessors provide only a few operations and are usually restricted to moves by one place. Figure 3.3 illustrates some possibilities for a one position movement in an 8-bit CPU, using *abcdefgh* as the initial register contents and *z* for the initial value in the carry flag where appropriate.

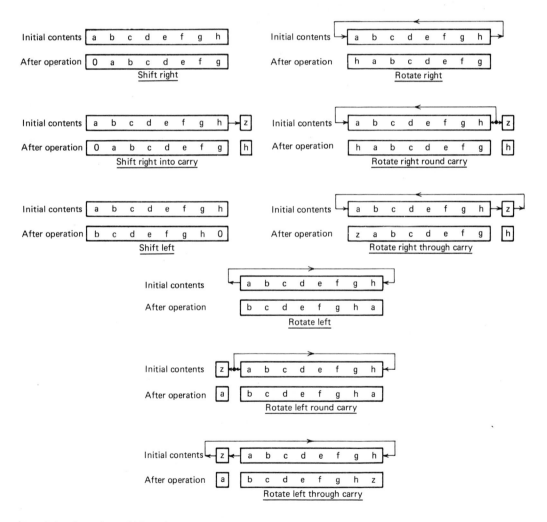

Fig. 3.3 One place shift and rotate operations

3.2.6 Processor control and other instructions

Most processors include a few instructions intended to assist in controlling their own operations. These are uniquely related to CPU design so have few common features; typical instructions include those halting the processor or setting the actions of the interrupt system.

There are also instructions which do not clearly fit any of the simple categories given. For example the 8080 instruction PCHL is to move the contents of the registers H and L into the 16-bit register PC. This appears to be a data transfer but behaves as a very powerful multiway branch which allows implementation of a *computed GOTO*.

3.3 Instruction execution

Figure 2.6 indicated the basic processor action showing the sequence of obtaining, decoding and executing instructions in the correct order. Execution of an instruction may require a process of several steps; the step sequences for a few 8080 instructions are indicated in Table 3.4.

Table 3.4 Execution steps for some 8080A instructions

Step (clock cycle)	Action
1	Output contents of PC to address bus
2	Increment contents of PC
3	Transfer (copy) instruction code from memory to IR
4	Copy r2 contents to an internal work register
5	Copy internal work register contents to r1

a) Instruction MOV r1,r2

Step (clock cycle)	Action
1	
2	} Fetch instruction, action identical to steps 1, 2, 3 of MOV
3	
4	Internal decoding by CPU
5	Output contents of PC to address bus
6	Increment contents of PC
7	Copy byte 2 (low data address) to internal Z register
8	Repeat step 5
9	Repeat step 6
10	Copy byte 3 (high data address) to internal W register
11	Output contents of W and Z onto address bus
12	Output contents of A to data bus, hold through next state
13	Signal memory write ($\overline{MW}$ goes low)

b) Instruction STA address

Step (clock cycle)	Action
1	
2	} Fetch instruction, action identical to steps 1, 2, 3 of MOV
3	
4	Copy register r contents to internal temporary register and add 1 to temporary register in ALU
5	Copy ALU result to register r

c) Instruction INR r

The breakdown of the instruction execution into steps shows that even complex instructions consist of simple actions in sequence. It is also clear that the number of steps in fetching and executing instructions varies; in simple processors each step takes one clock period, hence different instructions take different times to fetch and execute. For 8080 processors total instruction fetch, decode and execution times range from 4 clock periods to 18 clock periods, while for the 6800 the range is 2 to 12 clock periods. In more complex CPUs such simple timing does not hold and the time to fetch and execute a specific instruction is not constant.

It takes the CPU a finite time to execute an instruction. For some processors the time to execute a section of program is easily determined by adding together the times for each instruction in that section; for others determination of execution time may be difficult and it may not be constant.

3.4 The flags

The single bit flag registers are an important element of any processor system as they form the basis of all decision making. Examination of different CPUs shows a range of flags; the carry, zero and sign flags tend to occur in most designs. Several others occur in a significant proportion of designs. It is essential to check **the effect of each instruction on the flags** before using the flags to make decisions (branches) in a program; many CPUs, especially microprocessors, behave in unexpected ways and flag setting is inconsistent.

3.4.1   Carry flag

Most processors have a carry flag, whose main purpose is to indicate when the result of an arithmetic operation exceeds the size of register available to hold the result. This is possible in most arithmetic operations; while the flag shows simple overflow in addition there are several possible actions in other operations. For example in subtraction of a value from the accumulator, the carry is often used as a **borrow flag**. If the quantity subtracted from the accumulator is less than or equal to the original contents of the accumulator the borrow is 0; if the value subtracted exceeds the original accumulator contents the borrow is 1. However, the common design of circuit used for subtraction produces opposite values to those required in the carry position; many processors include an extra circuit to correct this but some, for example the 6502 and the RCA1802, do not.

3.4.2   Zero flag

This normally indicates the value of the result in the accumulator only. First examination of its behaviour is sometimes confusing as a zero flag is usually set to 1 to indicate a result of zero, and to 0 to indicate a result of not zero. The operations of flags are best shown by examples; again 8-bit examples are chosen and the flag actions are common to most CPU designs.

Example

Determine the values of the zero, Z, and carry, CY, flags after the following values are added in an 8-bit addition unit.

a)   01011010 added to 00101111
b)   10011110 added to 01100010
c)   00000000 added to 00000000

As in previous examples these are straightforward additions as shown below

(a)	(b)	(c)
01011010	10011110	00000000
00101111	01100010	00000000
0 10001001	1 00000000	0 00000000

In case (a), the 8-bit result is not zero so the zero flag is 0, (Z) ← 0. There is no carry from the 8-bit result so the carry flag is 0, (CY) ← 0. However in case (b) the 8-bit result is zero so the zero flag is set to 1, (Z) ← 1; the 9-bit result is not zero and the carry flag is set to 1, (CY) ← 1. Finally for case (c) both the 8-bit and 9-bit results are zero so (Z) ← 1 and (CY) ← 0.

3.4.3   Sign flag

The methods of representing signed numbers are described in detail in Chapter 6. At present it is sufficient to state that most common methods use the MSB of an n-bit number to indicate the sign, with 0 for positive and 1 for negative. The sign flag is then just a copy of the MSB of the n-bit result (i.e. the bit next to the carry in the $(n+1)$-bit result). For the previous example case (a) would give a sign bit of 1, (b) would leave it 0, and (c) would also leave it 0.

3.4.4   Other common flags

Several other flags are in common use although the selection varies from one processor to another. Many CPUs have an arithmetic **overflow** flag because, in signed arithmetic, the carry flag no longer indicates a result which is too large. Although such overflow may be inferred from a combination of other flags, many CPUs provide an overflow flag to assist in performing signed arithmetic.

Another common flag indicates **parity**; parity is a measure of the number of bits in a binary number which are either 0 or 1. A number has **even parity** if it contains an even number of bits which are 1 and it has **odd parity** if an odd number of bits are 1. A parity flag indicates whether the result of some operation has even or odd parity; in the case of the 8080 family the parity flag is set to 1 for even parity and to 0 for odd parity. In the previous examples case (a) would set the parity flag to 1, (P) ← 1, while cases (b) and (c) would give a setting of 0, (P) ← 0.

A final flag in many 8-bit CPUs is the **half-carry** which is used to assist the programmer using BCD representation. Two BCD digits are packed into one byte, and the half-carry flag indicates a carry from the low nibble to the high nibble. It is not usually tested directly but is used in conjunction with special instructions to adjust results in BCD calculations.

3.5   Subroutines

Subroutines are not essential to the successful operation of a processor system, but they offer many advantages and nearly all CPUs provide facilities to implement them. In most programs there are usually several points which require similar sequences of instructions. A typical example is the group of instructions required in many programs to output a number to some device such as a visual display unit, VDU. Such outputs occur at several points in most programs and one feature of subroutines is that the required sequence of instructions is only included once in the program no matter how many times it is used.

A subroutine is a sequence of instructions placed at some convenient position in the memory outside the main program area. At any point in a program the subroutine may be used by branching to it using a special subroutine call instruction. After executing the instructions in the subroutine, the program must continue correctly from the position immediately following the call instruction which caused the branch to the subroutine. As there may be many different calling points some mechanism is required which remembers the address of the required return point and jumps to it after completion of the subroutine.

There are several methods of implementing a subroutine call and return sequence; the most general is to use a **stack**. Stacks are areas of read and write memory, RAM, reserved by the programmer for temporary storage of working values; they usually appear to behave as **last in-first out, LIFO,** memories. The common method of defining the position in memory of a stack for use with subroutines is by holding the address in a special register in the CPU, the **stack pointer**, SP. Several different subroutine mechanisms have been devised; the form used by the 8080 family is described here as it is relatively simple yet powerful.

At the start of any 8080 program using subroutines the programmer includes an instruction which loads the stack pointer with a value one greater than the highest address in the area reserved for the stack (instruction LXI SP, $aaaa_H$). In many programs this is the only time an explicit instruction is given concerning the address of the stack. Entry to a subroutine is by executing the three byte instruction CALL $xxyy_H$, where $xxyy_H$ is the address of the first instruction of the subroutine. After the CPU has fetched all three bytes of the instruction, it performs the following sequence of actions.

i) Decrement the contents of the stack pointer.
ii) Copy the high byte of the program counter to memory, using the contents of the stack pointer as the address.
iii) Decrement the contents of the stack pointer again.
iv) Copy the low byte of the program counter to memory, using the stack pointer contents as the address.
v) Move the second and third bytes of the instruction into the program counter (force the branch to the subroutine).

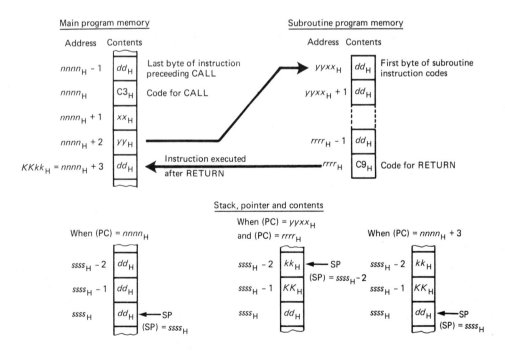

Fig. 3.4 Actions and memory contents for 8080 subroutine execution

The final instruction executed in a subroutine, not necessarily the one placed at the end, is the single byte return instruction, RET. This reverses the call sequence and its actions are as follows.

i)   Copy the contents of the memory location whose address is the stack pointer contents to an internal work register of the CPU.
ii) Increment the contents of the stack pointer.
iii) Copy the contents of the memory location whose address is given by the stack pointer contents to a second CPU work register.
iv) Increment the stack pointer contents.
v)   Transfer the contents of the work registers to the program counter (force the return branch).

The complete call and return sequence is illustrated by Fig. 3.4.
    This structure is very powerful because subroutines may be **nested**, that is one subroutine

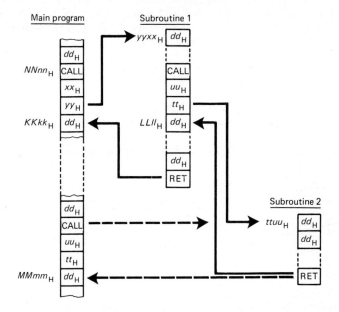

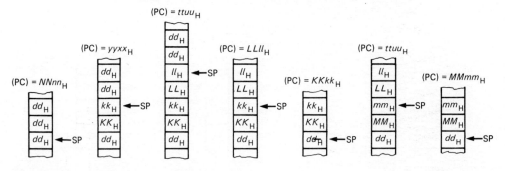

Fig. 3.5   Two level nesting of 8080 subroutines

can call another and so on. Each return will correctly branch to the instruction which follows the call associated with it. The only limit to the degree of nesting is the amount of RAM available for stack operations. Nesting is illustrated for two levels in Fig. 3.5; this diagram also indicates that the same subroutine may be called from different levels of nesting.

There are other instructions which use the stack as a temporary store; provided that they are used correctly no problems will arise. However any errors in use of the stack will produce program malfunctions which are often difficult to detect.

3.6 Programming.

The objective of programming is to put a sequence of binary numbers in memory so that when read as instructions by the CPU they cause the CPU to perform the operations set by some specification. One simple method of presenting the specification is as a flowchart. Although flowcharts are thought by some experts to lead to poor program development, they are used in many other fields, particularly engineering and business planning. This text only attempts to introduce programming to the extent necessary to describe the interactions between hardware and software, and to explain CPU design. Flowcharts are adopted to illustrate program actions. They are particularly useful in control or automation applications, because actual behaviour can be checked against that specified in such a chart. Figure 3.6 illustrates some typical flowchart symbols.

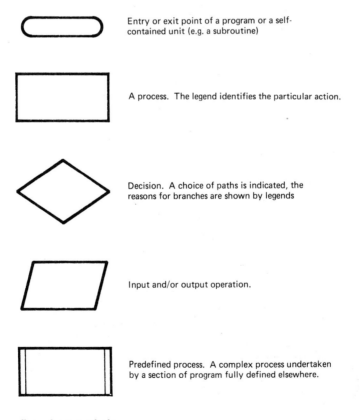

Entry or exit point of a program or a self-contained unit (e.g. a subroutine)

A process. The legend identifies the particular action.

Decision. A choice of paths is indicated, the reasons for branches are shown by legends

Input and/or output operation.

Predefined process. A complex process undertaken by a section of program fully defined elsewhere.

Fig. 3.6 Some flow chart symbols

The problem in generating the sequence of binary numbers which form a program to meet a specification is that for any non-trivial task the number of instruction codes required is very large. The creation of such a large pattern of binary numbers must be performed in a well organized manner if problems are to be avoided.

It is a good exercise to create binary programs without any aids for one or two very simple short tasks. This assists in understanding processor operation; also at some time many engineers will have to examine electrical signals in a running processor system and relate these to the ones expected. Some experience of this elementary level of programming is a useful background.

Example

Develop a program which takes two 8-bit numbers, x and y (unsigned positive integers), from specified memory locations with unrelated addresses. The numbers are multiplied together by adding x to itself y times and the result is left in the accumulator in which it is

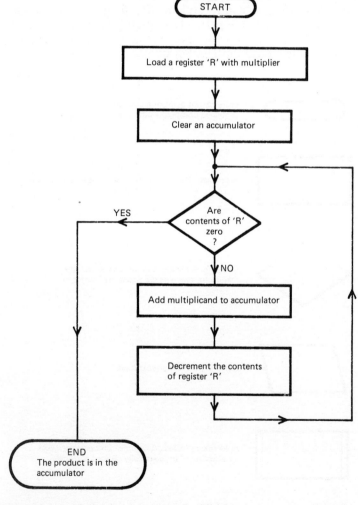

Fig. 3.7 Flowchart for multiplication by repeated addition

formed. It is assumed that the product is small enough to ignore overflow problems. Position the program so that the first instruction is at address 1000_H, and illustrate for 8080 and 6800 processors.

No attempt is made to adopt neat or clever solutions; Fig. 3.7 shows the basic flowchart for the program sequence. The addresses chosen for x and y are $20AA_H$ and $3A0D_H$; these are easily changed to other values.

Once a flowchart has been drawn, both the method of solving the problem and the order of program actions have been decided. (There may still be detailed choices to make, for example which register or memory location to use at some point.) It is now necessary to determine the exact sequence of instructions, and a simple method is a tabular one. A table with four columns is constructed; the columns are headed address, mnemonic, code and comment. Starting with the address which is to hold the first instruction code, the rows are numbered by placing consecutive addresses in the address column. The mnemonic names of the instructions are written in order of execution in the mnemonic column, allowing as many rows for a mnemonic as there will be bytes in the complete binary code for the instruction it represents. The comment column is used for future reference so that reasons for particular choices are clear.

Finally the binary instruction codes are determined by look-up using the listed instruction set. These are inserted in the code column; Tables 3.5 and 3.6 are the completed forms for the example. The codes are given in hexadecimal form; even the most elementary laboratory test systems usually incorporate the simple circuits required to allow codes to be input in either octal or hexadecimal form. Once the program has been developed, it is essential that its actions are checked by running it on a processor system using several sets of test values.

This tabular method of program generation would take an unacceptable length of time for

Table 3.5 Code preparation for 8080 example program

Address (hex)	Mnemonic	Code (bin)	Code (hex)	Comment
1000	LXI H,$20AA_H$	00100001	21	Point to multiplicand (*x*) address
1001	(AA)	10101010	AA	
1002	(20)	00100000	20	
1003	LDA $3A0D_H$	00111010	3A	Get multiplier (*y*)
1004	(0D)	00001101	0D	
1005	(3A)	00111010	3A	
1006	MOV B,A	01000111	47	Transfer multiplier to B
1007	XRA A	10101111	AF	Clear A (initialize result)
1008	INR B	00000100	04	Prepare for decrement before test
1009	L1: DCR B	00000101	05	Count down times multiplicand added to total
100A	JZ L2	11001010	CA	Jump to end if multiplier now zero
100B	(L2)	00010001	11	
100C	(L2)	00010000	10	
100D	ADD M	10000110	86	Add multiplicand (*x*) once
100E	JMP L1	11000011	C3	Loop to decrement and test
100F	(L1)	00001001	09	
1010	(L1)	00010000	10	
1011	L2: HLT	01110110	76	Stop (otherwise random values will be fetched as instruction codes)

Table 3.6   Code preparation for 6800 example program

Address (hex)	Mnemonic	Code (bin)	Code (hex)	Comment
1000	LDAA #00	10000110	86	⎱ Clear A (initialize result)
1001	(00)	00000000	00	⎰
1002	LDX 3A0D$_H$	11111110	FE	⎱
1003	(3A)	00111010	3A	⎰ Get multiplier (y)
1004	(0D)	00001101	0D	⎰
1005	INX	00001000	08	Prepare for decrement before test
1006	L1: DEX	00001001	09	Count down times multiplicand added to total
1007	BEQ L2	00100111	27	⎱ Jump to end if multiplier now
1008	(L2)	00000110	06	⎰ zero
1009	ADDA 20AA$_H$	10111011	BB	⎱
100A	(20)	00100000	20	⎰ Add multiplicand (x) once
100B	(AA)	10101010	AA	⎰
100C	JMP L1	01111110	7E	⎱
100D	(L1)	00010000	10	⎰ Loop to decrement and test
100E	(L1)	00000110	06	⎰
100F	L2: WAI	00111110	3E	Stop (otherwise random values will be fetched as instruction codes)

most processor applications. Generally programs are developed using computer programs to assist in code preparation. The main methods involve the use of **assemblers** or **compilers** which are discussed briefly in Chapter 13. A program written for an assembler is very similar in appearance to the tabular listing, it does not have the address and code columns. Programming methods influence the design of CPUs to some extent; in particular good compilers are more easily produced for CPUs with small but powerful general purpose instruction sets.

3.7   Problems

1 Which instructions could be used to place the value from an address $aabb_H$ into the A register (accumulator) of (a) an 8080, (b) a 6502, (c) a 6800?

Give all possible instructions in each case, indicating the values that must already be present in other registers or memory locations so that the correct behaviour is obtained.

2 The hexadecimal values represent 8-bit numbers being supplied as operands to the ALU of an 8-bit processor system. Determine the value left in the accumulator in each case.

a) $A5_H$ added to 33_H.
b) 59_H subtracted from 95_H.
c) 74_H subtracted from $2D_H$.
d) $B5_H$ added with carry to $6A_H$, initial carry = 1.
e) 65_H subtracted with borrow from 97_H, initial borrow = 1.
f) $A5_H$ AND with 33_H.
g) 59_H AND with $A6_H$.
h) 74_H OR with $4A_H$.
i) $B5_H$ OR with $6A_H$.
j) 65_H XOR with 97_H.

3 In Problem 2, what would the final values (when defined) of the carry, zero and sign flags be in each case?

4 In an 8080 program the first byte of CALL 3A05$_H$ is located at address 231E$_H$. The corresponding return is at 3AFF$_H$, and the subroutine has no internal branches so it always executes the instruction CALL 3D2C$_H$ at address 3A56$_H$. The return for this second routine is at 3D5A$_H$, and before the first call the stack pointer contains the value 5100$_H$.

At the points immediately before and following each CALL and RETURN determine the values in both the stack pointer and the program counter registers. Also draw a diagram showing the known contents of the stack and the position of the stack pointer at each of these points.

5 For any 8-bit processor for which you have a complete instruction set and a test system, prepare the following programs in tabular form and then test them for correct operation.

   a) Assume that a random sequence of five numbers has been placed in memory locations at consecutive addresses. The program is required to place the five numbers in the same locations, but they should be in ascending order of size.

   b) Multiply two 8-bit numbers (unsigned integers) together using repeated addition; leave the 16-bit result in two successive memory locations. The program must produce the correct result if either number is zero.

   c) Divide one 8-bit number (unsigned integer) by another, use repeated subtraction to form an 8-bit integer result and an integer remainder. Leave these results in two successive memory locations. The program must behave in a reasonable manner if either number is zero.

4 Processor system assembly

The interconnection of a CPU, memory and I–O devices to form a processor system using the conventional three bus architecture outlined in Chapter 2 requires the design of a number of circuits. These are **interface circuits** and they consist mainly of decoders (selectors), latches and buffers.

4.1 Selection circuits

Memory connections to processor bus systems are examined in detail; the techniques are easily adapted for connection of I–O devices. Connections for ROM and RAM units differ only in one feature, read-or-write controls are supplied to the appropriate control inputs of all RAM units but are absent from ROM units.

In the most simple systems, all memory devices (units) are chosen so that the individual words have the same number of bits (width) as the processor data bus. Also, initial examination is for cases when all memory units have the same length of 2^x words. Many examples use $x = 12$, units have $2^x = 4096 = 4\text{k}$ words, however, techniques introduced are general and apply to any size of memory unit. CPU address buses have m lines ($m > x$) denoted by A_0 (LSB), A_1, A_2, . . ., A_{m-1}(MSB). The A_0 line from the CPU is connected to the corresponding A_0 line of every memory unit, A_1 is connected to every memory A_1, and so on up to A_{x-1}. The design objective is to build a memory with 2^m locations. Because memory devices are designed to be assembled into larger systems, each has a selection input, usually an active low input called **chip select, $\overline{\text{CS}}$**. If a single memory unit is selected when A_x to A_{m-1} are all 0, by an appropriate chip select signal, and all other memory units are inactive, then the selected unit provides all 2^x memory locations which have addresses with A_x to A_{m-1} at 0. Let this be memory unit 0 and call the signal line providing its selection input S_0.

Table 4.1 Memory unit selection circuit requirements

Inputs						Outputs						
A_{m-1}	A_{m-2}	. . .	A_{x+2}	A_{x+1}	A_x	S_0	S_1	S_2	S_3	. . .	S_{y-2}	S_{y-1}
0	0	. . .	0	0	0	0	1	1	1	. . .	1	1
0	0	. . .	0	0	1	1	0	1	1	. . .	1	1
0	0	. . .	0	1	0	1	1	0	1	. . .	1	1
0	0	. . .	0	1	1	1	1	1	0	. . .	1	1
.					.	.						.
.					.	.						.
.					.	.						.
1	1	. . .	1	1	0	1	1	1	1	. . .	0	1
1	1	. . .	1	1	1	1	1	1	1	. . .	1	0

Similarly $A_x = 1$ with all A_{x+1} to A_{m-1} at 0 may be used to generate the selection input S_1 to memory unit 1, and so on. Table 4.1 outlines the requirements for a circuit, a decoder or selector, to generate S_0, S_1, . . ., S_{y-1} where $y = 2^{m-x}$. Table 4.2 is a specific example for $x = 12$, $m = 16$. Table 4.1 is obviously the truth table of an $(m - x)$-line to 2^{m-x}-line decoder

Table 4.2 Truth table for memory selection, $x = 12$, $m = 16$

Inputs				Outputs															
A_{15}	A_{14}	A_{13}	A_{12}	S_0	S_1	S_2	S_3	S_4	S_5	S_6	S_7	S_8	S_9	S_{10}	S_{11}	S_{12}	S_{13}	S_{14}	S_{15}
0	0	0	0	0	1	1	1	1	1	1	1	1	1	1	1	1	1	1	1
0	0	0	1	1	0	1	1	1	1	1	1	1	1	1	1	1	1	1	1
0	0	1	0	1	1	0	1	1	1	1	1	1	1	1	1	1	1	1	1
0	0	1	1	1	1	1	0	1	1	1	1	1	1	1	1	1	1	1	1
0	1	0	0	1	1	1	1	0	1	1	1	1	1	1	1	1	1	1	1
0	1	0	1	1	1	1	1	1	0	1	1	1	1	1	1	1	1	1	1
0	1	1	0	1	1	1	1	1	1	0	1	·1	1	1	1	1	1	1	1
0	1	1	1	1	1	1	1	1	1	1	0	1	1	·1	1	1	1	1	1
1	0	0	0	1	1	1	1	1	1	1	1	0	1	1	1	1	1	1	1
1	0	0	1	1	1	1	1	1	1	1	1	1	0	1	1	1	1	1	1
1	0	1	0	1	1	1	1	1	1	1	1	1	1	0	1	1	1	1	1
1	0	1	1	1	1	1	1	1	1	1	1	1	1	1	0	1	1	1	1
1	1	0	0	1	1	1	1	1	1	1	1	1	1	1	1	0	1	1	1
1	1	0	1	1	1	1	1	1	1	1	1	1	1	1	1	1	0	1	1
1	1	1	0	1	1	1	1	1	1	1	1	1	1	1	1	1	1	0	1
1	1	1	1	1	1	1	1	1	1	1	1	1	1	1	1	1	1	1	0

when all its enable inputs are active. The complete system for the $x = 12$, $m = 16$ case is illustrated in Fig. 4.1 for a CPU with two control lines $R/\overline{W}$ and ϕ (timing; transfer occurs while $\phi = 1$). The memory unit has a single read–write control input which is read when high, write when low; this is connected directly to the CPU $R/\overline{W}$ control line. If a four line control bus is used, the $\overline{WR}$ line is connected to this read/write input of all memory units and the decoder active low enable is supplied by the AND of $\overline{RD}$ with $\overline{WR}$. The read-or-write connection is simply omitted for those units which have been chosen to be ROM. A further description of the complete circuit is given by a **hardware memory map** (software maps will be introduced later) which shows the address ranges used for each memory unit. Figure 4.2 is the memory map for the example.

The simple decoder only accommodates memory units of identical size; however designers must frequently use memory units of different sizes within one system. It is impossible to consider every possible case, but two different approaches are examined. In the first method, every memory unit has all its address lines A_0 to A_{x-1} connected to the corresponding lines of the CPU; x no longer has the same value for all units. A decode circuit is devised with all address lines A_{xx} to A_{m-1} connected as inputs; xx is the value of x for the memory unit with the smallest number of address inputs. As for the previous design, this circuit is enabled by the appropriate control lines and generates the memory unit selection signals. Each memory unit has to be correctly selected only when an address in the range it covers is output on the address bus.

Example

A memory system for a CPU with a 16-bit address bus consists of two ROMs, each with fourteen address inputs, and five RAMs, each with twelve address inputs. These are to form a continuous block of memory with the ROMs starting at address zero and the RAMs immediately following; the unused addresses are to be left available for future extensions.

The CPU has address lines A_0 to A_{15}, the ROM has an upper address line A_{13} and the RAM upper address line is A_{11}. Hence lines A_0 to A_{11} are connected to all memory units and A_{12} and A_{13} are connected to the A_{12} and A_{13} inputs of both ROMs. A_{12} to A_{15} are inputs to the decode circuit which provides the selection controls and, assuming active low selection

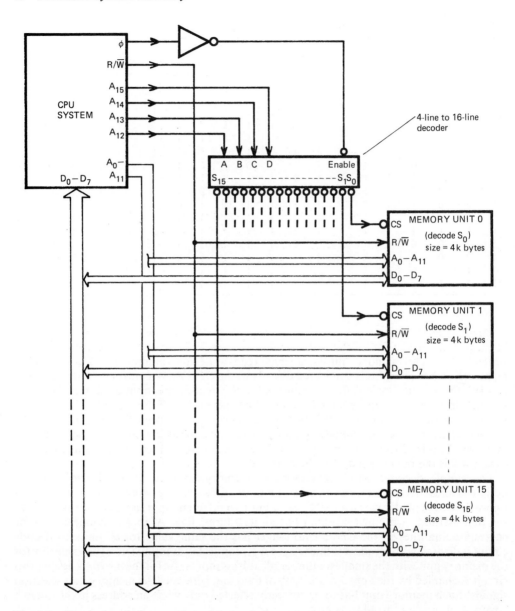

Fig. 4.1   Simple decode for a system with equal size memory units

Address Range   Selection

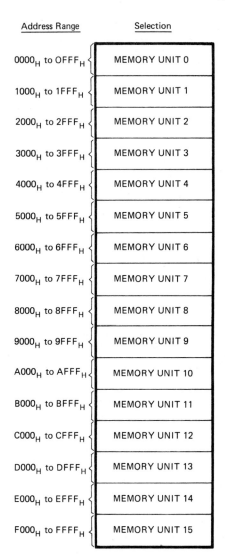

Address Range	Selection
0000_H to $0FFF_H$	MEMORY UNIT 0
1000_H to $1FFF_H$	MEMORY UNIT 1
2000_H to $2FFF_H$	MEMORY UNIT 2
3000_H to $3FFF_H$	MEMORY UNIT 3
4000_H to $4FFF_H$	MEMORY UNIT 4
5000_H to $5FFF_H$	MEMORY UNIT 5
6000_H to $6FFF_H$	MEMORY UNIT 6
7000_H to $7FFF_H$	MEMORY UNIT 7
8000_H to $8FFF_H$	MEMORY UNIT 8
9000_H to $9FFF_H$	MEMORY UNIT 9
$A000_H$ to $AFFF_H$	MEMORY UNIT 10
$B000_H$ to $BFFF_H$	MEMORY UNIT 11
$C000_H$ to $CFFF_H$	MEMORY UNIT 12
$D000_H$ to $DFFF_H$	MEMORY UNIT 13
$E000_H$ to $EFFF_H$	MEMORY UNIT 14
$F000_H$ to $FFFF_H$	MEMORY UNIT 15

Fig. 4.2 Hardware memory map for the system shown in Fig. 4.1

Table 4.3   Truth table for example memory selection

Inputs				Outputs							Device selected
A_{15}	A_{14}	A_{13}	A_{12}	S_0	S_1	S_2	S_3	S_4	S_5	S_6	
0	0	0	0	0	1	1	1	1	1	1	ROM 0 in all four cases
0	0	0	1	0	1	1	1	1	1	1	
0	0	1	0	0	1	1	1	1	1	1	
0	0	1	1	0	1	1	1	1	1	1	
0	1	0	0	1	0	1	1	1	1	1	ROM 1 in all four cases
0	1	0	1	1	0	1	1	1	1	1	
0	1	1	0	1	0	1	1	1	1	1	
0	1	1	1	1	0	1	1	1	1	1	
1	0	0	0	1	1	0	1	1	1	1	RAM 2 (first RAM)
1	0	0	1	1	1	1	0	1	1	1	RAM 3 (second RAM)
1	0	1	0	1	1	1	1	0	1	1	RAM 4 (third RAM)
1	0	1	1	1	1	1	1	1	0	1	RAM 5 (fourth RAM)
1	1	0	0	1	1	1	1	1	1	0	RAM 6 (fifth RAM)
1	1	0	1	1	1	1	1	1	1	1	No device selected
1	1	1	0	1	1	1	1	1	1	1	
1	1	1	1	1	1	1	1	1	1	1	

for all memories, Table 4.3 is the circuit truth table when the enable input to the decoder is active. Figure 4.3 is a diagram of this system with the selection circuit shown as a single block; the memory map is given in Fig 4.4.

From the example it is clear that the selection circuit is a combinational one but is not as simple as a conventional n-line to 2^n-line decoder. For example, the output S_0 is active, unit 0 selected, when four different values are present on the lines A_{12} to A_{15}; for a simple decode circuit an output is only active for one value of address at the inputs. One method of producing this circuit is to use a PROM, a programmable read only memory (Chapter 8), as a combinational circuit. Figure 4.5 illustrates this use for the example with the programming pattern included. The technique of constructing address decoding circuits using PROMs is a useful one for complex memory structures.

Often two sizes of memory unit are used in a system, usually because the most suitable ROM and RAM units for an application are of different sizes. A relatively simple decode circuit can be built in many such cases. The starting point is a conventional n-line to 2^n-line decoder designed as if the memory consists of equal size units all the size of the larger of the two types. This decoder directly supplies the selection inputs to the larger units. The smaller units are grouped together into blocks whose total size equals that of the larger unit (or is less than this if there are not enough smaller units to fill any block). The address lines not connected to the main decoder or to the smaller memory units are input to further separate decoders, one for each group of smaller units. The enable inputs to these second level decoders are driven by unused selection outputs from the first decoder. Figure 4.6 illustrates the previous example re-designed using this two level decode scheme; Fig. 4.4 is again the memory map.

The cascading of decoders may be extended to more than two levels, although care is required to ensure that circuit propagation delays do not cause problems. Such multiple level decoders are often used for memory mapped I–O devices because I–O devices are normally single or small groups of locations. For such small units a large amount of decoding is required and multiple level decodes often achieve this economically. When I–O is not memory mapped a separate I–O decode circuit is required. The design is similar to

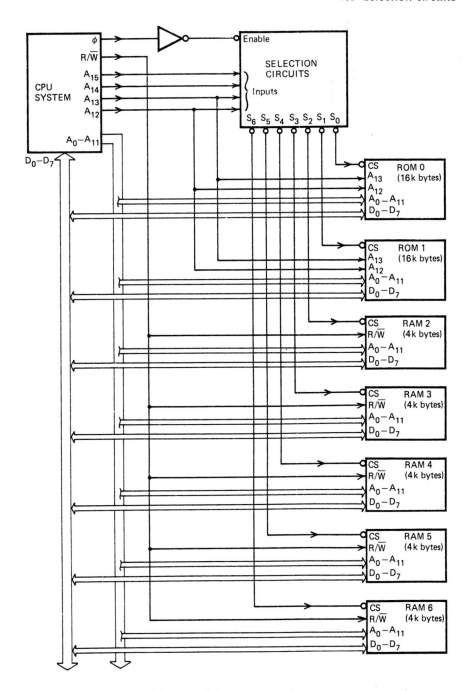

Fig. 4.3 Decode for a system with unequal size memory units

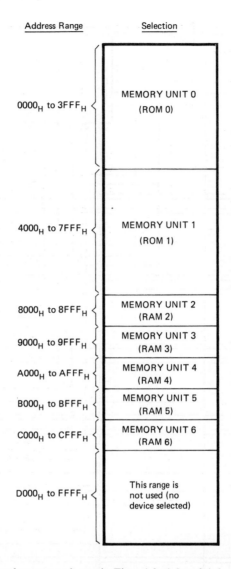

Fig. 4.4 Memory map for the system shown in Figs. 4.3, 4.5 and 4.6

that of memory decode circuits with the I–O decoder enable supplied by AND of $\overline{\text{IN}}$ with $\overline{\text{OUT}}$. (Alternatively separate input and output decode circuits may be used.)

4.2 Bus structures

The bus structures examined so far have differed only in the range of control lines. There are other possible sets of control lines; and bus structures other than three bus ones may be devised.

4.2.1 Control buses

Buses were introduced with four control lines, one for each of the required operations

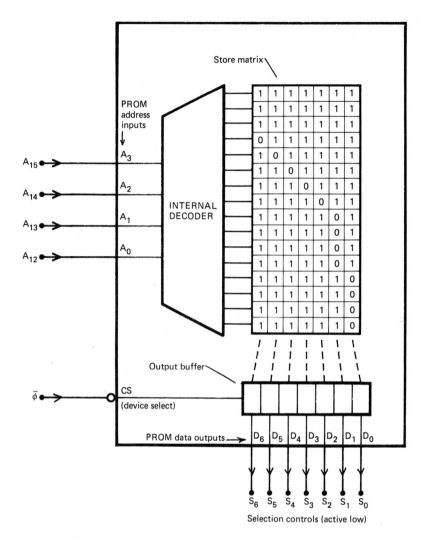

Fig. 4.5 Use of a PROM as a combinational decode circuit

memory read, memory write, input, and output. A wide range of alternative control buses are possible, obviously if I–O is memory mapped only two lines are required. These could be a read–write line (R/$\overline{\text{W}}$ or $\overline{\text{R}}$/W) with a timing control line as for the 6502 and 6800. Alternatively read and write control lines (e.g. $\overline{\text{RD}}$ and $\overline{\text{WR}}$) could be used.

There is some redundancy in the four line control system and it may be reduced to a three line one with no loss in capability. One method is to define memory read and input as both being read actions synchronized by a single read control line. Similarly, memory write and output may both be synchronized by a single write line. The third line indicates whether the particular transfer is an I–O or a memory transfer; one example is the 8085 which has $\overline{\text{RD}}$, $\overline{\text{WR}}$ and IO/$\overline{\text{M}}$ control lines.

In general, control bus designs vary significantly from one CPU manufacturer to another. The basic purposes of the bus remain the same and examination of the specification usually shows how the various transfer operations are controlled.

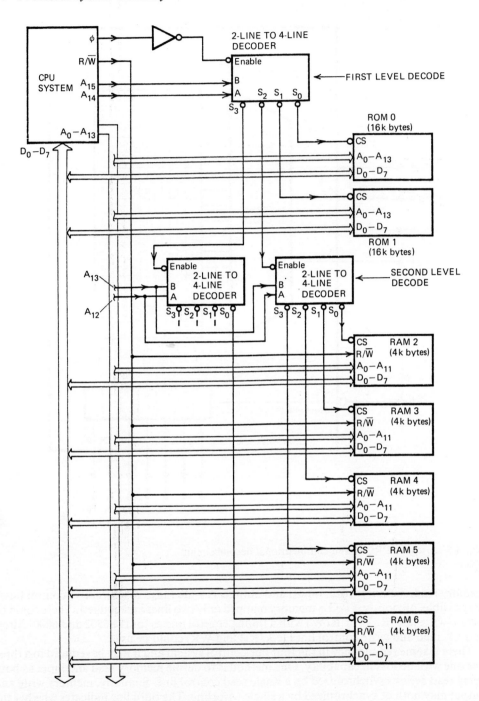

Fig. 4.6   Example of a two level decode system

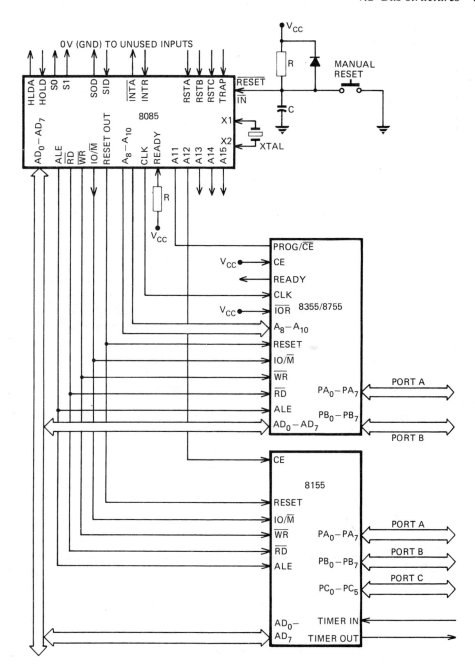

Fig. 4.7 A small 8085 based system

4.2.2 *Multiplexed buses*

When it was introduced, multiplexing was described as a method of sharing one data trans-mission system between several sources and destinations. The simple bus system does this by switching to one connection path and reserving it until the complete transfer is performed. Examination of simple three bus processors shows long periods when the bus system is not in use. One form of multiplexing requires fewer bus lines by using those lines which *are* provided for a greater proportion of time. A common method is **time division multiplexing,** in which the bus is rapidly switched from one task to another. Imple-mentation of time division multiplexing reduces the number of interconnection lines; use of fewer lines lowers the cost of the interconnection system and the cost of assembling inte-grated circuits.

Two different time division multiplexed bus systems are common. The approach adopted by Intel Corporation in many CPU designs (e.g. 8085, 8086, 8088, 8035) is to multiplex the data bus with the lower address lines, i.e. A_0 and D_0 are replaced by a single line AD_0, A_1 and D_1 are replaced by AD_1, and so on to AD_{n-1}. During a memory transfer, the address value A_0 to A_{m-1} is first output using the lines AD_0 to AD_{n-1} and A_n to A_{m-1}. While the AD lines are transmitting address values, an additional control line indicates that this is the function of the AD lines. The extra control may have several names; a common one is **address latch enable, ALE,** as it is often used to enable an external circuit to latch the address informa-tion. After the address has been output, the lines A_n to A_{m-1} continue to output the same address value but the lines AD_0 to AD_{n-1} act as the normal data lines D_0 to D_{n-1}. When systems are built with standard memory and I–O devices this bus has only minor advan-tages; extra latches are required to maintain address values during data transmission. How-ever, very compact systems can be constructed using special memory and I–O components that are directly connected to the bus. Figure 4.7 shows one such system using an 8085 CPU with EPROM, I–O and RAM.

An alternative form of multiplexed bus retains a separate data bus but the lines of the address bus are multiplexed. The number of address lines is halved and the address is output

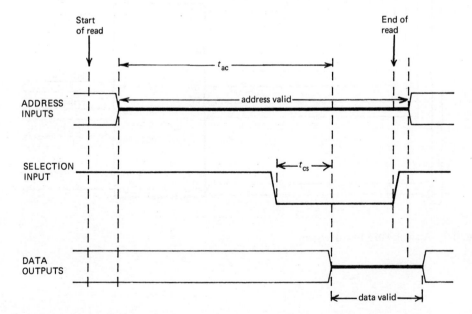

Fig. 4.8 Partial ROM timing specification for a read operation

in two parts in succession; this is compatible with many RAM devices. The only common microprocessor to use address multiplexing is the RCA 1802 family of CPUs. These have only eight address bus lines and the 16-bit address value is output in two stages, the high 8 bits first. The presence of the high or low half of the address is indicated by the state of a control line (TPA, timing pulse A). As in the case of address and data multiplexed bus systems, compact small systems may be constructed using address multiplexing.

4.3 Timing

The actions performed by any component in a processor system must occur at the correct time. Any circuit, no matter how fast, takes a finite time to respond to input signals and all operations within the system must allow for these delays. An essential part of system design is to ensure that all components have compatible timing specifications.

Figure 4.8 is a simplified partial timing specification for a read operation using a particular type of ROM. Figure 4.9 is a similar simplified timing specification for the corresponding memory read operation of a CPU. Examination of system timing will be illustrated using these devices as components of a processor system.

In the read cycle the CPU first outputs the address of the location to be accessed. The lower A_0 to A_{x-1} address lines are connected directly to the ROM, and lines A_x to A_{m-1} are connected to the decode circuit which is enabled by the read timing control signal. After the processor starts a read cycle, it will apply the correct address to the ROM and decoder within a time t_{add} (max). The ROM selection signal is supplied by the decode circuit which has a worst case propagation delay of t_{de} (max). Hence the memory selection signal will be applied to the ROM after the longer of the two decoder response times

$$(t_{add} \text{ (max)} + t_{de} \text{ (max)}) \quad \text{and} \quad (t_{rd} \text{ (max)} + t_{de} \text{ (max)}).$$

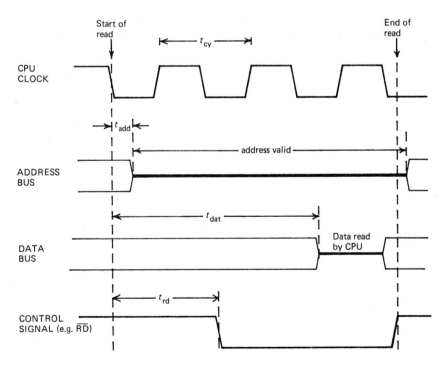

Fig. 4.9 Simplified CPU timing specification for a read operation

The ROM requires its address inputs to be correct at least a time t_{ac} (max) before valid data is required at its outputs. As the data must be available for the CPU within a time t_{dat} (min) from the start of the read operation, the following inequality must hold for reliable I:OM read operations:

$$t_{add} \text{ (max)} + t_{ac} \text{ (max)} < t_{dat} \text{ (min)}$$

Similarly inequalities for the selection input timing give

$$t_{add} \text{ (max)} + t_{de} \text{ (max)} + t_{cs} \text{ (max)} < t_{dat} \text{ (min)}$$

and
$$t_{rd} \text{ (max)} + t_{de} \text{ (max)} + t_{cs} \text{ (max)} < t_{dat} \text{ (min)}$$

These timing relations are the primary limits in this design; it is also necessary to check that the end of operation timing is correct although this rarely causes problems. That is, the memory must continue to output the correct data until it is certain that the CPU will have completed reading the value from the bus; also the memory must return its data outputs to an inactive condition before any subsequent operation requires the data bus.

Timing specifications exist for write, input and output operations as well as for read operations. In general, specifications are more complicated than the description given here; also there are no common standard forms of specification, for example timing parameters are defined in many different ways and by different symbols. However the basic principle, requiring all signals to be available at the correct time, always applies. The limits set by timing specifications may be used either to select particular devices from a range available or to select the processor clock speed. Often an integrated circuit manufacturer supplies a particular device with a choice of speeds, the faster versions being more expensive. Designers usually choose the lowest cost device which will operate as required.

Example

A particular type of ROM is available in three speed versions. Its general behaviour is described by Fig. 4.8 and that of the CPU to be used by Fig. 4.9. The following are the numeric values for the limiting times for all three ROM versions (V1, V2, V3). Determine the slowest version of ROM which may be used if the system clock frequency is to be 6 MHz and the decoder has a propagation delay $t_{de} = 15$ nsec.

		V1	V2	V3
ROM	t_{ac} (max)	350 nsec	250 nsec	150 nsec
ROM	t_{cs} (max)	150 nsec	100 nsec	100 nsec

CPU	t_{add} (max)	=	50 nsec
CPU	t_{dat} (min)	=	$(10 + 2 \times t_{cy})$ nsec
CPU	t_{rd} (max)	=	$(40 + t_{cy})$ nsec

t_{cy} is the period of the system clock in nanoseconds, that is 167 nsec for the specified clock frequency.

Using the inequalities developed gives

$$50 + t_{ac} \text{ (max)} \qquad < \quad 10 + 334$$
$$50 + 15 + t_{cs} \text{ (max)} \qquad < \quad 10 + 334$$
$$40 + 167 + 15 + t_{cs} \text{ (max)} \quad < \quad 10 + 334$$

Rearranging produces t_{ac} (max) < 294 nsec for the first, t_{cs} (max) < 279 nsec for the second and t_{cs} (max) < 122 nsec for the third. The third requirement is less easily met than the second and overrides it, the ROM selected must have t_{ac} (max) < 294 nsec and t_{cs} (max) < 122 nsec. This requirement is not met by version V1, but is met by V2 which is the slowest specification device which may be used for this application.

An alternative approach occurs when the processor clock frequency may be varied to suit specified or available memory and I-O components. Many of the processor timings include the clock period, t_{cy}, and it is usually possible to satisfy the inequalities by selection of the clock frequency.

Example

A particular ROM and CPU whose timings are described by Figs 4.8 and 4.9 have the following numeric values for the limiting parameters.

ROM	CPU
t_{ac} (max) = 400 nsec	t_{add} (max) = 50 nsec
t_{cs} (max) = 150 nsec	t_{dat} (min) = $(20 + 2 \times t_{cy})$ nsec
	t_{rd} (max) = $(50 + t_{cy})$ nsec

where t_{cy} is the period of the system clock. If the propagation delay of the decoder is t_{de} (max) = 20 nsec, determine the maximum clock frequency that may be used.
   Using the inequalities as previously gives

$$50 + 400 \qquad\qquad < \; 20 + 2 \times t_{cy}$$
$$50 + 20 + 150 \qquad < \; 20 + 2 \times t_{cy}$$
$$50 + t_{cy} + 20 + 150 < \; 20 + 2 \times t_{cy}$$

Rearranging gives $t_{cy} > 215$ nsec for the first, $t_{cy} > 100$ nsec for the second, and $t_{cy} > 200$ nsec for the third. Obviously the greatest must be taken, requiring $t_{cy} > 215$ nsec, that is the maxmum clock frequency is 4.65 MHz.

The particular inequalities developed only apply to devices behaving as specified by Figs 4.8 and 4.9, but similar inequalities may be developed for any devices on any bus system and for all operations (read, write, input, output). For any design of a processor system timing calculations are required; these must ensure correct operation for any components meeting manufacturer's specifications, not just for individually selected devices. That is, every system built should run without timing problems.

4.4   Alternative decoding schemes

Decoding schemes described so far involve a **complete decode**. That is, each address uniquely selects a single memory location, and conversely a specific memory location can only selected by a single value of address output by the CPU. Within these limits, no account is taken as to the actual presence or absence of a memory device at any location. For any large or general purpose system a complete decode must be used. However, in many microprocessor applications the processor system is built with much less than the maximum possible memory; it will never be extended to maximum size and is intended to operate with fixed software (usually firmware). In such cases various forms of **incomplete decode** may be used, provided that the possible problems are understood and avoided.
   In Section 4.1 decoding circuits for memory systems with blocks of different sizes were shown to be more complicated than those for systems with equal size memory units. A simple incomplete decode for a small memory system may be built by regarding all memory units as being of the same size, 2^x words, equal to or greater than the size of the largest unit. For a system with m address lines, a standard $(m-x)$-line to 2^{m-x}-line decoder will provide 2^{m-x} outputs; these outputs are connected to the selection inputs of the memory units. The circuit is essentially the same as that in Fig. 4.1 except that some of the memory units have fewer than x address inputs. Figure 4.10 shows such a system built with one ROM having

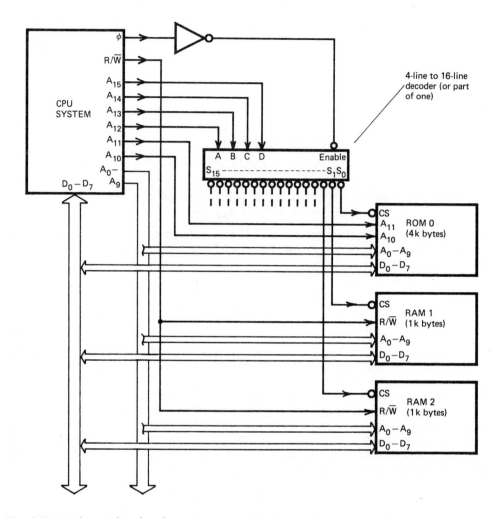

Fig. 4.10 An incomplete decode system

twelve address inputs and two RAMs each with ten address inputs. The memory map, Fig. 4.11, and its equivalent table, Table 4.4, for this circuit both show a peculiar feature of this design. Each RAM unit appears several times in the map, therefore an access to an address such as $12B3_H$ is to exactly the same real memory device as an access to addresses $16B3_H$, $1AB3_H$ and $1EB3_H$.

This multiple appearance of one memory device at several locations is sometimes called **fold-back** and imposes strict limits on programming. The usual technique is to consider the memory to be present at the lowest of the address positions at which it appears and never to access it at any of the other possible addresses. The memory is no longer one continuous block, there are gaps between the various units. In very small systems this technique may be extended even further, because it is not always necessary to connect the highest position address lines to any of the decode circuits. In the circuit of Fig. 4.10, the top two address lines, A_{14} and A_{15}, could be left unused and the 4-line to 16-line decoder replaced by a more simple 2-line to 4-line one. The reader is left to determine the effect this has on the memory map.

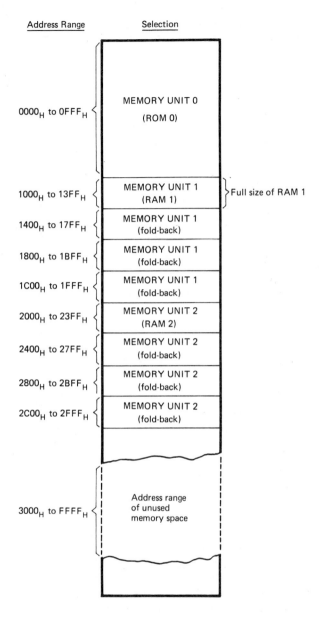

Fig. 4.11 Memory map for the system shown in Fig. 4.10

Table 4.4   Address decoding for simple incomplete decode

A_{15}	A_{14}	A_{13}	A_{12}	A_{11}	A_{10}	D	C	B	A	S_0	S_1	S_2	Device selected
0	0	0	0	0	0	0	0	0	0	0	1	1	
0	0	0	0	0	1	0	0	0	0	0	1	1	A separate quarter of
0	0	0	0	1	0	0	0	0	0	0	1	1	ROM 0 in each case
0	0	0	0	1	1	0	0	0	0	0	1	1	
0	0	0	1	0	0	0	0	0	1	1	0	1	All RAM 1 (first RAM)
0	0	0	1	0	1	0	0	0	1	1	0	1	All RAM 1 again
0	0	0	1	1	0	0	0	0	1	1	0	1	All RAM 1 again
0	0	0	1	1	1	0	0	0	1	1	0	1	All RAM 1 again
0	0	1	0	0	0	0	0	1	0	1	1	0	All RAM 2 (second RAM)
0	0	1	0	0	1	0	0	1	0	1	1	0	All RAM 2 again
0	0	1	0	1	0	0	0	1	0	1	1	0	All RAM 2 again
0	0	1	0	1	1	0	0	1	0	1	1	0	All RAM 2 again
0	0	1	1	X	X	0	0	1	1	1	1	1	
0	1	X	X	X	X	0	1	X	X	1	1	1	All cases unused
1	0	X	X	X	X	1	0	X	X	1	1	1	
1	1	X	X	X	X	1	1	X	X	1	1	1	

A second form of incomplete decode commonly used is a **linear decode**. This decode technique is most successful when the required memory devices are available with a choice of active low and active high selection inputs. Even when only one form of selection input is available, the scheme may be implemented using inverters to provide the opposite sense selection. As with other schemes, low address lines are connected to all memory units; these are assumed to be the same size. The remaining, high, address lines are used directly as the selection inputs to the memory units, one address line per memory unit. Figure 4.12 is an example of one linear decode for a system with five memory units, each with eleven address inputs. The effect of this decode is illustrated by Table 4.5, which is used instead of a memory map to emphasize the rather complex behaviour. The important feature to note is that two or more memory units may be selected simultaneously. This is not important during a write operation, although the programmer must be aware that it occurs, but during a read operation two devices will simultaneously output to the data bus. The minimum effect will be unpredictable, and damage to the devices is probable. Consequently the programmer must be fully aware of the effects of the decode and avoid the multiple selection areas. Another feature of this decode is that it greatly reduces the amount of memory that may be used. If x address lines are connected in parallel to memory units, leaving $m - x$ lines for decoder inputs, then only $m - x$ units may be connected by a linear decode, whereas 2^{m-x} may be connected by a complete decode.

Many incomplete decode schemes are possible; further, two or more schemes may be combined within a design and memory maps can be extremely complex. It is essential that programmers have a full knowledge of any incomplete decode adopted and its effects. In design care must be taken to ensure correct power on behaviour, that is there must be a single ROM holding the start-up program at the specified CPU start address.

In most descriptions of complete and incomplete decodes it has been assumed that each memory device has a single selection input, usually an active low chip select, $\overline{CS}$. Examination of specifications for available memory and I-O devices shows that this is common, but some devices have different selection controls. There are devices which have more than one selection input; also various names such as **chip enable, CE,** and **output enable, OE,** are used in addition to chip select with both active low and active high forms possible. While there are reasons for the different names, these are only relevant in more advanced con-

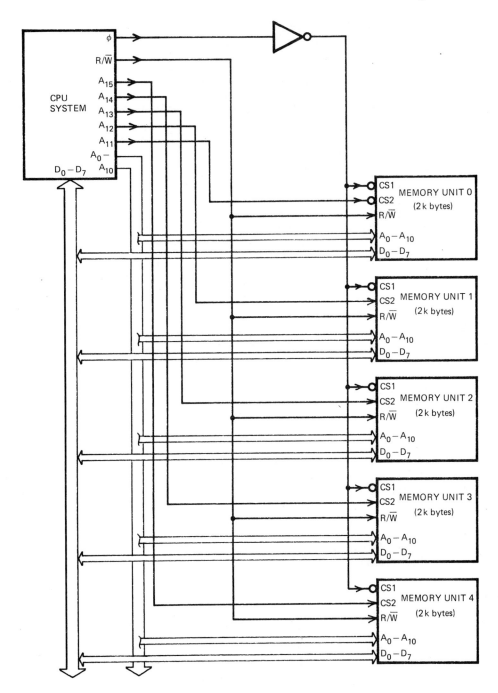

Fig. 4.12 A linear decode system

Table 4.5   Linear address decode

A_{15}	A_{14}	A_{13}	A_{12}	A_{11}	Device selected
\multicolumn{5}{c	}{CPU outputs}	

A_{15}	A_{14}	A_{13}	A_{12}	A_{11}	Device selected
0	0	0	0	0	Memory unit 0 (first)
0	0	0	0	1	No memory selected
0	0	0	1	0	Both memory units; 0 and 1 (hazard)
0	0	0	1	1	Memory unit 1
0	0	1	0	0	Both memory units; 0 and 2 (hazard)
0	0	1	0	1	Memory unit 2
0	0	1	1	0	Three memory units; 0, 1 and 2 (hazard)
0	0	1	1	1	Both memory units; 1 and 2 (hazard)
0	1	0	0	0	Both memory units; 0 and 3 (hazard)
0	1	0	0	1	Memory unit 3
0	1	0	1	0	Three memory units; 0, 1 and 3 (hazard)
0	1	0	1	1	Both memory units; 1 and 3 (hazard)
0	1	1	0	0	Three memory units; 0, 2 and 3 (hazard)
0	1	1	0	1	Both memory units; 2 and 3
0	1	1	1	0	Four memory units; 0, 1, 2 and 3 (hazard)
0	1	1	1	1	Three memory units; 1, 2 and 3
1	0	0	0	0	Both memory units; 0 and 4 (hazard)
1	0	0	0	1	Memory unit 4
1	0	0	1	0	Three memory units; 0, 1 and 4 (hazard)
1	0	0	1	1	Both memory units; 1 and 4 (hazard)
1	0	1	0	0	Three memory units; 0, 2 and 4 (hazard)
1	0	1	0	1	Both memory units; 2 and 4 (hazard)
1	0	1	1	0	Four memory units; 0, 1, 2, and 4 (hazard)
1	0	1	1	1	Three memory units; 1, 2 and 4 (hazard)
1	1	0	0	0	Three memory units; 0, 1 and 4 (hazard)
1	1	0	0	1	Two memory units; 3 and 4 (hazard)
1	1	0	1	0	Four memory units; 0, 1, 3, and 4 (hazard)
1	1	0	1	1	Three memory units; 1, 3 and 4 (hazard)
1	1	1	0	0	Four memory units; 0, 2, 3 and 4 (hazard)
1	1	1	0	1	Three memory units; 2, 3 and 4 (hazard)
1	1	1	1	0	Five memory units; 0, 1, 2, 3 and 4 (hazard)
1	1	1	1	1	Four memory units; 1, 2, 3 and 4 (hazard)

siderations of design. Devices with two or more selection inputs allow simplified decoding circuits to be used in some situations.

4.5 Loading

So far, descriptions of system assemblies have ignored the electrical drive capabilities and requirements of processor components. Any electronic circuit is only capable of providing a finite output current while retaining the logic levels at the outputs within specified limits. When using a bus system, the number of circuit elements connected to an output may become very large. It is necessary to check that outputs are capable of driving all inputs connected to them; even when it is not selected, a memory or I–O device appears as a load on the address and data buses.

It is normally assumed that the definitions of the voltages corresponding to logic 0 and 1 of any CPU, memory, I–O, or interface components are all compatible. This is usually the case but the parameters defining these levels must be checked. If components do not have compatible levels alternatives must be selected or level changing circuits incorporated.

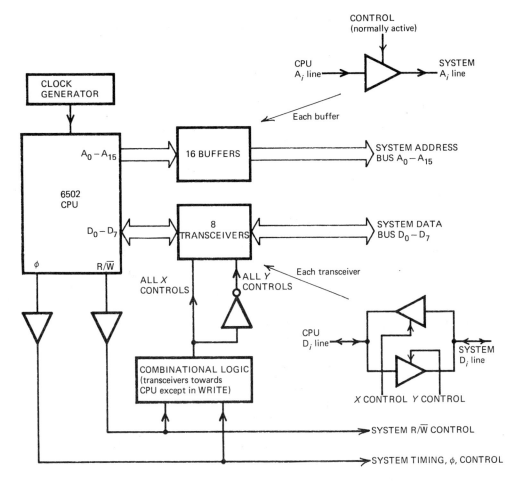

Fig. 4.13 Bus buffering for a 6502 based system

For small systems a check of component specifications usually shows that most designs operate within the allowed device loading limits. Larger systems often do not, in such cases, it is necessary to add buffering circuits. As the address bus is uni-directional, simple non-inverting logic buffers are usually adequate; they are chosen to be tri-state devices so that complex systems that have not been described yet may be built. The data bus is bi-directional and requires a bi-directional buffer, often called a **transceiver**, with the direction control of the transceiver operated by the CPU control lines. Figure 4.13 shows a simple buffer system for an 8-bit CPU; this example is drawn for a 6502, it is easily adapted to most 8-bit processor systems.

This system is only suitable for moderate size processor systems; during a memory read or an input operation, the memory or input device has to drive the data bus with all other memory and I-O devices connected. In large memory systems the individual memory devices are incapable of driving the whole memory and even the CPU buffers will probably be overloaded. The memory is divided into sections, or modules, each of which is fully buffered for connection to the bus so that the module appears as a single large memory unit as outlined in Fig. 4.14. Propagation delays in all buffer, control and decoding circuits must be included when determining circuit timing.

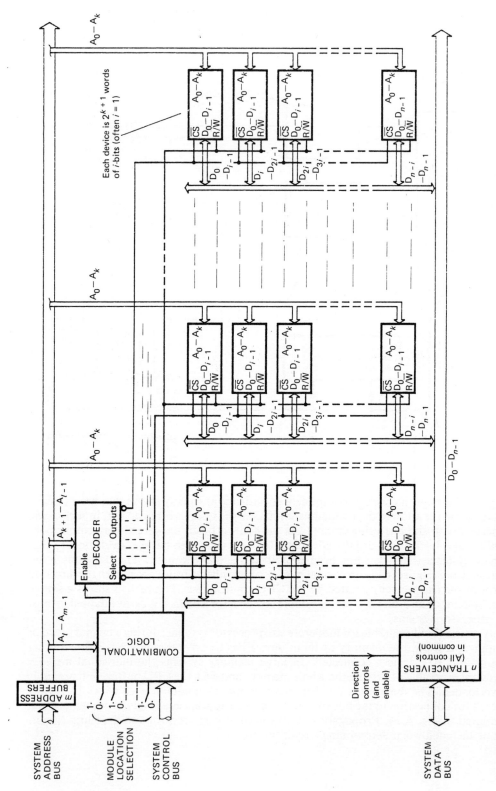

Fig. 4.14   Organisation of a memory module unit for large systems

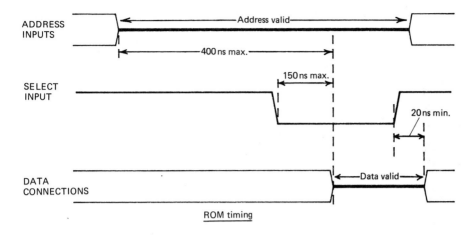

ROM timing

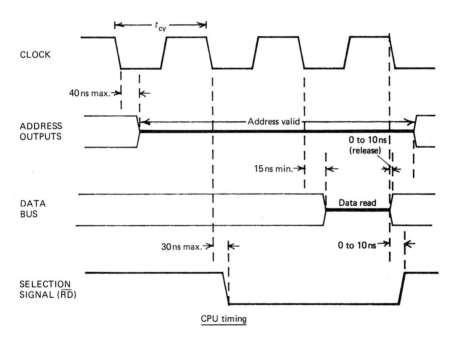

CPU timing

Fig. 4.15 Component timing specifications

4.6 System design

As with most design problems it is impossible to give a single set of design rules. Assuming that the types of CPU, memory, and I-O devices have been specified then system design requires the following.

a) Choice and design of the decode system if this is not restricted to a complete decode.

b) Checks that all component timings are within specification, and adjusting the clock frequency or component selection if they are not.

c)   Ensuring that no devices are operating outside their electrical loading specifications for voltage or current, and providing adequate buffer circuits when necessary.

If the designer has to select CPU, memory and I–O components then design becomes a very complex task. Some examples of particular designs are outlined in Chapter 15.

4.7   Problems

1 Design a complete decode system (to simplify design neglect read and write controls) for a memory system connected to a 16-bit address bus. The system has three ROMs, each of 4k words; five RAMs, each of 1k words; and a memory mapped I–O unit which behaves as an eight word RAM.

Give the memory map for your design.

2 Repeat Problem 1 using some form of incomplete decode to reduce the complexity of the decode circuit; give the revised memory map.

3 A simple *three-chip* system consists of a CPU, a ROM, and a RAM connected in a simple linear decode. Figure 4.15 shows the CPU and ROM timings for a memory read cycle. How fast can the CPU clock be run without risk of timing problems when reading from the ROM? (Assuming no upper limit to the CPU clock frequency unless worst case delay timings make a complete read cycle impossible.)

A single wait state, T* (an extra clock cycle), may be inserted every CPU read operation between the second and third clock cycles (i.e. after $\overline{RD}$ goes low). How fast can the CPU clock be run with this state included? Does this lead to a higher or lower possible maximum overall system speed?

4 Figure 4.7 is the manufacturer's suggestion for a minimum 8085 system using one ROM and one RAM with the CPU. (These are special devices which can use the multiplexed bus and as well as memory incorporate I–O sections.) Ignoring the I–O, the ROM is 2k words and the RAM is 256 words. Derive the memory map for this arrangement and comment on its form.

Part 2
Central Processing Units (CPUs)

5 Control units and control sequences

The control units of the processors described so far adopt a relatively simple implementation of the structure outlined by von Neumann in 1946. There are many methods of achieving this behaviour and many ways to modify the basic scheme to improve performance.

Every action in a processor system is synchronized to the clock within the control unit. The simple control loop can be expanded to the form in Fig. 5.1, which shows each differ-

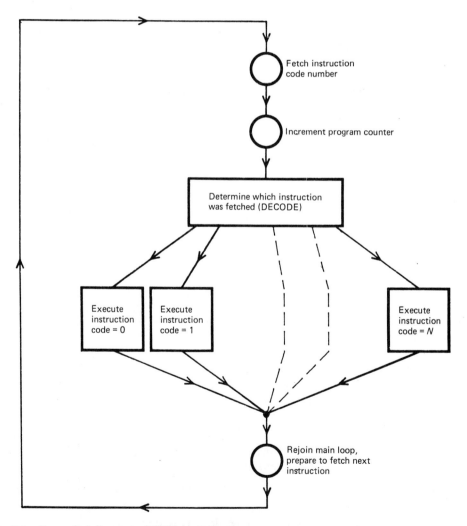

Fig. 5.1 Expanded diagram of CPU operating sequence

ent instruction as one branch of many parallel branches. When instruction execution requires several steps, the single step shown in a branch is replaced by the required number of steps. Direct design of a sequential control circuit to implement all these parallel branches using conventional techniques leads to a very complex circuit. Despite this difficulty most CPU control circuits were designed with this form until the mid-1960s, and the technique is still used in a few designs because it produces the fastest possible circuits using a specific type of circuit element. However, the design process is difficult and the resulting circuit is complicated; hence it is expensive to build, test and service. The control circuits of most modern processors are based on a design technique known as **microprogramming**, first proposed by M. V. Wilkes (1951).

5.1 Microprogrammed control

If each instruction in an instruction set is broken down into simple elementary steps, then examination of all the steps of all instructions for any particular CPU shows that in most designs there are very few different steps. Instructions differ mainly in the position to which multiplexers are set and in the order of performing steps. For example, the steps required in instructions for a simple 8-bit processor with the form *load A with the contents of address* $xxxx_H$ and *store contents of A at memory address* $xxxx_H$ are shown in Fig. 5.2. With the exception of setting transfer directions, the operations involved are nearly all the same ones with only their order differing.

A large proportion of CPU designs utilize this sequence of small steps by having a microprogrammed control unit. In such a unit each small step becomes a **microinstruction** and each microinstruction may be described by its own **microcode number**. The execution of any CPU instruction consists of executing a sequence of microinstructions which are in the form of a **microprogram**; a different microprogram is provided for each full machine code instruction. After an instruction operation code has been brought into the instruction register, the decoding process is essentially only the determination of the address of the microprogram for that instruction. The microprograms are held in a special ROM that is part of the CPU itself. There is a program within a program structure, almost a recursive design. Microprogrammed designs have several advantages, although some apply only to CPUs built of separate components and not to single circuit microprocessors.

a) The design of the instruction decode and execute units is more simple, and the resulting circuits are less complex, than those required if other design techniques are used.

b) By switching microprogram ROMs, one CPU may be made to emulate (imitate and execute instructions coded for) another. This is useful with large computers when an old machine is being replaced, existing programs can be made to run immediately without change on the new system. If part of the microprogram store is RAM the system is even more versatile.

c) It is possible to devise systems where the user may add special instructions for a particular application. This is useful when a processor is dedicated to some special task requiring frequent rapid execution of unique operations. Such a requirement is common when the processor is being incorporated as a control unit in an item such as an automatic machine tool.

d) Many design errors can be corrected, or improvements made late in the development of a CPU, without extensive circuit modifications.

e) Diagnostic tests to find problems during design and in service are more easily established.

The main disadvantage of microprogrammed designs is that using a particular type of

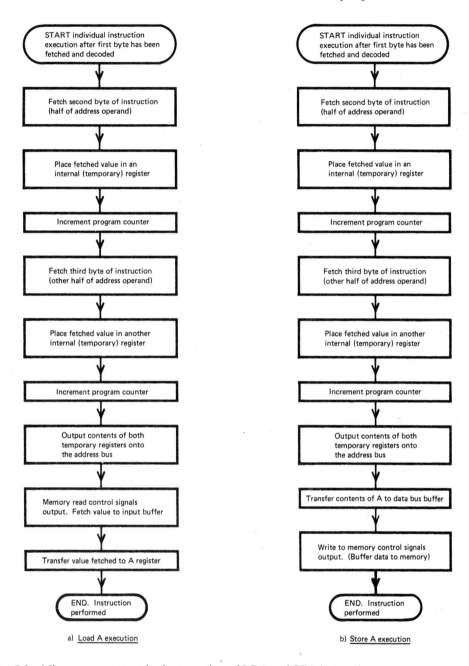

Fig. 5.2 Microprogram steps in the execution of LDA and STA instructions

component they tend to run more slowly than well designed systems which are not microprogrammed.

Most CPUs combine microprogrammed control with some fixed control circuits. For example, the microprogrammed section does not begin to operate until the instruction has been fetched and decoded. As all instructions have to be fetched and decoded, this is a task for which efficient dedicated circuits are used. Another way in which the microprogrammed form may be slightly changed is by using only part of the instruction code to identify the microprogram for an instruction. A small, not necessarily fixed, number of bits are retained for other purposes; this allows certain sections of the CPU to be controlled so that they act in one of several different ways while running one particular microprogram.

A typical example is the use of one bit in instruction codes to select some feature of an operand; a single microprogram can then be used for two similar tasks. For example many instruction codes for the 8086 CPU, a 16-bit processor, include a bit denoted by w. Although the CPU has a 16-bit word length, execution is often faster if only 8 bits are moved from one point to another when there is no requirement to use 16 bits. The 8086 move immediate instruction has the code form

$$1011wccc \qquad \text{data byte 1} \qquad \text{data byte 2}$$

Here ccc is a code specifying the register to receive the data and w is the word or byte control. If $w = 1$ then 16 bits of data are required and the instruction is 24 bits long; if $w = 0$ then only 8 bits of data are required and the instruction is only 16 bits. This saves time in instruction fetch and internal CPU transfers, provides flexibility for the programmer, and saves space in memory.

Control sections of CPUs can be very complex in order to produce fast and versatile systems. However, close examination will show that many modern designs include some degree of microprogrammed control.

5.2   Control loop modifications

Processor operation has been described in terms of a repeated fetch, decode and execute loop. Facilities are usually provided to modify this behaviour, and most of the lines in typical control buses which have been ignored so far are concerned with such modifications. One essential feature is a start-up mechanism to enter the control loop correctly and put the system into a known condition when power is turned on, or when the user wishes to reset the

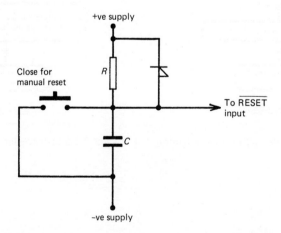

Fig. 5.3   Typical combined power-on and manual reset circuit

system. In most cases the reset mechanism operates when a specified logic level is applied to the RESET input of the CPU. A common choice is an active low control; with this input a simple RC circuit and a switch will provide both power-on reset and a user reset control as illustrated in Fig. 5.3. Generally a reset performs very few actions; usually the program counter is forced to some specific value and one or two internal control bistables are put into a known condition. All other internal CPU registers and flags will be in unknown conditions (few CPU designs clear registers and flags during reset) and the programmer must set known conditions after any reset. At power-on any RAM and other bistable devices in a processor system will be in random conditions; however, a user reset only affects the CPU and will not change the states of other components.

In addition to the reset, there are three common types of control input which modify the basic control loop. One type slows down the system, a second introduces distinct pauses to allow some other circuits to perform some task, and the third type allows an external event to initiate complete breaks in program sequence. Figure 5.4 shows a simplified state diagram for an 8080 CPU when none of these features are included. This diagram specifies a simple sequential circuit which is easily designed; however, when all the additional features are included the diagram becomes that in Fig. 5.5 which is much more complex.

Microprocessors in particular are provided with a mechanism allowing their actions when accessing memory or I-O devices to be slowed by applying signals to a control input. The CPU designer, particularly the designer of an integrated circuit CPU, has little control over

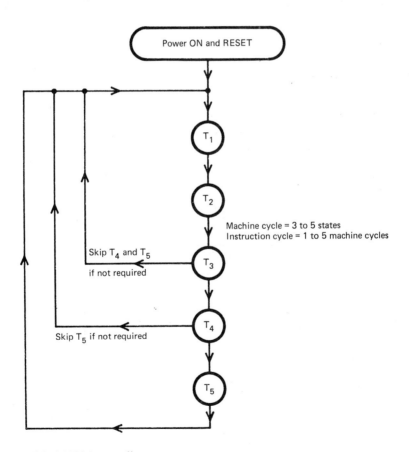

Fig. 5.4 Simplified 8080A state diagram

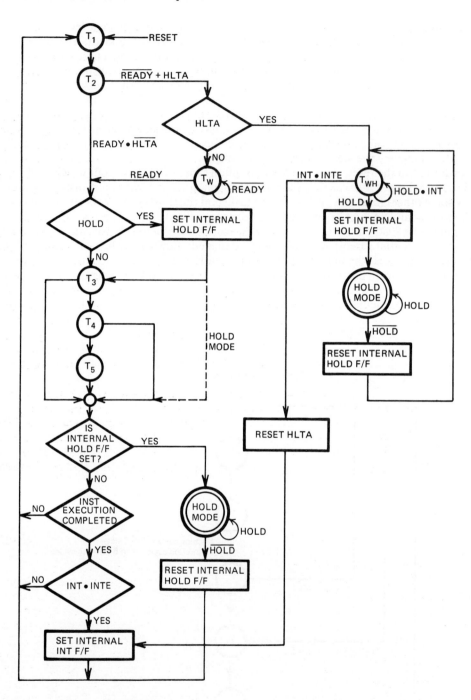

Fig. 5.5   Full 8080A state diagram

the memory used. In many cases the CPU can perform memory access operations faster than the memory devices which a user may wish to incorporate in a system. For example EPROMs (Chapter 8) are slower than many RAM devices but have many useful features: a system designer may mix EPROMs and RAM while requiring the system to operate as quickly as possible. In such cases the access time must vary according to the memory device, and hence the address, being used for an operation.

Whenever the CPU accesses a memory location, the operation is output the address, set the data bus correctly, then output the control signal. Each step in the sequence usually corresponds to one period of the clock, and a simple method of slowing down the system is to insert an extra clock cycle, a WAIT state, in the sequence. During the wait state the CPU does nothing except maintain conditions on the bus system constant. This extra clock cycle is usually inserted by a signal into the CPU on an additional control line; timing synchronization may necessitate the use of additional circuits.

The facility to provide a distinct, usually relatively short, pause in the execution of a running program is necessary if more than one device is to have the ability to output to the address and control buses. There are many reasons for requiring such actions; in principle these consist of more than one CPU sharing part or all of the memory and I-O system. A general purpose CPU is very versatile, but there are many functions which it does not perform efficiently. Improvements may be made by fitting additional special purpose CPUs to the system. Such CPUs are capable of only a limited range of actions but perform these actions efficiently. When a program reaches a point requiring an action by the extra CPU, the main CPU must release the bus system and pause while the second CPU performs the required action. Many special extra processors exist; the most simple are **direct memory access (DMA)** controllers, while others perform complicated numeric operations or handle elaborate input and output systems.

The third form of control modification arises when some external event occurs requiring a response by the processor, regardless of the time of the event relative to the current position in the program. To react to an event at any time requires an input signal to the CPU which causes it to break off its current sequence of actions and commence operations relevant to the input. The input for such a signal is an **interrupt input**; these inputs are provided in most CPU designs, and processor systems without interrupt capability are of limited power.

5.3 Interrupts

When external inputs are supplied to a processor system several situations arise. Some inputs are always available; for example, the outputs from measuring devices indicating quantities such as position, voltage, temperature, etc. can usually be read by a running program at any point where the present value is required. Alternatively occasional inputs, typically out of range switches, alarms in equipment controlled by a processor, a user pressing a key, will exist only when these events occur; in most cases a rapid response is required. Either the running program must frequently examine such inputs, or a mechanism must be available which enables the processor to respond to the external event.

If the inputs are obtained only when the processor executes an input instruction, these inputs are under **program control**. The alternative mechanism requires an additional CPU control input which causes the CPU to stop its present action, examine the input and perform any operations necessary; this input is an interrupt input. Inputs connected to a processor through an interrupt mechanism are handled under **interrupt control**.

Interrupts create many problems in processor system operation and should only be used when program control cannot be implemented or is difficult to implement. There are no absolute rules, but the common reasons for requiring interrupts are to obtain fast response to an external event or to handle very rare events. When an input requiring a response is supplied to a processor system, an important feature is the **latency**. Latency is the maximum possible time that could elapse between the input occurring and the processor responding. Under program control, latency can be very long because it is the maximum time interval between two executions of the instruction examining the particular input. This depends upon the frequency the programmer has chosen to include such instructions but, if the system is to perform any useful task, there will probably be over twenty instructions between successive input instructions; indeed higher values are more realistic. When interrupt control is used, a much faster response, that is a shorter latency, is possible although the response is not immediate.

The CPU must respond quickly to an interrupt, but in most cases it should be possible to restore the system to the condition which existed before the interrupt. This allows the CPU to continue with the task that was interrupted without error when this is necessary. To satisfy this requirement the CPU must be able to store its current status and, as it would be difficult to store the status when an instruction is partially completed, the instruction in progress must be fully executed. The latency will be the length of time taken to execute the slowest instruction; this is the value usually given in the specification for a CPU. The real latency is somewhat longer, because the system will have to execute several instructions to react as required.

When there are several sources of interrupt, the CPU must be able to identify the source which caused the interrupt. A further useful feature for an interrupt system is a mechanism allowing a programmer to protect an area of program from interrupts, that is to switch the interrupt system on and off.

Interrupt systems vary from one CPU to another; the form used in the 8080 is described because it is powerful, meets most requirements, yet is relatively simple. The CPU has a single interrupt input, INT; an associated output, $\overline{\text{INTA}}$; and there is an internal flip-flop whose state determines acceptance or non-acceptance of interrupt request signals. Control of the flip-flop within a program is by executing enable interrupt, EI, and disable interrupt, DI, instructions. At power-on, or reset, the flip-flop is forced into the disabled condition to allow programmers to set up the stack, important variables, etc., before any interrupt is accepted. Once the system is running normally an EI instruction may be executed, and subsequently whenever the interrupt input is held at logic 1 the program will be interrupted after completion of the instruction in progress. It is necessary to hold the interrupt input at 1 because it is only examined during the last clock period in the execution of an instruction.

The CPU responds to the interrupt by performing a special instruction fetch. This is the same as a normal instruction fetch except that the timing signal is supplied by the control line $\overline{\text{INTA}}$ instead of $\overline{\text{RD}}$, the program counter is *not* incremented, and no useful value appears on the address bus. The device which generated the interrupt signal must force an instruction code onto the data bus when $\overline{\text{INTA}}$ is low. Any instruction may be supplied and multiple byte instructions will be given the correct number of $\overline{\text{INTA}}$ signals. In general, only a branch instruction, usually a subroutine call, will be of use. To simplify the circuits required, the 8080 has a special one byte call instruction, RST n (RESTART n, where n is any value from 0 to 7). This may be used within programs but is primarily provided for interrupt use. The code is $11NNN111_2$, where NNN is the binary equivalent of n. This one byte instruction behaves exactly as the three byte subroutine call instruction except that the branch address is $0000000000NNN000_2$, it is a call to one of eight specific locations.

When an interrupt is accepted the CPU disables further interrupts. Figure 5.6 illustrates a typical single interrupt connection to an 8080; note that the interrupt input must be maintained by a latch if it may be of short duration. Figure 5.7 outlines typical software required to handle such an interrupt. The processor must complete the current instruction, perform the RST 7 instruction and then several others before it begins to execute the actions required to deal with the interrupt. The real system latency is greater than that given in the CPU

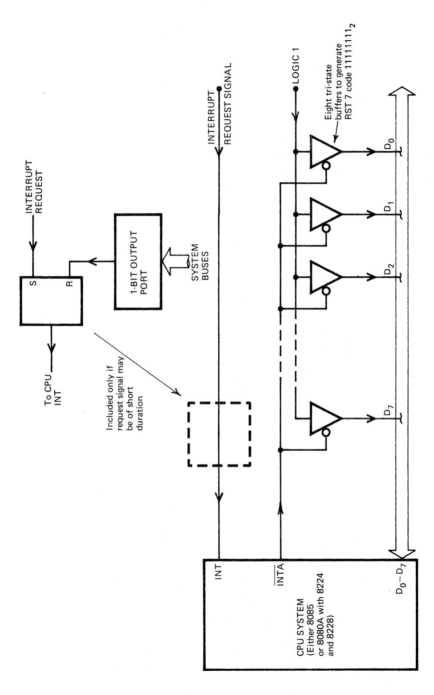

Fig. 5.6 Single interrupt connection to an 8080 CPU

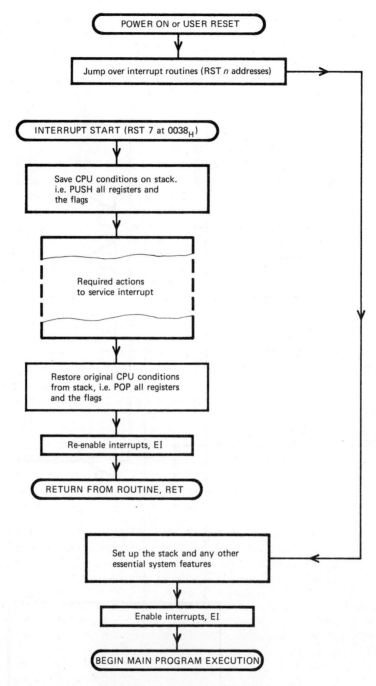

Fig. 5.7 Software outline for an 8080 system with a single interrupt

specification. Before returning to the interrupted program the cause of the interrupt must be removed; if it is not, the processor will be interrupted again as soon as the enable interrupt instruction is executed. The system could be trapped in a loop continually executing the interrupt actions. Often the responses to an interrupt will clear the signal; for example, if a limit of travel switch on a machine controlled by the processor causes the interrupt, then the service subroutine would probably reverse the process which caused the switch to operate. In other cases, such as a user pressing a key, the service routine will probably loop until the signal has gone (key release) before executing the return. However, a deliberate clearing action is sometimes necessary; one case is when a short interrupt signal is maintained by a latch, the latch must be cleared before interrupts are re-enabled.

The 8080 interrupt system is easily extended to several (seven or eight) sources with a simple combinational encoding circuit. This circuit produces a 3-bit code indicating which interrupt input is active; additionally an OR function in the encoder provides an output when any interrupt is active. The encoding function is often required, not only for interrupt systems, and several integrated circuit forms are available (e.g. type 74LS148). The 3-bit code becomes the value n in the RST n instruction code supplied by the interrupt circuits, as illustrated in Fig. 5.8. This circuit implements a **vectored interrupt**; when interrupted, the processor branches to an address related to the cause of the interrupt. The interrupt route is directed, that is vectored, by the hardware. In processor systems which have a single interrupt receipt of a signal simply causes a branch to a predetermined address. It is necessary to connect all the signals to the CPU interrupt input with an OR function. When responding to an interrupt, the service routine must first examine all possible interrupts to determine which was responsible for the interrupt request.

Note that the 8080 system RST 0 address is 0000_H, the same as RESET. Except that registers and flags do not change RST 0 behaves as a reset, and this restricts the use of the RST 0 position of the interrupt vector. In addition, vector addresses are only eight locations apart; usually simple JUMP or CALL instructions are placed at these addresses to redirect to locations with more space available.

If a system has several interrupts, there is a possibility that two or more will occur simultaneously. To the processor *simultaneously* means within the latency period. In Fig. 5.8 the encoder is a combinational logic circuit, and its design requires consideration of the 3-bit output to be produced when two or more inputs occur simultaneously. The most simple case is to rank the inputs in some order of importance and output the code for the one of highest order (priority). The encoder becomes a priority encoder and the interrupt system is a **vectored priority interrupt** system.

Priority interrupt systems are relatively easy to implement, but several decisions are still required. For example, in Fig. 5.7 interrupts are re-enabled just before exit from the service routine. When there are several interrupt sources it may be necessary for the service routine for one interrupt to be itself interrupted by some other source. This requires the enable interrupt, EI, instruction to be placed at an early point in the service routine. A more complex arrangement would only allow a higher priority interrupt to interrupt one already being serviced. Further, just as all interrupts may be enabled or disabled, it is convenient to have a mechanism, an **interrupt mask**, which allows individual interrupts to be enabled or disabled by decisions within a running program.

A priority system is useful in some situations, but if interrupts are frequent those given high priority will obtain more attention than lower ones. If all sources are to be treated equally then either the priorities must be adjusted according to the number of times an interrupt has been serviced or an alternative scheme must be used. One possibility is construction of a queue mechanism to service interrupts in their order of arrival. This may be created in several ways; one method is to use a small first in–first out memory while another is to create the queue through software. Provided that an interrupt may only appear once in the queue, the interrupt which occurs most frequently obtains maximum service but others obtain a

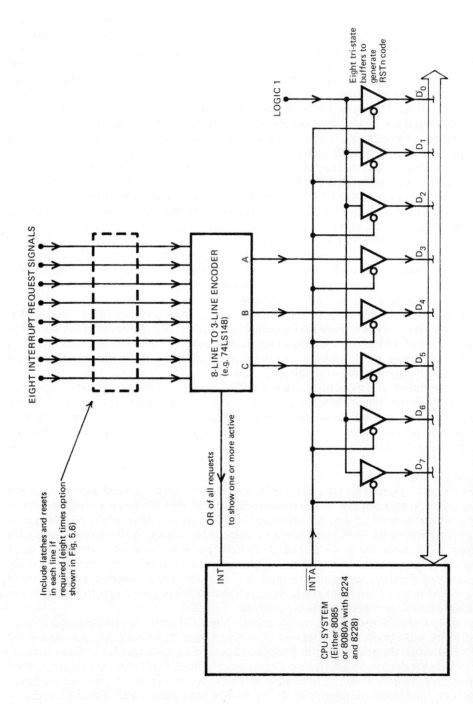

Fig. 5.8   Vectored interrupt system for an 8080 CPU

reasonable response. A third scheme, which tends to achieve a more equal rate of servicing interrupts, is one based on polling.

Polling is commonly used for inputs under program control, and may also be used by interrupt systems. In a polling scheme the input request signal lines are examined in some fixed sequence until one is found which is active. This position in the sequence is noted, the input is serviced, and then the system restarts examining, that is polling, the inputs, beginning immediately after the one just serviced. When the last input is reached, the system loops to examine the first again. An interrupt polling system may be implemented in hardware or software. It operates as if all interrupts are connected to the processor through an OR function. When an interrupt is detected, all possible sources are polled; examination starts with the one which follows the source serviced during the last interrupt. Under polling, frequent interrupts obtain more attention than infrequent ones, but every input is examined within one polling loop.

In some processor applications there are events which are so important that they must be serviced rapidly. Many CPUs have a separate TRAP or NMI (non-maskable interrupt) input. This is an interrupt with higher priority than all others and it cannot be disabled by the user; it must be used with care. These interrupts tend to be used for catastrophic events, for example failure of the processor's supply. There is usually sufficient stored energy in the power supply capacitors for the system to execute several thousand instructions after power source failure. If a power fail detection unit on the incoming power line activates an NMI interrupt, the service routine can save important information in a non-volatile (power independent) store.

Complex input structures may be built with some inputs under program control and others under interrupt control. The various inputs under either form of control may be allocated different priorities, or queued, or polled, or a mixture of several methods used. Further, the arrangements may be changed by decisions of the program while running. Possibilities are so great that large computers often have a smaller computer to manipulate and organize inputs. Even for microprocessor based systems, special integrated circuits are available to manipulate interrupts.

There are two other forms of interrupt which have not been described. One is a **software interrupt**; when this facility is available, the programmer may include an instruction which, if executed, produces an effect similar to that of an external interrupt. This can be useful in complex software when error conditions arise which require operator intervention. The other form is an **internally generated interrupt.** In large processor systems programs may attempt to perform actions which are not allowed. One example is in systems with hardware division circuits; a program may execute the division instruction when the contents of the register holding the divisor are zero. While the programmer could include instructions to test for such conditions before every division operation, this would slow the program. Provision of additional hardware which detects such actions removes the need for such instructions and speeds execution. The error condition may be indicated by simply setting a flag and not performing the division. An alternative is that the hardware generates an interrupt; such interrupts are generated internally from the CPU's own actions, not by external sources.

5.4 CPU performance improvements

Faster, larger and cheaper processor systems are always in demand. Within the basic von Neumann architecture, many improvements may be made to the simple designs described so far (possible alternative architectures are introduced briefly in Chapter 16). Often, improvements produce more symmetrical (systematic) designs requiring fewer special circuits to control individual small features. Many features previously found only in large CPUs are now appearing in microprocessors.

Direct methods of improving performance include increasing parallelism so that more actions occur simultaneously, and provision of circuits (hardware) to perform tasks undertaken by software in simple systems. It is convenient to examine the improvements as they affect separate functions of the control unit, although similar techniques are used in most sections. The ALU is a major element of the CPU and is considered separately in Chapter 7.

5.4.1   Instruction set and word length

The instruction set of a CPU directly affects the control unit design. In simple terms, large instruction sets require many control circuits or a large microprogram ROM with a large address range. Consequently, increasing the number of instructions increases control unit complexity and cost; however, provision of hardware and a single instruction for a commonly required operation which otherwise needs several instructions will greatly improve system speed. A specific example is provision of hardware to perform multiply and divide with each operation executed by a single instruction.

If the processor is designed in a systematic manner the instruction set can become simple, small, yet very powerful and easy to use. This is because instructions become much more general in nature, and a single instruction may be used for many similar tasks. Most 8-bit CPUs are rather poor in this respect; at the time they were developed the limitations of integrated circuit manufacture restricted designers. Ideally any instruction takes the form

OPERATION (operand 1), (operand 2), . . ., (operand *n*)

The operation defines a single action that may be executed, for example increment, add, branch, etc. Some operations may require no operands, some one operand, some two, and so on. Usually any real system restricts the maximum number of operands to two or three, although instruction sets with more exist.

The operands specify the sources or destinations for data items involved in the operation, and the complete instruction code is determined using both the operation and the operands. Operands are closely associated with the concept of **addressing mode**, introduced as an element of programming in Chapter 14. Provision of several methods of obtaining or storing a quantity used as an operand (several addressing modes) can assist in efficient programming. The implementation of these addressing modes requires provision of appropriate elements in the control unit. If a uniform method is developed for operand specification and all addressing modes may be used whenever an operand is required, the control unit becomes much more symmetrical and its design is less complex (fewer special cases have to be implemented by extra circuits). This requires that no registers or memory locations serve special functions, and all may be used as accumulators as well as simple word stores. Such an approach is too general but moves towards this ideal simplify the design of control units.

Examples of non-symmetrical features are found in all CPU designs, particularly most 8-bit microprocessors. A simple illustration is the instruction XCHG for the 8080 processor. This has no specified operands but several are implied. The instruction exchanges the contents of the D register with those of the H register; simultaneously the contents of E and L registers are exchanged. This is a very useful instruction but it is a special case; there are no other 8080 instructions which exchange contents of 8-bit registers.

The number of bits in the instruction word affects the ease with which the instructions can be encoded and decoded. Generally the encoding limits set by a short word length may be overcome by use of multiple word instructions. Often a variable number of words are used for an instruction, although this increases control system complexity. After fetching the first word the control system must recognize how many more words are required and fetch the correct number. Most simple 8-bit CPUs reduce problems of multiple byte instructions by having the first byte as the actual code, any subsequent bytes contain only numeric values. In such cases the microprogram can fetch these bytes as data; the address is taken from the program counter rather than from some data index register, also the program counter must be automatically incremented.

In addition to affecting the range of instruction codes possible, an increase in processor word length increases the number of actions performed simultaneously (i.e. there are more parallel actions). Each time an item of data is transferred to or from memory or an I–O device, the number of bits transferred in one operation is equal to the word length. Hence the greater the word length the more bits that are transferred simultaneously. Similarly, more bits are manipulated in a single ALU operation. In general, program execution will be faster as the word length is increased but not in direct proportion to the word length. The reason for a smaller increase is that in some circumstances only a few bits are required, and the extra bits in the word are unused. Using any fixed word length, some bits in a memory system are wasted by programs because many words are only partly utilized; the proportion of unused memory elements tends to rise as the word length is increased. Improved system performance by increasing word length is achieved at greater cost as more memory elements are required to overcome the reduced efficiency of memory use; also the larger data bus increases interconnection costs. For any particular application there will be an optimum word length; this optimum is continually rising because memory costs are falling.

5.4.2   Instruction fetch

An obvious feature of simple processors is that during instruction fetch all the ALU circuits, instruction decode, and the execution circuits are doing nothing. Similarly, during ALU operations once the operands have been retrieved from memory the bus system is often unused. A simple but significant improvement in speed is obtained by **instruction overlap**, a form of **pre-fetch**. If the final steps in executing an instruction do not require the bus system, for example many arithmetic and logic instructions, then the next instruction

Table 5.1   Execution steps for 8080 instructions showing overlap

Steps (clock cycle)	Action	Overlap (next instruction)
1	Output contents of PC to address bus	—
2	Increment contents of PC	—
3	Copy instruction code from memory to IR	—
4	Register r contents to internal TMP register, A contents to latch; both are inputs to ALU	—
5	Internal operations	Output contents PC to address bus
6	Copy output of ALU to A	Increment contents of PC

(a)   Instruction ADD r

Steps (clock cycle)	Action	Overlap (next instruction)
1	Output contents of PC to address bus	—
2	Increment contents of PC	—
3	Copy instruction code from memory to IR	—
4	Contents of A to ALU and rotated	—
5	Internal operations	Output contents PC to address bus
6	Copy output of ALU to A	Increment contents of PC

(b)   Instructions RLC, RRC, RAL, and RAR

code can be fetched while these final steps are in progress. The 8080 adopts a limited form of this in several instructions; Table 5.1 illustrates the execution steps of two such instructions.

This overlap produces some improvement in processor performance, and it is used to a significant extent in the 6502 CPU. This is why with a relatively low maximum clock frequency the 6502 CPU executes programs as rapidly as other 8-bit CPUs operating with higher clock frequencies. A more powerful pre-fetch system is a **pipeline**; this is a special first in–first out, FIFO, memory within the CPU. The first popular microprocessor to adopt this technique was the 16-bit 8086 processor. Figure 5.9 is an outline of the 8086 structure and indicates that the CPU may be considered to be in two parts. The execution unit (EU) undertakes the normal instruction decode and execution tasks; an additional section, the bus interface unit (BIU), handles transfers from the CPU to memory and I-O devices and includes the pipeline (instruction stream byte queue).

At start-up the processor fetches the first instruction normally, then decodes and executes it. At any time when the BIU detects that the bus system is not in use, it fetches the next instruction word from memory and puts it into the pipeline. The BIU continues to do this whenever there is space in the pipeline. When the EU requires its next instruction it takes it from the pipeline if the instruction is there; if not a normal instruction fetch is performed. The pipeline contents are automatically moved upward when the EU takes an instruction, the next instruction becomes available for the EU and space is created for the BIU to enter further instructions into the pipeline. In cases of a normal fetch, the complete fetch, decode and execute sequence takes no longer than it would if there was no pipeline. However, when the instruction is taken from the pipeline it is already in the CPU and only has to be trans-ferred to the instruction register. In these cases the fetch time is very short, almost negligible. Obviously a conditional branch instruction which is obeyed is followed by a normal fetch from memory, and the pipeline is reset to the empty condition.

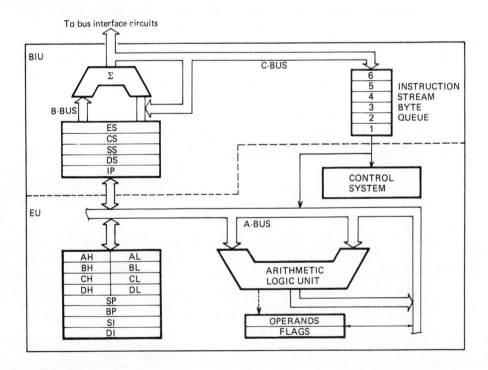

Fig. 5.9   Intel 8086 CPU structure

Pipelining instructions can lead to a great increase in processor speed; the only disadvantage in a few cases is that the fetch time is not constant and it can be difficult to predict the exact time to execute a section of program. Although software timing loops are useful in some applications with small microprocessors, precise timing in more complex systems should be achieved with hardware timers; variable execution time is not a serious problem.

5.4.3   Instruction decode

The instruction decode operation is relatively simple; depending on control unit design, instruction codes select either which execution circuit to activate or which microprogram to execute. In principle this can be achieved with a simple fast combinational circuit, although decoding may be more complex in some processors. For simple systems, decode improvements are probably uneconomical but in larger systems they may be worthwhile. Figure 5.10 is an outline of the 80286 CPU, an advanced development of the 8086, and it indicates that as well as a pipeline for instructions some decoding is performed on instructions in advance of the instruction transfer to the execution unit.

5.4.4   Instruction execution

While instruction fetch and decode may be speeded by overlap or pipelining, the speeding of execution is more complicated. There are two major actions which take time: one is data transfer (fetch and store of values) between CPU and memory or the I–O system; the other is the execution of arithmetic operations, which are examined in Chapter 7. The movement of data in a processor system takes a significant proportion of program execution time. Good internal CPU design combined with sophisticated memory and I–O structures can lead to significant improvements. The I–O in complex systems is usually handled by additional units, sometimes even by complete I–O processor systems, and then I–O has only limited effect on system performance. The major improvements possible are in memory systems, their organization, and CPU to memory system communications.

Memory organization ideally requires connection of an extremely large, very high speed memory to a CPU with a compatible address bus. However, the cost is prohibitive and the need to manipulate large addresses can reduce processor system speed. Instead, complex memory structures with sophisticated memory management schemes are devised. One simple structure has already been illustrated; the use of a pipeline for instructions. This may be extended to more complex structures such as data scratchpads and cache memories. These tend to make small sections of data and stacks more rapidly available to the CPU, rather as a pipeline places instructions closer to the control unit. The overall design aim is to use a small, very fast memory to keep costs low and the address size small. This memory is combined with a much larger but slower memory, so that the memory size appears to be that of this large, slow memory but the memory speed is close to that of the small fast one. Memory components, structures and their management are considered further in Part 3.

Even with complex memory structures and management, the size of memory directly connected to the CPU is tending to increase as memory costs continue to fall. The increased size of the address bus and manipulation of addresses affects the processor operation, and additional features are provided in many CPUs to improve performance. Complex separate memory management units are used in large systems, but a simple start to address manipulation is found within the 8086. The address bus is 20 bits wide; with a data word length of only 16 bits, manipulation of addresses becomes cumbersome. In practice programs only occasionally branch by large amounts and, since items of data are usually stored close together, much of the time the processor may operate with a reduced address range. In the 8086, addresses are manipulated in two parts by dividing memory into segments of 64k words with all internal CPU registers limited to 16 bits. The EU, essentially the ALU plus

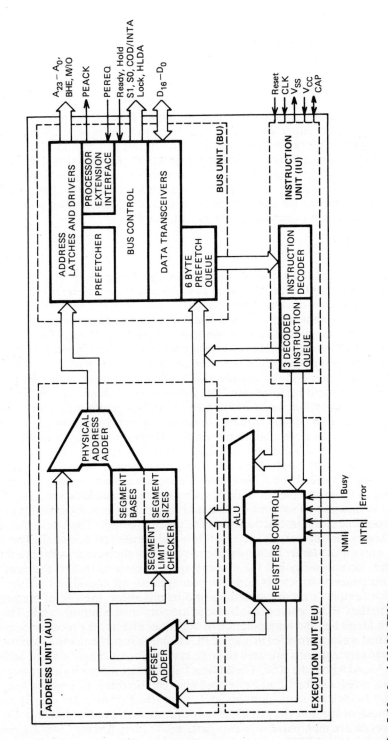

Fig. 5.10   Intel 80286 CPU structure

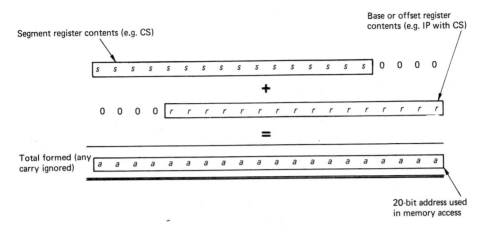

Fig. 5.11   Formation of an 8086 address by the CPU

instruction decode and execution sections of the CPU, usually operates with only 16-bit addresses. The complete 20-bit address is computed by the BIU, which combines the base address from the EU with the appropriate segment address from one of the four segment registers in the BIU. This combination is illustrated in Fig. 5.11. The BIU operates automatically after the programmer has loaded the correct values into the segment registers. When necessary, the full address may be used (at the cost of some inefficiency) instead of one offset by the segment base. For example, there are two subroutine CALL instructions; the short call has code $E8_H$ followed by a 16-bit address while the long call has code $9A_H$ followed by two 16-bit addresses (essentially it includes its own segment base which is used to reload the code segment, CS, register). Note that there are corresponding different short and long return instructions which must be used correctly; the form of return must be the same as that of the call.

5.4.5   Additional CPU hardware features

When designing a complete processor assembly of CPU, memory and other components it is always possible to perform some tasks by either hardware or software. A trade-off may be made between the increased cost of providing a hardware unit and the greater time taken by software to perform some task. This trade-off can also occur in the design of the CPU itself, with a more complex and expensive control unit undertaking tasks which the user would otherwise have to perform in software. An obvious example already suggested is the provision of a multiplication circuit.

More complex processors undertake many other tasks, for example the 80286 includes memory protection circuits. Processors are often used in a multi-task or multi-program mode, that is they perform two or more functions apparently simultaneously by jumping between separate programs (or sections of programs) and rapidly executing small amounts of each in turn. It is essential that the programs, their data and stacks do not interfere with one another. To do this each memory transfer, especially each write, should be checked to see that the current program is accessing an address in an area allocated for its own use. The overhead in programming when this is performed in software is prohibitive and only limited checks are made. In Fig. 5.10, an outline of the 80286, there is a section labelled *address unit (AU)*; this is a hardware unit which performs the address computation tasks of the BIU in the 8086. It also contains registers which the programmer may load to specify the regions of memory available to a particular program. Any attempt by a running program to access a location outside the specified limits will set an error condition; this may be used as an interrupt. This is another example of an internally generated interrupt.

5.5   Comments

By careful programming, even the most simple processor system can perform most tasks required by a user; however, the length of time taken to execute programs may be unacceptable. Additionally, the programming effort to make a system perform adequately with a processor which has too little power is usually too great to be economical.

More complex hardware can be used to improve system performance and to reduce programming effort. This tends to increase the cost of each unit built, but often decreases the initial design cost. Hardware costs are falling and will probably continue to do so for some years, allowing more elaborate hardware to be incorporated in processor systems. Tasks previously always performed in software are increasingly undertaken in hardware.

5.6   Problems

1 Design a processor system using any 8-bit CPU which allows the use of wait states and for which you have a full specification. The memory is in four equal size blocks, each of 16k bytes, but one block is a device which is relatively slow. The system designed must insert a wait of one clock cycle when the slow block is accessed (but not when any other is accessed) so that it has time to respond.

2 Using extra components, modify the vectored interrupt system of Fig. 5.8 so that an interrupt with higher priority than one already being serviced will be accepted. Outline the software required to implement such a scheme.

3 A processor has eight interrupt sources connected through individual latches to a simple OR gate; the gate output is the single interrupt input. The latch outputs also appear as a single memory mapped 8-bit input port so that they may be examined. The clear controls for the latches are supplied from a single memory mapped 8-bit output port. Describe with the aid of flowcharts the software required: (a) to handle the interrupts through a polling scheme; (b) to queue interrupt requests in the order of arrival.

6 Number representation and arithmetic operations

Before designs of arithmetic circuits can be examined, the functions they perform must be understood. This requires some knowledge of the storage of numbers in processor systems and examination of the processes to be performed on the numbers. A bit pattern in a register or memory location of a processor system may be regarded as a code which represents one of many possible quantities. This quantity will depend upon the use made of the pattern by the program running; possibilities include codes for alphabetic characters, CPU instruction codes, and simple positive integers from 0 to $2^n - 1$ for a word length of n bits. For example, the bit pattern 01001000 in an 8080-based system could represent the letter H in ASCII code (Appendix B), the instruction MOV C,B, or the number with decimal value 72. For a 6800 system the same pattern could still represent letter H or 72 decimal, but the instruction represented would be ASLA; and in a 6502 system the pattern again represents H or 72 decimal but the instruction is PHA.

The representation of numbers as positive integers in the range from 0 to $2^n - 1$ is too great a restriction when processor systems are used to perform calculations. One extension is to use two or more words to represent a larger range of positive integers. Further techniques allow a wide range of numbers to be represented, not just positive integers. Each type of number may be represented in many different ways, and problems arise when programs or data from more than one source are linked together. Some attempts at standardization exist, for example the IEEE 754 standard for floating point numbers, but standards are not universally used.

Several common number representations are described here; this is not a comprehensive list of all types, nor are all forms of each type described. In particular, binary representations of decimal numbers (BCD and packed BCD) have been ignored.

6.1 Unsigned integer

A group of n bits is used to represent the positive integral values from 0 to $2^n - 1$ as simple binary numbers. Usually ALU designs are such that the arithmetic circuits will operate using integers with n equal to the CPU word size. However, instructions are usually provided to make multiple word length arithmetic simple, and programmers may devise schemes in which a fixed number, N, of memory locations hold integers with $(n \times N)$ bits. Commonly double or quadruple length arithmetic is performed, especially with 8-bit microprocessors which have a rather short word length for many calculations.

Figure 6.1 is the flow diagram of a routine which adds together two multiple byte unsigned integers using an 8-bit CPU. Table 6.1 is two assembly language listings of general purpose subroutines which behave as Fig. 6.1; Table 6.1(a) is for an 8080 type processor and Table 6.1(b) is for a 6502.

6.2 Signed integer

If one number is subtracted from another, cases with negative results will arise. Either such results must be rejected or a method of representing negative numbers must be devised. Once negative numbers can be represented by a binary pattern, subtraction no longer

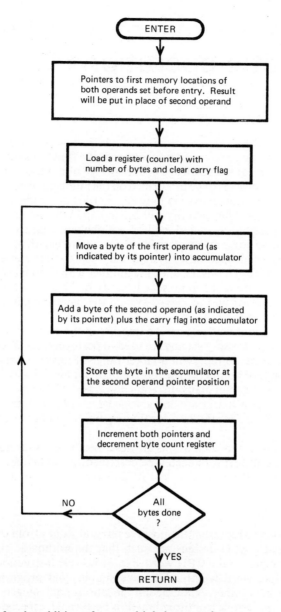

Fig. 6.1   Flowchart for the addition of two multiple byte numbers

requires special circuits. Provided that positive numbers can be converted to equal magnitude (size) negative ones and *vice versa*, and that the addition unit can handle both positive and negative numbers, subtraction of one number from another is just a case of change the sign of the second number and then add it to the first. Many methods of representing numbers as integers with both positive and negative values allowed have been devised; most rely on using one bit of the number as a sign indicator. In nearly all cases the MSB is used to represent the sign with 0 for positive and 1 for negative. Even with this restricted form there are several representations of signed integers.

Table 6.1 *N*-byte addition subroutines

; Subroutine to add two *N*-byte numbers, each stored least
; significant byte first (at lowest address). On entry pair
; D–E must already hold the address of the lowest byte of
; the first number and pair H–L must hold the address of the
; lowest byte of the second number. The result is left in
; place of the second number and the carry flag indicates
; overflow when it is left set at 1.

NAD:	MVI C,*N*	; In actual use replace *N* by number
		; of bytes
	XRA A	; Clear initial carry flag
NAD05:	LDAX D	; Get byte of first number
	ADC M	; Add byte of second number plus
		; carry (from previous addition)
	MOV M,A	; Save result byte
	INX H	; } Move on index pinters
	INX D	; }
	DCR C	; Decrement byte counter
	JNZ NAD05	; Jump (loop) unless all bytes done
	RET	

(a) Routine for 8080.

; Subroutine to add two *N*-byte numbers, each stored most
; significant byte first (at lowest address). On entry page
; zero addresses (*NUM1*) and (*NUM1*) + 1 must already hold the
; address of the highest byte of the first number and page
; zero addresses (*NUM2*) and (*NUM2*) + 1 must hold the address
; of the highest byte of the second number. The result is
; left in place of the second number and the carry flag
; indicates overflow when it is left set at 1.

NAD	LDY #(*N* − 1)	; In actual use replace *N* by number
		; of bytes (load Y with *N* − 1)
	CLC	; Clear initial carry flag
NAD05	LDA (*NUM1*),Y	; Get byte of first number
	ADC (*NUM2*),Y	; Add byte of second number plus
		; carry (from previous addition)
	STA (*NUM2*),Y	; Save result byte
	DEY	; Decrement index pointer (also
		; byte counter)
	BPL NAD05	; Jump (loop) unless all bytes done
	RTS	

(b) Routine for 6502.

When one bit of an *n*-bit number is reserved for the sign, then only $(n-1)$ bits are available to store the numeric part (magnitude or size) of the number. Consequently *n*-bit signed numbers hold values from $-(2^{n-1}-1)$ through 0 to $+(2^{n-1}-1)$. Note that there are only (2^n-1) different signed integers in this range, whereas the *n* bits can store 2^n different values. The *missing number* arises because zero is not usually considered to have a sign. However, if one bit of a pattern is reserved for use as the sign of a number then the number zero must be allocated a sign. The choice of method used to represent signed numbers affects how signed zero is represented and the *missing number* will differ from one representation to another.

A final feature necessary for correct behaviour of any signed number system is that double negation must produce the original number. That is, if the process to change a number to one of the same magnitude but opposite sign is performed twice in succession, the result must equal the initial value.

6.2.1   Signed magnitude (sign-and-magnitude)

The magnitude (size) of the number is given by all the bits of the number except the MSB; these magnitude bits are taken as a positive binary integer. The MSB is the sign bit, and indicates positive values when it is 0 and negative values when it is 1. For example 42 decimal is 101010_2, hence in 8-bit signed magnitude representation:

$$+ 42 \text{ decimal is} \qquad 00101010_2$$
$$- 42 \text{ decimal is} \qquad 10101010_2$$

The negation operation is simple and consists of inverting the sign bit; double negation reproduces the original number. Signed zero appears twice, because all zeros represents positive zero and the MSB (sign bit) 1 with all other bits 0 is negative zero. In this system the *missing number* is accounted for by two codes for zero.

Signed magnitude representation is useful in some situations, but more complex circuits are required to perform arithmetic operations than in cases when one of the complement representations is used. Complement relations rely on a *trick* for the simple implementation of addition and subtraction circuits. Correct results are only obtained when **all numbers have exactly the same, fixed, number of bits**.

6.2.2   Ones-complement

This is not often used although it does have some useful features. If n bits are used to represent the numbers $-(2^{n-1}-1)$ through 0 to $+(2^{n-1}-1)$, then in ones-complement the value $-X$ is obtained by subtracting X from $2^n - 1$. This is very easily formed as $(2^n-1)-X$ is just $\overline{X}$, where $\overline{X}$ is the binary number X with all the bits inverted.

Example

Use 8 bits to represent the decimal numbers $+42$ and -42 in ones-complement.

$$+ 42 \text{ decimal is} \qquad 00101010_2$$

Now inverting gives the ones-complement so

$$- 42 \text{ decimal is} \qquad 11010101_2$$

For 8 bits, $2^8 = 256$ so $(2^8 - 1) = 255$ and $255 - 42 = 213$. In simple unsigned binary, 213 decimal is 11010101 ($= 128 + 64 + 16 + 4 + 1$) which demonstrates that inversion produces the ones-complement in this case. The general case can be proven that inversion of each bit of an n-bit number X produces $(2^n - 1) - X$.

Two important features to note are that the correct value of sign bit appears automatically in the MSB position and that double negation reproduces the original value; that is $-(-X) = +X$. As $-X = (2^n - 1) - X$ in ones-complement, $-(-X)$ is

$$(2^n - 1) - \{(2^n - 1) - X\} = (2^n - 1) - (2^n - 1) + X = +X.$$

If the all zeros code represents positive zero, then the ones-complement, that is negative zero, is the all ones case. Thus the ones-complement representation has two different zeros. The all ones version of zero may cause problems when used with some circuits which perform arithmetic operations; such cases have to be identified and removed.

The main disadvantage of ones-complement is that when numbers in this representation are added or subtracted as simple n-bit unsigned binary numbers, the result is not the required ones-complement value in certain cases. While such cases are easily predicted, extra features must be incorporated in arithmetic circuits to correct such results.

6.2.3 Twos-complement

This is the most commonly used complement form as it leads to simple arithmetic circuits in most situations, especially for addition and subtraction. When a number is represented by n bits, the twos-complement of the number X is equal to $2^n - X$. This is relatively easy to form; the ones-complement is $(2^n - 1) - X = (2^n - X) - 1$ and is therefore one less than the twos-complement. Consequently, to form the twos-complement invert all the bits in the number (form the ones-complement) then add one to the resulting n-bit binary number to obtain the twos-complement. There are other *tricks* which may be used to produce the twos-complement value; the one described is easily implemented in both hardware and software.

Example

Again using 42 decimal ($= 00101010_2$), form the 8-bit twos-complement.

$$
\begin{array}{rl}
+42 \text{ decimal is} & 00101010_2 \\
\text{the ones-complement is} & 11010101_2 \\
\text{add 1} & 00000001_2 \\
\text{the twos-complement is} & 11010110_2
\end{array}
$$

As for ones-complement, the correct sign automatically appears in the MSB position. Double negation also behaves correctly; using the result of the previous example:

$$
\begin{array}{rl}
-42 \text{ (twos-complement) is} & 11010110 \\
\text{the ones-complement is} & 00101001_2 \\
\text{add 1} & 00000001_2 \\
\text{the twos-complement is} & 00101010_2
\end{array}
$$

The result is the original binary value equal to $+42$ decimal.

Twos-complement form has the very useful feature that if numbers in this form are added or subtracted as simple binary integers (i.e. the whole number, including sign, is just treated as an unsigned integer by the addition or subtraction process), then the correct result is obtained in twos-complement form. The only exceptions are cases when the result is outside the range that can be held in the number of bits available.

The reason this system behaves in this simple manner is that the complement is $2^n - X$ but the largest unsigned integer in n bits is $2^n - 1$; hence if 2^n appears as part of a result it will overflow from the arithmetic operation. The types of case which usually give problems in other representations are of the form $Y - X$ and $-Y - X$ with X and Y both positive. Considering $Y - X$, if $X^* = 2^n - X$ then $Y + X^* = Y + 2^n - X = 2^n + (Y - X)$. Ignoring the overflow of 2^n, which cannot be held in n bits, the result is $Y - X$, that is $Y + X^*$ is the same as $Y - X$.

Example

Using twos-complement representation with 8-bit numbers, perform calculations to evaluate the decimal expressions: (a) 87–42   (b) 32–42   (c) 42–42

Use the previous result that in twos-complement $+42$ is 00101010_2 and -42 is 11010110_2. Also $+87$ is 01010111_2 and $+32$ is 00100000_2.

(a) $+87$ is   01010111
      -42 is   11010110
      ─────────────────
      sum   1 00101101
      ═════════════════

Ignoring the overflow, the result is 00101101_2, which is the twos-complement representation of $+45$ decimal as expected.

(b) $+32$ is   00100000
      -42 is   11010110
      ─────────────────
      sum   0 11110110
      ═════════════════

The MSB of 1 indicates that the result is negative; note this and complement the result to find the magnitude.

            result   11110110
            invert   00001001
            add 1   00000001
   twos-complement   00001010

The magnitude of the result is 00001010_2, which is ten; with the sign this result has the expected value of minus ten.

(c) $+42$ is   00101010
      -42 is   11010110
      ─────────────────
      sum   1 00000000
      ═════════════════

Ignoring overflow, the result is the expected value of zero.

The one feature of twos-complement which differs from the other forms considered is the representation of zero. All zeros represents zero; if this is complemented the result (ignoring any overflow) is the same value of all zeros. Thus there is only a single representation of zero. There is now a *missing number* which is the binary value with MSB one and all other bits zero. This value also reproduces itself when complemented. It can be used to represent the value $-(2^{n-1})$ which may arise in some calculations; however, it is probably better to regard it as an unallowed result and indicate it as out of range when it occurs.

6.2.4   Offset representation

This form of signed integer is also known as **biased** or **excess-N** representation. It has some special uses and is a method by which all values may be manipulated as unsigned positive values for many purposes. The numbers $-(2^{n-1}-1)$ through 0 to $+2^{n-1}$ are represented by adding an offset, bias, or excess of $N = (2^{n-1}-1)$ to the value, thus obtaining positive values from 0 to (2^n-1). In many systems an offset of 2^{n-1} is added rather than $(2^{n-1}-1)$ and the range becomes -2^{n-1} through 0 to $+(2^{n-1}-1)$. For offset representations the MSB may still be regarded as a sign bit but, unusually, 0 appears for negative numbers and 1 for positive ones.

Example

Again using $+42$ decimal in 8-bits and choosing an offset of $(2^{n-1}-1)$, derive the binary equivalents of $+42$ and -42 decimal.
   The offset is $2^7 - 1 = 127$ decimal hence as $127 + 42 = 169$ then in this case

$$+42 \text{ decimal is} \qquad 10101001_2$$

For -42 the decimal value is $127 - 42 = 85$ hence

$$-42 \text{ decimal is} \qquad 01010101_2$$

Offset representation requires careful interpretation of the results of calculations but has advantages when determining which of two numbers is the larger and by how much. It is rarely used for simple integer quantities but is used as a component of some of the floating point representations to be considered.

6.3 Fixed point

If only integer values are represented in any processor system the range of calculations which can be performed is very limited. One improvement is to use binary numbers which include a point at some position. For example, the 8-bit number $1101 \cdot 0110$ is equivalent to the decimal value $13 \cdot 375$. However, when logic storage circuits are used to hold binary values only two states are available. Consequently only ones and zeros can be represented and there is no simple method of storing the point. Numbers in this form can be held provided that the position of the point is always in the same, **fixed**, place and this place is known. Such numbers are called fixed point numbers and are occasionally used in computer systems. They provide a method of storing fractional values which may be necessary when division is used. Also numbers in fixed point are stored to constant absolute accuracy, unlike floating point numbers. Use of fractional fixed point numbers tends to occur in rather special applications, typically real-time control, and they are not examined in detail here.

Note that integers are just a very important special case of fixed point number with the point fixed just to the right of the LSB.

6.4 Floating point

This is the most common method used to represent numeric values which cover a wide range; it is also known as exponential or scientific notation. Many different formats (specifications) are possible but all have the general form that the number is arranged as a binary number, usually a fraction, multiplied by some fixed value (base radix) raised to a power given by an exponent. For any single format the point is usually placed in the same position relative to the most significant (first) one in the binary number and the exponent is adjusted to force this one to the required position. In general the number will be in some form such as $\pm 1ddd \cdot ddd \ldots d \times R^{\pm eeeeee}$.

The part $1ddd \cdot ddd \ldots d$ holding the significant digits of the number is given several names. The most common is **mantissa** (although the form used often does not meet the true mathematical meaning of this quantity); other common names are **fraction** and **significand**. For convenience this part will be referred to as the mantissa. R is the **base radix** (or just radix) and $\pm eeeeee$ is the **exponent**, which is a signed integer value.

A very large number of different formats are possible, because many decisions have to be made regarding the manner of fitting the various components of the number into the available bits. The number of bits used is usually large; it is necessary to represent the overall sign, the digits of the mantissa, the sign of exponent, and the digits of the exponent. Consequently floating point numbers usually have at least 24 bits with 32, 48 or 64 bits commonly used. As the position of the point and the value of R are the same for all numbers in any particular format, information regarding these does not have to be stored.

For a given number of bits the following decisions must be made in devising a format.

a)   The number of bits for the part representing the exponent. Hence the number of bits left will hold the mantissa and the two sign bits.
b)   The value of the base radix R which is to be raised to the power given in the exponent.
c)   The position at which the point is placed in the mantissa.
d)   The method of representing the overall sign.
e)   The method of representing the exponent sign.
f)   The order of the various items in the binary pattern.

With so many decisions, a wide range of formats is possible; examination of common formats shows that a rather narrow range of choices is made in practice. The division into the mantissa and exponent is usually such that between five and twelve bits are used for the exponent, the choice being influenced by the total number of bits available. As large a range of exponent values as possible is useful, but this must not be so large that the number of bits left are insufficient to specify the mantissa to an adequate degree of accuracy.

The choice of base radix for the exponent affects the choice of point position. In nearly all cases the radix, R, is chosen to be two. This seems to be the best choice for general use but $R = 2^N$ is sometimes used; in particular many designs by one large manufacturer (IBM) have $R = 2^4 = 16$.

There are several sensible positions for the point, but the two most common are just before and just after the most significant digit in the mantissa. That is, when the radix is 2 these two positions give numbers in the forms

$$\pm 0 \cdot 1dddd \ldots ddd \times R^{\pm eeeeee}$$

and
$$\pm 1 \cdot dddd \ldots ddd \times R^{\pm eeeeee}$$

For each movement of the point one place to the right as it is being correctly positioned, one must be subtracted from the exponent, each move one place left requires the addition of one to the exponent. This process of moving the point until correctly positioned is called **normalization**. A disadvantage of a base radix other than two is that the position of the leading one relative to the point will vary. When the radix is 2^N every change by one in the exponent moves the point by N places, that is it can only be moved in multiples of N places. Consequently in many cases the point cannot be placed immediately next to the most significant one, and some leading zeros will be stored for many values, this wastes available memory space.

As the first digit in most floating point representations is always 1, many formats do not store this leading 1. If it is not stored, it is known as a **hidden bit** or said to be **implicit**, an extra storage bit is effectively obtained in such cases. The 1 must be restored before any calculations are performed using the number.

The overall sign is usually associated with the mantissa and, although complement forms are sometimes used, signed magnitude is more common. A single bit then indicates that the whole number is either positive or negative, and this sign bit may be positioned at any fixed point in the word. The method of representing the exponent sign is more varied, with all possible forms of signed integer used. There is a trend towards using offset representation for exponents because, when performing calculations with floating point numbers, the difference in size of two exponents is often required. Offset form is particularly well suited to determining differences in integers regardless of their relative size or sign.

Finally, the order of the components in floating point numbers usually consists of the overall sign in the most significant position. This may be followed by either the signed exponent and then the mantissa, or by the mantissa and then the signed exponent. There is at least one format in use which has the mantissa split in two and the exponent positioned between the two parts of the mantissa. In the case of the exponent preceding the mantissa, it is also possible to choose to place the overall sign between the exponent and the mantissa.

6.5 Specific floating point formats

Floating point numbers are best illustrated by some particular examples of formats in common use.

6.5.1 IEEE 754 formats

These formats are important because many integrated circuit manufacturers are adopting them. The IEEE 754 standard has several formats and specifies minimum numbers of bits for exponent and mantissa in each format rather than a fixed number of bits. The most frequently encountered implementations use minimum numbers of bits and are single pre-

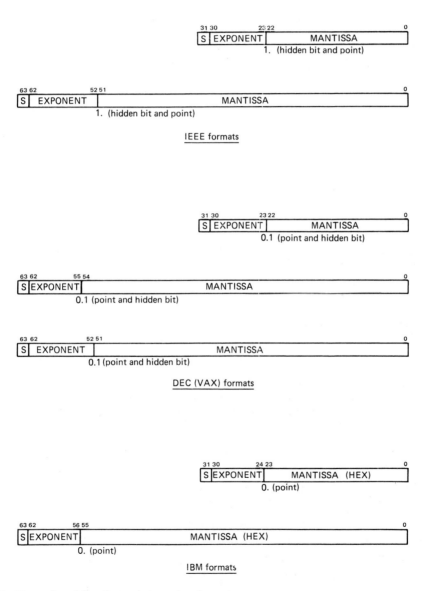

Fig. 6.2 Examples of floating point number formats

cision or short real (32 bits) and double precision or long real (64 bits). They are very similar in form except for the number of bits, so only the single precision format is illustrated by detailed examples.

These two formats have mantissas with the most significant 1 immediately to the left of the point, and this 1 is hidden (not actually stored). Both use signed magnitude, a single bit (the MSB) gives the overall number sign. The sign bit is followed by the exponent in offset form, with $2^{k-1} - 1$ as offset where k is the number of exponent bits. Exponents of all zeros and all ones are reserved for special purposes. For the short format $k = 8$ and for the long one $k = 11$. Figure 6.2 illustrates the storage of numbers in these formats and Table 6.2 outlines the ranges of values stored.

6.5.2 DEC formats for VAX machines

The VAX series of machines manufactured by Digital Equipment Corporation (DEC) support four floating point formats. There is a short single precision format using 32 bits, two double precision formats with 64 bits, and a quadruple one with 128 bits. All the VAX formats are similar in construction, differing only in the number of bits used for each component of the number. Again only the single precision form is illustrated in detail.

All formats use a signed magnitude mantissa with the sign in the MSB position. The sign is followed by a biased exponent with an offset of 2^{k-1} where k is the number of exponent bits. $k = 8$ for the 32-bit and one 64-bit format, $k = 11$ for the other 64-bit format, and $k = 15$ for the 128-bit version. The mantissa is normalized with the leading 1 just to the right of the point, and this leading 1 is not stored (a hidden bit). The 32-bit and 64-bit formats are illustrated by Fig. 6.2, with the ranges of values included in Table 6.2.

6.5.3 Formats for IBM 370 machines

Formats originally devised for the 360 series of machines are used by International Business Machines (IBM) in several ranges of machines, particularly the 370 series. There are three floating point formats, short using 32 bits, long with 64 bits, and extended with 128 bits. All are similar in construction, although the extended form has some slightly unusual features. Once more only the single precision form is illustrated in detail.

The formats use a signed magnitude mantissa with the sign in the MSB position followed by the exponent. The radix adopted is 16 rather than the more common value of 2, and all formats have a 7-bit exponent in biased form with an offset of $2^6 = 64$. Therefore the range allowed by radix plus exponent is 16^{-64} to 16^{63}. As the radix is 16, the mantissa is regarded as a hexadecimal number and is normalized so that the most significant hexadecimal digit is just to the right of the point. Consequently in binary form the leading digit of the mantissa is not always 1. The 32-bit and 64-bit formats are again illustrated by Fig. 6.2 with the ranges of values included in Table 6.2.

6.5.4 Floating point examples

To illustrate the formats described, binary representations of $+42 \cdot 913$ and $-42 \cdot 913$ in IEEE, DEC(VAX) and IBM(370) 32-bit formats are briefly derived. First separately form the binary equivalents of the integral and fractional parts of the decimal number.

$$42 \text{ decimal} = 101010_2$$
$$0 \cdot 913 \text{ decimal} = 0 \cdot 11101001101110100101111000110 1 \ldots_2$$

Hence the binary equivalent of $42 \cdot 913$ decimal is

$$101010 \cdot 11101001101110100101111000110101 \ldots$$

Table 6.2 Ranges of floating point numbers

Format	Range of binary values	Approximate decimal range	Approximate significant decimal digits
IEEE 32-bit	$1{\cdot}000\ldots \times 2^{-126}$ to $1{\cdot}111\ldots \times 2^{127}$	$1{\cdot}2 \times 10^{-38}$ to $3{\cdot}4 \times 10^{38}$	7
IEEE 64-bit	$1{\cdot}000\ldots \times 2^{-1022}$ to $1{\cdot}111\ldots \times 2^{1023}$	$2{\cdot}2 \times 10^{-308}$ to $1{\cdot}7 \times 10^{308}$	16
DEC VAX 32-bit	$0{\cdot}100\ldots \times 2^{-127}$ to $0{\cdot}111\ldots \times 2^{127}$	$2{\cdot}9 \times 10^{-38}$ to $1{\cdot}7 \times 10^{38}$	7
DEC VAX 64-bix (short exp.)	$0{\cdot}100\ldots \times 2^{-127}$ to $0{\cdot}111\ldots \times 2^{127}$	$2{\cdot}9 \times 10^{-38}$ to $1{\cdot}7 \times 10^{38}$	16
DEC VAX 64-bit (long exp.)	$0{\cdot}100\ldots \times 2^{-1023}$ to $0{\cdot}111\ldots \times 2^{1023}$	$5{\cdot}6 \times 10^{-309}$ to $9{\cdot}0 \times 10^{307}$	15
IBM 370 32-bit	$1{\cdot}000\ldots \times 2^{-260}$ to $1{\cdot}111\ldots \times 2^{248}$	$5{\cdot}4 \times 10^{-79}$ to $7{\cdot}2 \times 10^{75}$	7
IBM 370 64-bit (short exp.)	$1{\cdot}000\ldots \times 2^{-260}$ to $1{\cdot}111\ldots \times 2^{248}$	$5{\cdot}4 \times 10^{-79}$ to $7{\cdot}2 \times 10^{75}$	15

Notes (a) Ranges are not as great as the basic formats allow. Some values are reserved for special use.
(b) Ranges of magnitude are given, both positive and negative values are allowed.

IEEE 754 format This has the point to the right of the leading one, and normalization requires five left moves of the point. Before removal of the leading one, the mantissa is

$$1{\cdot}0101011101001101110100101111100011101\ldots$$

The exponent value is the number of left moves of the point offset by $2^7 - 1 = 127$, that is the exponent is $127 + 5 = 132$ which in 8 bits is 10000100_2. The sign bit is zero for a positive number so the complete representation is

$$0100\ 0010\ 0010\ 1011\ 1010\ 0110\ 1110\ 1001$$

DEC(VAX) format Normalization in this case gives a mantissa of

$$0{\cdot}101010111010011011101001011111100011101\ldots$$

after six left movements of the point. As the offset is $2^7 = 128$, the exponent is $128 + 6 = 134$ which is 10000110 in 8 bits. Including the sign bit of zero for a positive number, the complete representation is

$$0100\ 0011\ 0010\ 1011\ 1010\ 0110\ 1110\ 1001$$

IBM(370) format The number is first represented in hexadecimal form; converting from binary gives

$$2A{\cdot}E9BA5E35\ldots$$

Normalization requires two left movements of the point, producing

$$0{\cdot}2AE9BA5E35\ldots$$

As the offset is $2^6 = 64$, the exponent is $64 + 2 = 66$ which is 1000010 in 7 bits. Adding the sign bit of zero for positive, and expanding each hexadecimal digit as 4 bits, gives the full representation as

$$0100\ 0010\ 0010\ 1010\ 1110\ 1001\ 1011\ 1010$$

For all three formats the negative value $-42{\cdot}913$ is obtained by inverting the sign bit only. The results for the six cases are summarized in Table 6.3.

Note that even though there are several differences between IEEE and DEC formats, the binary patterns for the example in Table 6.3 only differ in the exponent part. Also, in determining the fractional binary value for decimal $0{\cdot}913$, the infinite length binary value had to be restricted to fit the format; the choice of truncation or rounding in such cases is an essential feature of the full specification of the particular floating point format.

The method illustrated shows how the binary value is constructed, but is not sufficiently general for use in computer systems. For example, it would be extremely difficult to derive the binary equivalent of $5{\cdot}718 \times 10^{17}$ by this method. In general, the decimal value should be put in a normalized exponential notation with a base radix of ten. The base radix should be converted to two, making the necessary adjustments to the numeric (mantissa like) term to obtain an integral exponent.

Table 6.3 Summary of 32-bit floating point example values

Number	Format	Representation
$+42{\cdot}913$	IEEE	0100 0010 0010 1011 1010 0110 1110 1001
$+42{\cdot}913$	DEC(VAX)	0100 0011 0010 1011 1010 0110 1110 1001
$+42{\cdot}913$	IBM(370)	0100 0010 0010 1010 1110 1001 1011 1010
$-42{\cdot}913$	IEEE	1100 0010 0010 1011 1010 0110 1110 1001
$-42{\cdot}913$	DEC(VAX)	1100 0011 0010 1011 1010 0110 1110 1001
$-42{\cdot}913$	IBM(370)	1100 0010 0010 1010 1110 1001 1011 1010

6.6   Effects of number representation

It has already been shown in Table 6.2 that even a floating point representation has maximum and minimum values that it can represent. There are also limits of precision in all types of representation. Fixed point formats represent numbers only to the accuracy of the least significant bit, however, this is a constant known amount. In floating point, the accuracy of the numbers varies, and is a function of their magnitude; such numbers are not equally distributed throughout their range of allowed values.

Fundamentally, problems arise because any set of numbers which can be used in a processor system is a finite set of 2^n different numbers when n bits are used. These 2^n numbers are only a subset of the infinite set of all real numbers. For example, the outlines given for floating point formats cannot exactly represent zero. Most specifications reserve a special bit pattern for zero (all zeros is the most common choice), and the circuits which perform arithmetic operations include features to handle zero as a special case. Errors occur because any attempt to represent a real number by a value belonging to some subset of all real numbers will usually be inexact. The difference between the real number and the nearest value in the subset is an error in the representation of the number; such errors cause problems.

The purpose of representing numbers as a binary pattern is to enable a processor system to be used to perform calculations. That is, the arithmetic operations of addition, subtraction, multiplication and division are to be performed using numbers in a specified format. The operations are well defined for normal numbers upon which no restrictions are placed; when numbers are restricted to fit within a rigid format the errors and limits in representation will cause problems.

There are many special problem cases to be considered. Generally these will have been foreseen and the full format specification will describe the action to be taken when such problems arise. Usually a number of hardware or software **flags** act as specific problem indicators. Every time an arithmetic operation is performed, the flags are forced to values so that each indicates if the error it represents arose or was absent. The user (programmer) must check the flags and take any appropriate action. In addition to the carry and zero flags described in Chapter 3, common flags show overflow, that is the result is too large for the format, and attempt to divide by zero which, unless deliberately stopped, could cause some arithmetic circuits to loop forever.

The complete specification of any particular format is a large detailed document. It is beyond the scope of this discussion to examine such specifications fully; when using a particular format, especially a floating point one, refer to the full specification. However, many problems which may arise for a format with a particular arithmetic operation are apparent when the operation is examined carefully.

6.6.1   Addition and subtraction operations

For all forms of fixed point number (including integers) the only problems that may arise are overflow and underflow. These are essentially the same; underflow is just a negative result with too large a magnitude. With unsigned numbers underflow occurs when the result is below zero. In most other cases the allowed number range is $-(2^{n-1}-1)$ through 0 to $+(2^{n-1}-1)$, and both overflow and underflow occur when the magnitude of the result exceeds $(2^{n-1}-1)$. In such cases detection of overflow needs care.

Example

Add + 87 to + 87 in 8-bit twos-complement form.

From a previous example + 87 decimal was 01010111 in 8-bit twos-complement, hence

+ 87 decimal	01010111
+ 87 decimal	01010111
sum	10101110

This result is a perfectly valid binary number, but in twos-complement it represents a negative quantity. In 8-bit signed form only seven bits represent the magnitude, which is in the range 0 to 127 decimal. When the result of an addition or subtraction overflows the seven magnitude bits, a carry-out from these bits is added into the sign bit, causing it to become incorrect. This effect occurs in most signed fixed point formats and extra circuits are required in the arithmetic unit to identify such cases and set the appropriate overflow flag.

In floating point formats the addition and subtraction processes are much more complex. Generally the exponents of the two numbers will differ (i.e. the points do not line up). Before performing the operation, the number with the smaller exponent must be identified and the number right shifted (point left shifted), moving in zeros as leading digits. Each place shifted causes one to be added to the exponent and shifting continues until both numbers have the same exponent. After shifting a number its mantissa may require rounding. The signed mantissas are then added or subtracted as required by the signs of each number and the operation being performed. The result may no longer have the point in the correct place and must be normalized to complete the operation.

Overflow and underflow are possible in floating point addition and subtraction, but are not as easily determined as in the case of these operations with fixed point numbers. Several other problems can arise, particularly when the overall effect of a calculation is to determine the difference between two numbers which are very close in magnitude. Large errors can arise in such cases, and skilled programming is essential if meaningless results are to be avoided.

6.6.2   Unary minus

This is simply the operation of negation, that is changing the sign of a number. Negation is considered as an arithmetic operation on a single operand, because expressions such as $A = -B - C$; $A = -B$; and $A = -B \times C$ are allowed in conventional mathematics. When writing computer programs similar expressions may arise, and unary minus allows their evaluation without the need for the two source operands normally required by the subtraction process. Without unary minus a dummy operand of zero would be inserted, for example $A = -B$ would become $A = 0 - B$.

Provided that the numbers represented by the format cover a range $-X$ through 0 to $+X$, with a negative equivalent for every positive value and *vice versa*, no problems will arise. Symmetry about zero does not exist for one value in offset representation and leads to minor problems. Also, generation of the all ones code for zero in ones-complement may cause some difficulties.

6.6.3   Multiplication operations

In principle, multiplication is just repeated addition, therefore only the problems associated with addition should arise. Multiplication is rarely performed by repeated addition and, although the problem cases are essentially the same as those in addition, they are sometimes more difficult to detect.

Overflow and underflow occur much more frequently in multiplication than in addition and subtraction. In general, if two *n*-bit numbers are multiplied together the result is a number with (2*n*) bits. It is usual to require the result of a calculation to be in the same format as the initial numbers (operands); hence in fixed point arithmetic, cases of multiplication with any one of the most significant *n* bits of the result not zero are overflow cases. Floating point form is much more flexible; a double length result is still obtained but may be rounded off at the appropriate number of bits. Final adjustment of a floating point result is a little more complicated, because in addition to rounding some normalization may be necessary.

When using floating point format, the rounding of numbers and results has a significant effect in many cases. For example, the result of one stage of a calculation may produce a very small result instead of zero because of rounding effects. If this is multiplied by a very large value a result of significant size may occur.

6.6.4 Division operations

Just as multiplication is repeated addition, so division is repeated subtraction. However, with integer formats division is the only operation which in general does not produce integral results. The most suitable method for performing integer division is to produce an integral result and an integral remainder. The result of division is the nearest integer to the correct (non-integer) result which has a magnitude less than that of the correct result.

In all formats, division by zero will give problems. Simple repeated subtraction would eventually cause overflow to occur, however most arithmetic circuits do not operate this way. It is common to test for attempts to divide by zero before any division operation; if such an attempt is found a divide by zero flag is set and the operation is not attempted.

6.7 Comments

A general outline of the representation of numbers for use with circuits performing binary arithmetic has been given. Further, some consequences of representing numbers in particular formats have been indicated. Many possibilities have not been discussed and full descriptions of format specifications have not been given. More details may be required to make full use of a particular format.

6.8 Problems

1 Form the 8-bit equivalent representations of the following decimal values. For each number derive the signed magnitude, ones-complement, twos-complement, and offset representations.

$$+12 \quad -37 \quad -104 \quad +75 \quad +1 \quad -3$$

2 It was stated in Section 6.2.2 that simple addition or subtraction using numbers in ones-complement does not always give results which are the correct values if assumed to be in ones-complement. Find an example of one such case. Also find a case in which an addition or subtraction produces the all ones version of zero.

3 Form the 32-bit floating point equivalents of the following decimal values in the format stated.

a) $52871 \cdot 261$ in IEEE format.
b) $0 \cdot 00003885$ in DEC(VAX) format.
c) $37801 \cdot 63$ in IBM(370) format.
d) $-9 \cdot 261 \times 10^{17}$ in IEEE format.

4 Perform the following calculations in 8-bit twos-complement commenting on the results.

a) $+12 + 75$ b) $+75 - 37$
c) $-104 - 37$ d) $-104 - 104 + 97$

5 For any single 8-bit processor, devise a subroutine to subtract one N-bit number from another ($N = n \times 8$, where n is an integer). The numbers are already in N-bit twos-complement before entry to the routine. State clearly whether numbers are to be stored least significant or most significant byte first. How does the routine indicate overflow and underflow?

6 Use any 32-bit floating point format for which you have an adequate specification. Derive representations in that format for the decimal numbers 327·056 and 19·782. Using these binary representations compute both 327·056 + 19·782 and 19·782 − 327·056.

7 Describe all the steps in the process required to multiply one floating point number by another. Illustrate the description by multiplying the binary equivalents of the decimal numbers 43·19 and −0·017 in one specified format. Convert your result to decimal and determine the extent to which it is in error.

7 Arithmetic and logic units

The essential processes for calculations and for logical manipulations consist of combining two numbers by a specific rule for the operation. Some operations, for example inversion and unary minus, involve only one number while others require three or more numbers. However, sequences of operations each with two initial numbers allow all possible calculations to be performed.

When the number of bits and the format (identical size and format initial numbers assumed) have been defined, an arithmetic or logic operation takes the form *combine n-bit pattern A with n-bit pattern B by a fixed rule*. The result will be an N-bit pattern (N and n are not always equal) representing the output numeric value formed according to the rules for the selected process. There will usually be an additional set of F output bits which are indicators, **flags**, showing important features of the result; typical flags show overflow, zero, etc. Hence it is possible to prepare a table of every combination of all 2^n values of A with all 2^n values of B and show the resulting $(N+F)$ bits for all cases. This is a truth table, and consequently any arithmetic or logic operation can be performed by a combinational logic circuit; the two n-bit number patterns provide the $2n$ circuit inputs and the result is given by the $N+F$ circuit outputs. The various different arithmetic and logic functions could be performed by having M additional inputs whose values define the operation, for example with three inputs (controls), a small but useful range of actions could be produced as illustrated in Table 7.1. Figure 7.1 illustrates the general form of this hypothetical ALU.

Combinational logic design is a straightforward task, and this ALU is simple in concept. However, for numbers with a reasonable value of n the circuit with $2n+M$ inputs and $N+F$ outputs becomes impractical to design by conventional truth table and minimization techniques. Further, even if the design is completed the resulting circuit is almost impossible to construct; for example it will probably require some gates with nearly $\frac{1}{2}(2n+M)^2$ inputs. Consequently somewhat *ad hoc* techniques are adopted to design ALU circuits with separate circuits often provided for different operations. Addition, subtraction and logic circuits are often combined into one unit, but multiplication and division usually require either one or two separate units within the ALU.

In the following descriptions of ALU circuits it is assumed that the circuit inputs represent two n-bit numbers which are in the same format. This format will be either unsigned integer or twos-complement. Floating point and mixed format operations are discussed

Table 7.1 Effect of control inputs for a simple ALU

Control inputs			Action of ALU
0	0	0	ADD the two input numbers
0	0	1	SUBTRACT input B from input A
0	1	0	ADD the two input numbers with carry
0	1	1	SUBTRACT input B from input A with borrow
1	0	0	AND the two input numbers
1	0	1	OR the two input numbers
1	1	0	XOR the two input numbers
1	1	1	INVERT (ones-complement) input A

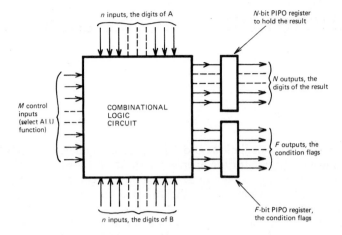

Fig. 7.1   Outline of a combinational logic ALU

briefly later, because operations with these are generally performed by a sequence of actions using circuits which manipulate integers.

7.1   Addition circuits

For numbers with n small, a truth table for addition may be produced; the size of the table quickly becomes excessive as n is increased to a useful value. An alternative approach is to examine manual addition of numbers, this is particularly simple for binary numbers, as illustrated by Fig. 7.2 for the 8-bit numbers $A = 00100111_2$ and $B = 10101110_2$. The process

STEP	Digit position	Digits of A		Digits of B		Carry from last step	Carry to next step	Sum at this position
1	D_0 (LSB)	1	+	0		NONE	0	1
2	D_1	1	+	1	+	0	1	0
3	D_2	1	+	1	+	1	1	1
4	D_3	0	+	1	+	1	1	0
5	D_4	0	+	0	+	1	0	1
6	D_5	1	+	1	+	0	1	0
7	D_6	0	+	0	+	1	0	1
8	D_7 (MSB)	0	+	1	+	0	0	1

final 0 indicates no overflow

Fig. 7.2   Steps in the manual addition of binary numbers

Table 7.2 Truth table for a full adder

Inputs			Outputs	
Carry-in C_{i-1}	Digits		Sum S_i	Carry C_i
	A_i	B_i		
0	0	0	0	0
0	0	1	1	0
0	1	0	1	0
0	1	1	0	1
1	0	0	1	0
1	0	1	0	1
1	1	0	0	1
1	1	1	1	1

is broken into steps; starting from the LSBs, the corresponding digits of each number are added together and any overflow, **carry-in**, from the previous step is also added. This produces a **sum** in the same position and a **carry-out** to the next step. The process is relatively simple, and the action required in a single step may be evaluated for all possible inputs; this is described by Table 7.2. The circuit which meets this truth table is a **full adder**; one of many possible full adder circuits is shown in Fig. 7.3.

Early computer systems used a single full adder, and a sequential control circuit performed the addition one pair of digits at a time, as in manual addition. Such a circuit is a

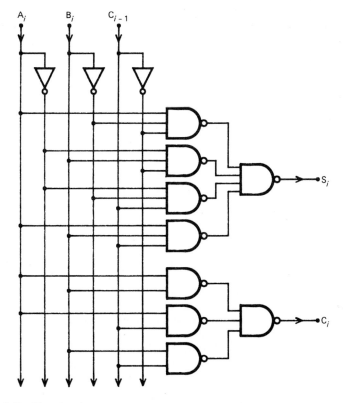

Fig. 7.3 One full adder circuit

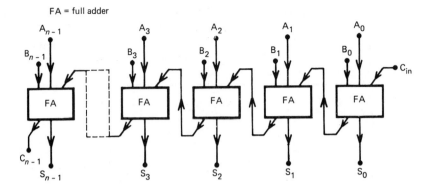

Fig. 7.4 Ripple-carry addition circuit

serial addition unit. As components are now much cheaper, smaller, and have significantly better reliability, these circuits are no longer in general use because they are inherently slow. A simple alternative is to provide a separate full adder for each step in the addition; the carry-out from one position is connected to provide the carry-in to the next. This circuit is sometimes called a **parallel addition unit**, although a better name is a **ripple-carry adder**. The carry may propagate from one stage to the next, and a carry originating in one stage may ripple through several stages (all stages in extreme cases). This circuit is illustrated in Fig. 7.4; it is an example of the **cell** or **iterative technique** of combinational logic design. In this approach a relatively simple unit, a **cell**, is identified and reproduced many times. The complete circuit is formed by interconnecting the cells in a suitable network. A minor modification to the technique allows a small number of different basic cell designs to be used rather than a single type.

While the ripple-carry adder has a performance that is much faster than that of a serial adder, it still has some undesirable features. In principle, any combinational logic circuit may be designed and constructed as a **three-level circuit**. That is, any output of a three-level circuit only arises as the result of signals passing through a maximum of three gates between any input and the output. This is apparent if any of the standard combinational logic design techniques is examined, because the usual process is to reduce the circuit specification either to a sum of products or to a product of sums. The resulting expression may be used directly to construct a three-level circuit, or manipulated to define a three-level circuit constructed entirely of NAND gates or entirely or NOR gates. In cases when both true and complement values of each input are available (e.g. when they originate from values stored in bistables), a two-level circuit is possible. Obviously the ripple-carry adder is not a three-level circuit; for example in 8 bits, if 00000001 is added to 11111111 then the carry will have to ripple through all eight full adders. Each full adder could be a three-level circuit; a complete n-bit adder then has three levels for each stage giving a total of $3n$ levels for the final carry-out. When using an arithmetic circuit, a processor system must wait after setting the correct inputs until the correct output is certain to exist before it can make use of the output and proceed with the next step in instruction execution. If a circuit has $3n$ levels, the processor must wait for the time a signal may take to pass through $3n$ gates, that is it must wait for at least $3n$ worst case gate propagation delays.

For small values of n the time is not excessive, but even for 8 bits the time for 24 delays is often unacceptable; for the larger word lengths used by many computers the resulting delay must be avoided in some way. A considerable effort has been expended in designing fast addition circuits; it is only possible to illustrate a few of the more common approaches here.

To increase addition speed it is necessary to break the carry-in to carry-out chain. A

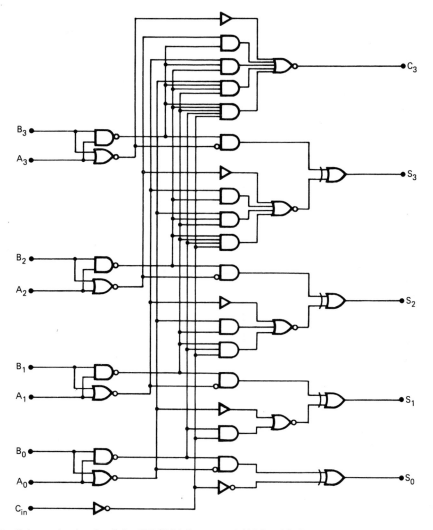

Fig. 7.5 Schematic circuit of the 74LS83A integrated (4-bit adder)

simple but effective method is to determine the largest size numbers, each *m* bits, for which
a three-level addition circuit may reasonably be designed and constructed; a direct design.
That is, all the sum outputs and the final carry-out are produced within three gate delays of
connecting the inputs. Figure 7.5 is a schematic circuit of the commonly used 74LS83A
integrated circuit, a fast 4-bit adder. Strictly this includes some four-level circuits, but it is
still much faster than a ripple-carry circuit. Once designed, the three-level *m*-bit adders are
used as cells for a ripple design as shown in Fig. 7.6. There are only three delays for every
m bits, and the worst case delay is $3n/m$ gate delays (assuming *m* to be a factor of *n*).

In this design the requirements of producing carries within the *m* stages do not exist; the
sums are generated directly from the inputs. Clearly S_0 is a Boolean function of A_0, B_0, and
C_{in}; that is

$$S_0 = \text{fn} (A_0, B_0, C_{in})$$

Similarly
$$S_1 = \text{fn} (A_0, B_0, A_1, B_1, C_{in})$$
$$S_2 = \text{fn} (A_0, B_0, A_1, B_1, A_2, B_2, C_{in})$$

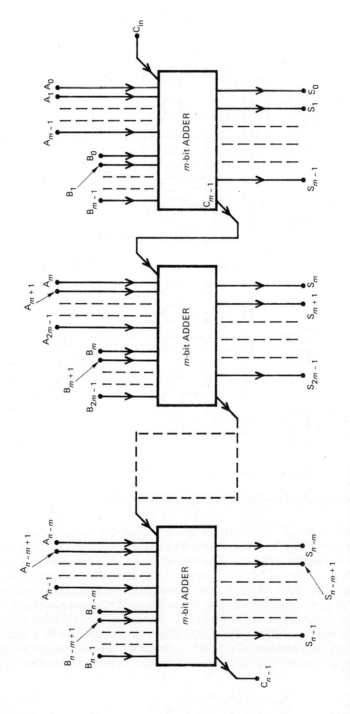

Fig. 7.6 Ripple connection of *m*-bit parallel addition units

etc. to

$$S_{m-1} = \text{fn}\ (A_0,\ B_0,\ A_1,\ B_1,\ A_2,\ B_2,\ \ldots,\ A_{m-1},\ B_{m-1},\ C_{in})$$

and

$$C_{out} = \text{fn}'\ (A_0,\ B_0,\ A_1,\ B_1,\ A_2,\ B_2,\ \ldots,\ A_{m-1},\ B_{m-1},\ C_{in})$$

The maximum value of m is set by the maximum number of inputs which can reasonably be achieved in constructing the gates used in the circuits to generate S_{m-1} and C_{out}. For an m-bit adder this number will be almost $\frac{1}{2}m^2$ and will limit m to a value in a range of about 3 to 8, depending upon the internal design of the logic gates. The final carry-out has the same inputs as the sum, S_{m-1}, although it is a different function. It is a form of **look-ahead carry**, that is it is produced much earlier than if it arose from a simple ripple-carry circuit.

The literature contains many designs of addition circuits incorporating look-ahead techniques; the most common one is based partly on cell design techniques. This is the circuit usually called a look-ahead carry adder which is described here. Many other designs may be found in the suggested further reading; note that similar designs may have minor circuit variations, so Boolean expressions in the references may not be identical.

The object of any look-ahead adder design is to generate the carry for any stage in a simple manner, using only a few levels of logic. If the ith stage of an adder is examined, then it will have inputs A_i and B_i, the ith digits of the numbers, and a carry-in C_{i-1}, which is the carry-out of the previous, lower, stage. The stage will produce a sum bit, S_i, and a carry-out, C_i. Two other quantities are now introduced; one is the generate function, G_i, which is 1 only if the stage has a carry-out of 1 regardless of its carry-in. The second is the propagate function, P_i, which is 1 if the stage propagates a carry; that is $P_i = 1$ if the carry-out will be the same as the carry-in. These functions are easily determined in terms of A_i and B_i, they are

$$G_i = A_i \cdot B_i$$
$$P_i = A_i \oplus B_i$$

Circuits for G_i and P_i are easily constructed, and form ideal cell units. In general, three levels of logic are required for a cell which produces P_i, Fig. 7.7 shows a typical cell producing both G_i and P_i. It is easily proved that the following identities satisfy Table 7.2, the truth table for a full adder.

$$S_i = A_i \oplus B_i \oplus C_{i-1}$$

hence

$$S_i = P_i \oplus C_{i-1}$$

and

$$C_i = A_i \cdot B_i + (A_i \oplus B_i) \cdot C_{i-1}$$
$$= G_i + P_i \cdot C_{i-1}$$

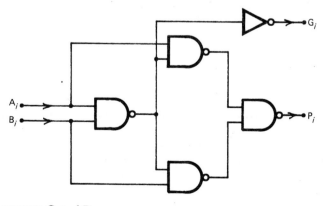

Fig. 7.7   Cell to generate G_i and P_i

This last equation forms a Boolean recursion relation. Expanding gives the first few equations:

$$C_0 = G_0 + C_{in} \cdot P_0$$
$$C_1 = G_1 + G_0 \cdot P_1 + C_{in} \cdot P_0 \cdot P_1$$
$$C_2 = G_2 + G_1 \cdot P_2 + G_0 \cdot P_1 \cdot P_2 + C_{in} \cdot P_0 \cdot P_1 \cdot P_2$$
$$C_3 = G_3 + G_2 \cdot P_3 + G_1 \cdot P_2 \cdot P_3 + G_0 \cdot P_1 \cdot P_2 \cdot P_3 + C_{in} \cdot P_0 \cdot P_1 \cdot P_2 \cdot P_3$$

The general expression for the ith carry is

$$C_i = G_i + G_{i-1} \cdot P_i + G_{i-2} \cdot P_{i-1} \cdot P_i + \ldots$$
$$+ G_{i-k} \cdot P_{i-k+1} \cdot P_{i-k+2} \cdot \ldots \cdot P_i + \ldots + C_{in} \cdot P_0 \cdot P_1 \cdot \ldots \cdot P_i$$

These equations are used to produce a set of carry units which generate every carry directly from G_i and P_i. The sum of any stage is just $P_i \oplus C_{i-1}$, so a set of exclusive-OR cells form the sum units and the complete look-ahead adder is constructed as outlined in Fig. 7.8.

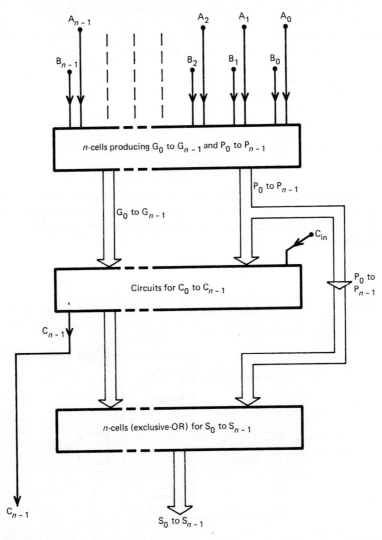

Fig. 7.8   Outline of a carry look-ahead adder

In the circuits for the carries of an m-bit adder (the most significant stage produces carry C_{m-1}), the maximum number of Boolean variables in any AND term is $m+1$. The maximum number of terms to be combined in an OR function is also $m+1$. This quantity $m+1$ is much less than the estimated value of $\frac{1}{2}m^2$ required for gates used in a direct three-level design for an adder. Consequently many more single bit addition stages may be constructed within fixed component limits using the carry look-ahead design than may be built for the direct design. Assuming no inverted inputs are available, a direct design will have three levels and hence three delays. The carry look-ahead circuit will have eight levels giving eight delays but, for the same limit to gate inputs, will add at least twice the number of bits if $m>3$. When a ripple construction is used to double the number of bits for a direct design, the total delay increases to six gate delays. Further examination of the two approaches shows that fewer gates are required in the look-ahead design; also many sections of the circuit are identical cell units which are ideal for integrated circuit manufacture.

Summarizing, the look-ahead design produces a less complicated and lower cost circuit than a direct three-level design; the penalty is a slightly slower overall performance. In general, the wide range of parallel adder designs that have been produced offer different compromises between speed and cost. The ripple-carry circuit is the slowest but least expensive and least complicated; a direct three-level design is the fastest but also the most expensive and complex.

7.2 Subtraction

Complement mechanisms were described in Chapter 6, and it was shown that using them subtraction may be performed by an addition process. Consequently a sequence of complementing a number and then adding it to another will perform subtraction, and a special subtraction circuit is not necessary. As most ALU systems include the unary logical operation which inverts all the bits of a number (forms the ones-complement), the process of subtracting some value Y from another value X when both are represented in n-bit twos-complement may be performed by a program with a few simple steps.

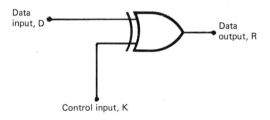

Data input, D	Control input, K	Output $R = D \oplus K$	Comments
0	0	0	$R = D$ when control $= 0$
1	0	1	
0	1	1	$R = \bar{D}$ when control $= 1$
1	1	0	

Fig. 7.9 An exclusive-OR gate as a controlled inverter

a)   Put the binary pattern representing Y into an accumulator.
b)   Invert all the bits of the accumulator holding Y (form the ones-complement).
c)   Increment the contents of the accumulator holding the inverted value (form the twos-complement, Y^*).
d)   Add the binary pattern representing X to the accumulator holding Y^*; it now contains $X - Y$.

This software process is necessary when a processor instruction set has no subtraction operation; also the steps may be the control sequence for a sequential subtraction circuit. However, examination of the process shows that all that is being done is the inversion of all bits and the addition of 1. The exclusive-OR gate may be used as a controlled inverter as illustrated in Fig. 7.9. When the control input is zero, the data output is the same as the data input; when the control input is 1, the data output is the inverse of the data input.

By using n controlled inverters with all their control inputs connected to a common input, a combined addition and subtraction circuit is formed. The LSB adder must be a full adder with the control input also connected as its carry-in; this produces the *add 1* for the twos-complement. The circuit is illustrated in Fig. 7.10 with a ripple-carry adder, although any design of addition circuit may be used. When the control input is 0 the unit performs the operation $X + Y$, and when the control is 1 it performs $X - Y$ with the inputs and result in n-bit twos-complement. An extra exclusive-OR gate forms the correct carry/borrow from the MSB carry-out. Examination shows that not only does this circuit add and subtract n-bit twos-complement numbers, but if the inputs are interpreted as n-bit unsigned positive integers then the result including the MSB carry/borrow is correct in $(n + 1)$-bit twos-complement. This result is suitable for use in multiple word arithmetic when the carry/borrow from operations on one pair of words is used in the addition or subtraction of the next most significant pair of words.

To assist in performing multiple word arithmetic, most processor instruction sets include the instructions *add with carry* and *subtract with borrow* (Chapter 3). The addition and subtraction circuit is simply modified by including an extra control input and one AND gate to perform these functions; this gate is indicated inside the broken line in Fig. 7.10. Note that controlled inverters could be included in the inputs connecting number X to the adder allowing the operations $-X + Y$ and $-X - Y$ to be performed as well as $+X + Y$ and $+X - Y$.

7.3   Multiplication

It is more difficult to build multiplication circuits than addition and subtraction ones; multipliers are rarely found in the smaller 8-bit microprocessors because of the large number of components required. There are probably even more multiplier designs than there are addition circuit designs. Consequently only a brief introduction to a few multiplier designs can be given here.

A complication arising in multiplication is that the general result of multiplying two n-bit numbers is a number with $2n$-bits. This extra length causes several problems, provision of space for the extra bits is the most immediate. With differing word sizes the input and output formats must differ, whereas it is more convenient to have inputs and output in the same format. Signed arithmetic using complement notation is no longer straightforward as the complement *trick* relies on use of a fixed word length.

As for all arithmetic circuits, a basic multiplier circuit is a combinational logic one; however, for useful word length the circuit cannot be designed and built using simple methods. There are two main approaches to multiplier design; one is a serial form using a parallel adder which will already exist in an ALU, and the other is to attempt some form of combinational design by cell techniques. The serial approach is convenient to consider first; it may be used to design a sequential logic control circuit, or a microprogram, or it may be the

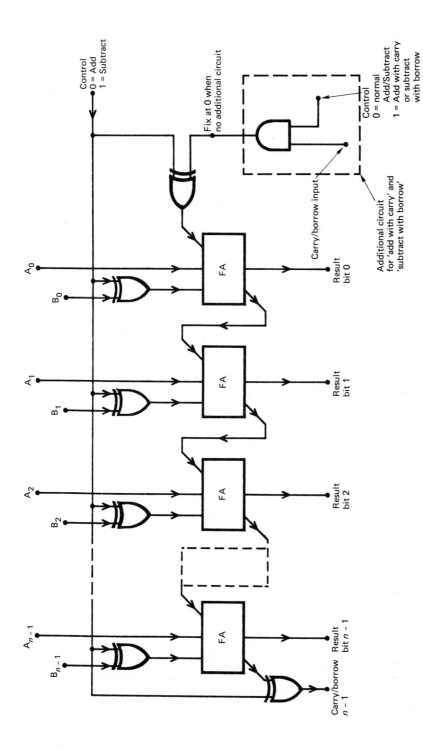

Fig. 7.10 Combined addition and subtraction circuit

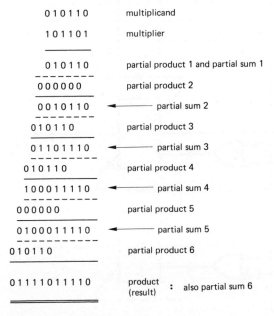

```
    0 1 0 1 1 0          multiplicand

    1 0 1 1 0 1          multiplier
    ─────────
    0 1 0 1 1 0    ⎫
    0 0 0 0 0 0    ⎪
    0 1 0 1 1 0    ⎬  partial products
  0 1 0 1 1 0      ⎪
  0 0 0 0 0 0      ⎪
0 1 0 1 1 0        ⎭
─────────────
0 1 1 1 0 1 1 1 1 0    product    =  sum of partial products
═════════════          (result)
```

a)   Simultaneous addition of partial products

```
    0 1 0 1 1 0          multiplicand

    1 0 1 1 0 1          multiplier
    ─────────
    0 1 0 1 1 0          partial product 1 and partial sum 1
    - - - - - - - -
    0 0 0 0 0 0          partial product 2
    ─────────
    0 0 1 0 1 1 0     ◄──────── partial sum 2
    - - - - - - - -
  0 1 0 1 1 0            partial product 3
  ─────────
  0 1 1 0 1 1 1 0   ◄──────── partial sum 3
  - - - - - - - - -
0 1 0 1 1 0              partial product 4
─────────
1 0 0 0 1 1 1 1 0  ◄──────── partial sum 4
- - - - - - - - -
0 0 0 0 0 0              partial product 5
─────────
0 1 0 0 0 1 1 1 1 0 ◄──────── partial sum 5
- - - - - - - - - -
0 1 0 1 1 0            partial product 6
─────────
0 1 1 1 0 1 1 1 1 0    product    :  also partial sum 6
═════════════          (result)
```

b)   Separate addition of partial products

Fig. 7.11   Shift and add multiplication

basis of a software subroutine for processors without a multiplication instruction. Manual multiplication of the 6-bit numbers 010110 and 101101 would probably be performed as in Fig. 7.11a. The simultaneous addition of all **partial products** is not suitable for a serial machine approach; formation of a running total or **partial sums** as in Fig. 7.11b is more convenient. Multiplication of unsigned binary integers by this process is very simple; it is a sequence of **shift and add** operations. Many multiplier designs are based on shift and add techniques; all are similar although there are many detail variations in the implementations.

Figure 7.12 outlines the hardware configuration for one particular shift and add technique. Many arithmetic units will not have a double length accumulator, and in such cases

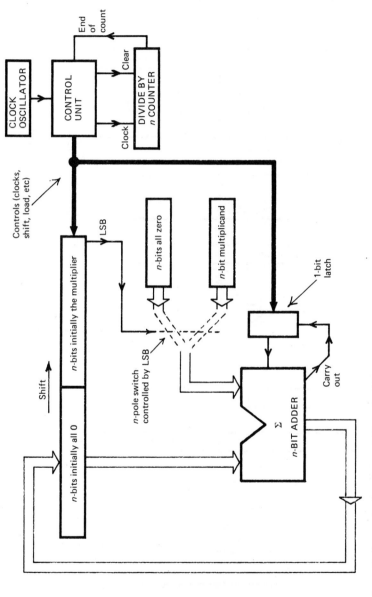

Fig. 7.12 Schematic form of a hardware shift and add multiplier

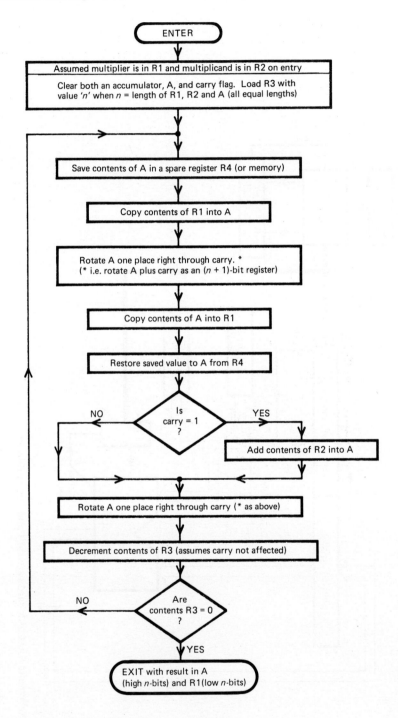

Fig. 7.13 Flow diagram for shift and add multiplication

the extra half of the double length accumulator is formed using a register or memory location to extend the accumulator. The design illustrated would use a register for the lower half of the accumulator, but other designs may use a register as the upper half. Assuming the two numbers to be initially loaded into registers R1 and R2, with a single length accumulator, A, and a register R3 reserved for counting, the required sequence of operations is shown in Fig. 7.13. This figure may be used either as the basis of a specification for a sequential logic circuit to perform multiplication or as a flow diagram for software. The flow diagram may either specify a subroutine to be used with a processor without a multiply instruction, or describe a microprogram for an instruction in a CPU control unit. The number of steps in performing an *n*-bit multiplication is obviously large; shift and add multipliers are slow (but faster than simple repeated addition). One software implementation is illustrated in Table 7.3; this is a listing of a subroutine for an 8080 processor. By using register C to hold the initial multiplier, and to form the accumulator extension, the number of data transfer and shift instructions is significantly reduced.

Table 7.3 Shift and add multiply subroutine for 8080

; Multiply subroutine; on entry the multiplicand must be
; in D and the multiplier in C. On exist the result is left
; in registers B and C. (B holds the high byte).

MUL:	MVI E,8	; Load bit counter
	XRA A	; Clear A and initial carry
	MOV B,A	; Clear high result byte
MUL05:	MOV A,C	; Multiplier to A
	RAR	; Current multiplier bit to carry
		; previous result LSB into MSB
	MOV C,A	; Save shifted multiplier plus part
		; of low result
	MOV A,B	; Partial result to A
	JNC MUL10	; Jump if multiplier bit was 0
	ADD D	; Add in multiplicand if bit was 1
MUL10:	RAR	; Result LSB to carry, result MSB moved
		; into register from carry
	MOV B,A	; Save partial result
	DCR E	; Decrement bit counter
	JNZ MUL05	; Jump (loop) unless all bits done
	RET	

There are several possible design improvements in serial multipliers; one approach is to examine two or more bits of the multiplier at a time. This reduces the number of shift and add cycles required for a fixed word length, although the individual steps in these **multiple _shift** designs are more complex. The actions required in a multiplier examining two bits at a time are described in Table 7.4. The case of both bits 1 which produces the most difficult situation may be speeded up by subtracting the multiplicand once before any shifting, and

Table 7.4 Actions for multiplier bits used two at a time

Multiplier bits		Action before shifting
0	0	No action required
0	1	Add multiplicand
1	0	Add twice multiplicand
1	1	Add multiplicand, add twice multiplicand

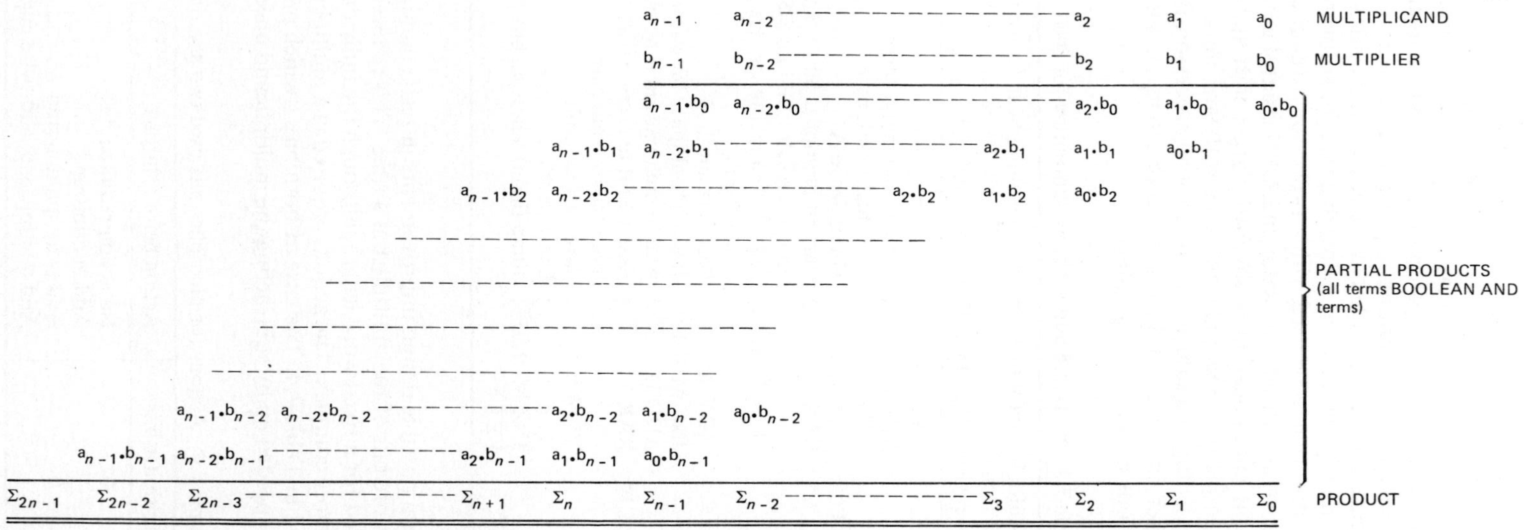

a_{n-1}	a_{n-2}				a_2	a_1	a_0					MULTIPLICAND
b_{n-1}	b_{n-2}				b_2	b_1	b_0					MULTIPLIER
	$a_{n-2}.b_0$				$a_2.b_0$	$a_1.b_0$	$a_0.b_0$					
$a_{n-1}.b_0$	$a_{n-2}.b_1$				$a_1.b_1$	$a_0.b_1$						
$a_{n-1}.b_1$	$a_{n-2}.b_2$			$a_2.b_1$	$a_0.b_2$							PARTIAL PRODUCTS (all terms BOOLEAN AND terms)
$a_{n-1}.b_2$	$a_{n-2}.b_2$			$a_2.b_2$	$a_1.b_2$							
$a_{n-1}.b_{n-2}$	$a_{n-2}.b_{n-2}$		$a_2.b_{n-2}$	$a_1.b_{n-2}$	$a_0.b_{n-2}$							
$a_{n-1}.b_{n-1}$	$a_{n-2}.b_{n-1}$		$a_2.b_{n-1}$	$a_1.b_{n-1}$	$a_0.b_{n-1}$							
Σ_{2n-1}	Σ_{2n-2}	Σ_{2n-3}	Σ_{n+1}	Σ_n	Σ_{n-1}	Σ_{n-2}	Σ_3	Σ_2	Σ_1	Σ_0		PRODUCT

$\Sigma_0 = a_0.b_0$

Σ_1 = LSB of arithmetic sum ($a_1.b_0$ plus $a_0.b_1$)

Σ_2 = LSB of arithmetic sum ($a_2.b_0$ plus $a_1.b_1$ plus $a_0.b_2$ plus carry from Σ_1 column)

Σ_3 = LSB of arithmetic sum ($a_3.b_0$ plus $a_2.b_1$ plus $a_1.b_2$ plus $a_0.b_3$ plus multiple carries from Σ_2 column)

etc.

Fig. 7.14   General form of binary multiplication

then adding one to the next pair of multiplier bits to be examined (propagating carries). The action add three times the multiplier is effectively replaced by subtract it once and add it four times.

For higher speeds a combinational multiplier design is required; some form of cell design is almost essential. The general form of multiplication in Fig. 7.14 shows that a large number of two input AND terms are required; the resulting quantities are added together **arithmetically** (i.e. it is not a Boolean OR summation). If a large array of AND gates is constructed and their outputs are connected into a network of half and full adders, as illustrated for 5 bits in Fig. 7.15, then a combinational multiplier is formed. This is one example of an array or matrix multiplier; it is probably the most simple of the array and tree structures which have been developed. The circuit is a ripple-carry one with consequent long delays; the worst case is $2n$ adder delays for n-bit multiplication. Improved designs exist which adopt various look-ahead techniques to reduce the propagation delay.

Various techniques for multiplication of signed integer values have been developed. The most simple approach is to determine the sign of result and save it before performing the multiplication; the result sign is simply the exclusive-OR of the input number sign bits. The multiplicand and multiplier are then both forced to positive magnitude values which are multiplied; the result is adjusted to the required format with its correct sign. Processes operating directly on signed integers, usually twos-complement, have been devised. The best known technique is by Booth; this allows numbers in n-bit twos-complement to be multipled, giving a result in $2n$-bit twos-complement.

7.4 Division

Division circuits are in general more complicated than multiplication ones. If a serial approach is adopted in a similar manner to that used in multiplication then, after initial set up, the sequences for division and multiplication of unsigned integers show relatively small differences. Figure 7.16 illustrates a division sequence with an overall structure similar to the multiplication sequence in Fig. 7.13; the test then add operations are replaced by subtract then test. In the case of microprogrammed or software routines for division, entirely separate multiply and divide routines are developed in most cases. However, for a hardware design the two functions may be combined to reduce component duplication. Combinational division circuits may be built but are not common; however, some approaches to division use fast combinational multipliers.

When restricted to unsigned integers, serial division methods follow a process of subtract then shift. The divisor which was left shifted at initial setup is subtracted from the dividend, and the sign of the result is checked. If the result is negative, the subtraction should not have been performed and the divisor must be added back (restored) to the dividend before it is shifted. This sequence is called **restoring division**. More advanced serial designs intercept the result of the subtraction before it is written into the accumulator and test its sign. If it is negative, the transfer to the accumulator is blocked, which removes the requirement of performing a restoring addition. Techniques similar to multiple bit examination in multiplication have also been devised.

Examination of many running computer programs shows that division is performed much less frequently than any other arithmetic operation. Professional programmers are aware that the division operation is usually the slowest, and write programs with as few divisions as possible. Consequently, when designing an ALU one approach is to use available resources to produce the fastest possible addition and multiplication circuits and then perform division by a sequence of multiplication processes. For floating point numbers a simple method is to form the reciprocal of the divisor and then multiply by this. Obviously this is not suitable for integer arithmetic, because reciprocals are less than the smallest non-zero integer. The mantissa of a normalized floating point number lies in a restricted range,

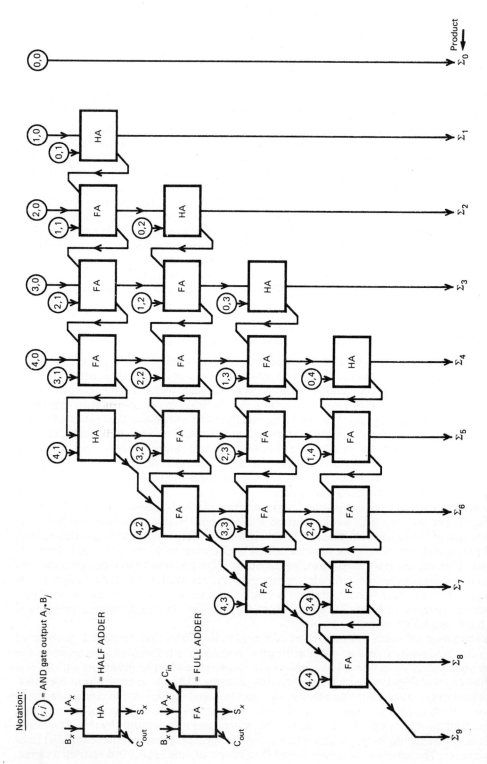

Fig. 7.15   One form of circuit for a matrix multiplier

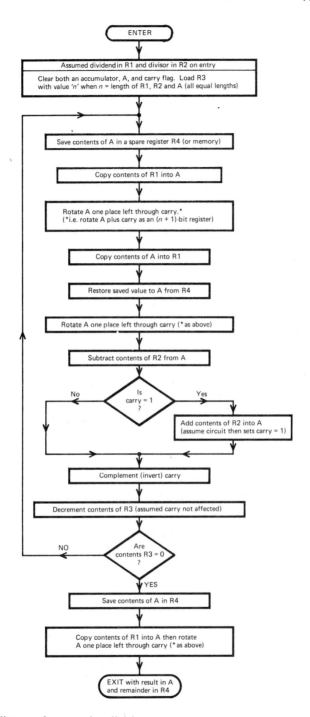

Fig. 7.16 Flow diagram for restoring division

usually 0·5 to 1·0, or 1·0 to 2·0 decimal equivalents. About three to five bits following the leading 1 of the mantissa for which a reciprocal is required are used as a ROM address. The contents read from this ROM address are the initial value for an iteration formula involving only addition, subtraction and multiplication. By careful choice of formula, the reciprocal can be produced within the accuracy allowed by the word length after only a few iterations. One simple derivation of $1/X$ uses

$$R_0 = \text{initial trial for } 1/X$$
$$e_i = X \times R_i$$
$$R_i = R_{i-1} \times (2 - e_{i-1}) = i\text{th iteration result}$$

Clearly $e_i = 1$ if R_i is exactly the reciprocal of X. Iterating from a reasonable initial value, R_0, produces a rapid convergence of e_i to 1. Ignoring inaccuracies arising in performance of the calculations, the number of bits of R_i which are correct doubles on each iteration.

7.5 Logic and shift operations

Circuits for logic operations are more simple than those for arithmetic ones, because no inputs to a circuit for one pair of bits come from the circuit for another pair. Figure 7.17 is the ith stage of a circuit to implement the operations AND, OR, INVERT, and exclusive-OR (XOR), with two control inputs used to select the function. The circuit is relatively simple, and in many ALU designs these functions are combined with the addition unit for the ith digit pair; for example the circuit for G_i is $A_i \cdot B_i$ therefore AND is often already available.

Shifting or rotating within the ALU usually requires shift registers and the appropriate control circuits, although two registers and combinational multiplexers may be used in principle. Standard shift register designs are often used, although in many MOS microprocessors the registers are dynamic devices with the shift easily implemented. For high speed and multiple shifts a large matrix of switches known as a **barrel shifter** is used.

7.6 Non-integer and mixed arithmetic

Generally, the requirement for arithmetic with non-integer numbers is met by performing a sequence of integer arithmetic operations. Fixed point numbers with both operands in the same format may use the same circuits as integers. The results will be correct except that after multiplication and division the position of the point will have to be determined and the result shifted an appropriate amount left or right to restore the initial format.

For floating point numbers the arithmetic process is usually broken into a sequence of steps. The sequence may be executed by a hardware control unit, or a microprogram, or user supplied software. The exact sequence of steps will depend on the format in use.

Example

Add the two numbers with equivalent decimal values 42·913 and 25·726 when a 32-bit IEEE format is used.
The IEEE format for 42·913 was derived earlier and is

0100 0010 0010 1011 1010 0110 1110 1001

The representation of 25·726 is

0100 0001 1100 1101 1100 1110 1101 1001

i)   The numbers are separated into their exponents and unsigned magnitude values of the mantissas with the leading 1 restored. Both mantissas are lengthened by adding two leading

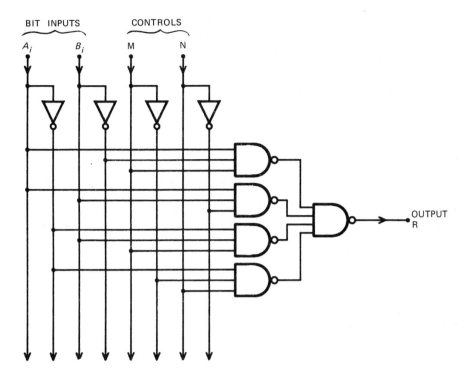

Fig. 7.17 Multifunction logic cell

CONTROLS			OUTPUT
N	M	ACTION	R
0	0	AND	$R = A_i.B_i$
0	1	OR	$R = A_i + B_i$
1	0	INVERT	$R = \bar{A}_i$
1	1	EXCLUSIVE-OR	$R = A_i \oplus B_i$

zeros and several trailing zeros (only four are shown here, this is rather few). For the two numbers chosen:

$$\text{Exponent of } 42 \cdot 913 \text{ is } 10000100$$
$$\text{Exponent of } 25 \cdot 726 \text{ is } 10000011$$

Mantissa of 42·913 is

$$00\ 1010\ 1011\ 1010\ 0110\ 1110\ 1001\ 0000$$

Mantissa of 25·726 is

$$00\ 1100\ 1101\ 1100\ 1110\ 1101\ 1001\ 0000$$

(The point is after the third digit, the most significant digit of 1, but the mantissas are treated as integers).

ii) The exponent of the second operand, the addend, is subtracted from that of the first, the augend. The sign and magnitude of the difference, D, are required. $D = +1$ for the example.

iii)   If D is negative, shift the mantissa of the augend by $|D|$ places right, moving in zeros; when D is positive, shift the mantissa of the addend in this way. For the example $D = +1$, and the addend mantissa becomes

$$00\ 0110\ 0110\ 1110\ 0111\ 0110\ 1100\ 1000$$

The larger of the exponents, E (the one for the number not shifted), is the initial exponent of the result. $E = 10000100$ for the example.

iv)   The overall signs of the augend and addend are examined; the mantissa of any negative number is converted into its twos-complement value, with the first of the leading zeros added becoming the sign bit. Neither example number is negative so no changes are required.

v)   Add the mantissas, now in twos-complement, as integers (this is the only step for which subtraction of floating point numbers differs from addition). The example gives

$$01\ 0001\ 0010\ 1000\ 1110\ 0101\ 0101\ 1000$$

vi)   The sign of this total, S, is the sign of the result. If the sign is negative, complement the result to give its magnitude; this is not necessary for the example as $S = 0$.

vii)   The result is examined for the position of the leading 1, (the MSB is now always zero) and the number is normalized so that the most significant 1 is in the third digit position. If the second most significant bit is 1, the whole number is shifted right one place moving in 0 as the MSB and incrementing the exponent, E. When the leading 1 is the third bit from the left, no changes are required. If the leading 1 is further right, the number should be shifted left R places until the 1 is in the third bit position. The value R must be subtracted from the exponent, E. However, if R exceeds some particular value set in the format specification, the result must have had very few significant digits and should be treated as a special case, probably forced to zero. The action will depend on the full floating point format.

At this point the exponent, E, must also be examined for overflow or underflow and any error flags set if either occurs, as the result is out of range.

The example result requires a move one place to the right, so E is incremented to 10000101 and the mantissa becomes

$$00\ 1000\ 1001\ 0100\ 0111\ 0010\ 1010\ 1100$$

viii)   The results for sign, exponent, and mantissa are now combined to produce the final result in the floating point format; the correct rounding or truncation rules must be followed. For the example, $42 \cdot 913_{10} + 25 \cdot 726_{10}$ this gives

$$0100\ 0010\ 1000\ 1001\ 0100\ 0111\ 0010\ 1011$$

As a check this result is unpacked; this gives the binary value $+1000100 \cdot 10100011100101011$. Conversion of this produces the approximate decimal equivalent of $+68 \cdot 639$ as expected.

Mixed arithmetic is not often undertaken in hardware, it is usually left to the programmer to devise methods of performing it by converting all operands for an arithmetic process to the same format. In most cases formats are ranked in order of complexity; unsigned integer is the most simple, followed by signed integer, fixed point then floating point. Most software systems assume that, when two numbers in different formats are combined by an arithmetic operation, the result will be produced in the more complex of the two formats. Consequently, mixed format arithmetic is usually performed by converting the number in the less complex format into its nearest equivalent in the more complex format and performing the operation in this format.

7.7 Some alternative circuit techniques

ALU circuits are combinational ones, although arithmetic processes are sometimes broken into a sequence of simple combinational steps executed by a sequential control circuit. Any combinational design method may be used, but only standard textbook minimization methods and cell techniques have been examined.

One design technique that is suitable for arithmetic circuits is to use a ROM, or an assembly of several ROMs, as a combinational circuit. The ROM contents are the truth table for the required circuit, the address inputs form the circuit inputs and the data outputs are the circuit outputs. In most cases the ROM is permanently enabled, and it then acts as a combinational circuit. Table 7.5 illustrates the pattern to be used in a ROM with 16-words each of 4-bits which performs the multiplication of two 2-bit numbers, obviously this is a simple case but the method is easily extended. Depending upon speed requirements either bipolar or MOS devices may be used. The present economic limit with bipolar devices is probably about 4k-words allowing circuits with twelve inputs to be constructed. For MOS devices the corresponding limit is about 256k-words giving circuits with eighteen inputs. The number of outputs is set by the word length of individual devices combined with the number of devices that it is reasonable to connect so have all the same address inputs.

The ROM technique relies on mass production of identical memory cells which is a low cost process. It may in some cases be extremely wasteful, even if cheap. For example the LSB of the result of multiplication is always just the AND of the LSBs of the two input numbers. In a ROM circuit such as that in Table 7.5 when the numbers each have n-bits then 2^{2n} memory cells are required to generate this LSB.

Integrated circuit devices with alternative programmable techniques are available. These include both user programmable devices such as programmable logic arrays (PLAs, FPLAs, PALs) and devices fixed during manufacture, for example uncommitted logic arrays (ULAs). In most cases these implement conventional sum of products minimizations or are forms of cell technique.

Table 7.5 ROM contents for 2-bit by 2-bit multiplier

Address inputs				ROM data			
A_3	A_2	A_1	A_0	D_3	D_2	D_1	D_0
0	0	0	0	0	0	0	0
0	0	0	1	0	0	0	0
0	0	1	0	0	0	0	0
0	0	1	1	0	0	0	0
0	1	0	0	0	0	0	0
0	1	0	1	0	0	0	1
0	1	1	0	0	0	1	0
0	1	1	1	0	0	1	1
1	0	0	0	0	0	0	0
1	0	0	1	0	0	1	0
1	0	1	0	0	1	0	0
1	0	1	1	0	1	1	0
1	1	0	0	0	0	0	0
1	1	0	1	0	0	1	1
1	1	1	0	0	1	1	0
1	1	1	1	1	0	0	1

Note that A_3A_2 forms multiplicand, A_1A_0 forms multiplier $D_3D_2D_1D_0$ forms results.

7.8   Problems

1 An 80-bit word length parallel addition unit is constructed using look-ahead carry modules of 8-bits. Each module adds two 8-bit numbers, producing the sum outputs within 15 nsec and the final carry-out within 12 nsec. These modules are connected together in a simple ripple scheme to produce the 80-bit adder. Determine the worst case propagation delay for the complete adder.

2 The specification for the 74LS83A indicates that the worst case propagation delays for the sum outputs are all the same value, 24 nsec. The maximum delay for the final carry-out is 17 nsec when a digit input changes, but is 22 nsec when the carry-in causes a change in the carry-out. If a circuit to add 32-bit numbers is built using 74LS83A devices in a ripple configuration as in Fig. 7.6, what time must elapse after connection of the inputs before the outputs may be safely used by other circuits?

3 Prove that the additional circuit included in Fig. 7.10 will correctly perform the operations *add with carry* and *subtract with borrow*.

   Also perform in detail (show values at unit inputs and outputs) the actions undertaken by the circuit in Fig. 7.10 with $n = 4$ for the 4-bit calculations $(+3)+(+3)$, $(-3)+(-2)$, $(-3)-(-3)$ and $(+2)-(+3)$ when the decimal numbers in parentheses are represented in 4-bit twos-complement. Complete each calculation in three cases. One case is for the operation which ignores the carry/borrow data input. The other two cases are the *add with carry* form when the carry/borrow input values are 0 and 1 respectively.

4 Combinational logic integrated circuits are available which multiply two 4-bit numbers. Using such devices and 4-bit full adder integrated circuits (e.g. 74LS83A devices) as cells, devise a network to multiply two 8-bit numbers.

5 Using the flow diagram in Fig. 7.16, perform the division of 10110111_2 by 00001010_2, working in 8 bits. Obtain an integer result and integer remainder. Convert the original values and the results to decimal equivalents to indicate that the results are correct.

6 Devise a sequence of operations to multiply together two numbers represented in a specified 32-bit floating point format. Demonstrate that the process operates correctly by converting the decimal numbers 47·329 and 0·00735 into the format and multiplying them by the process described. Convert the result to a decimal value and comment on the accuracy achieved.

Part 3
Memory Components
and Systems

8 Memory components

The memory of a processor system is frequently the most expensive hardware section and is often the unit which limits the overall system performance. If the processor has a basic von Neumann structure then the memory will be used to store the program, data and program work areas (stacks, intermediate variables, etc.). While the programmer may restrict certain areas of memory to performing specific functions, the architecture of most simple processor systems imposes no limitations on the use of memory.

Initially read and write types of memory are considered as these are the most general-purpose ones. Any device which may be forced into either one of two different stable conditions, **states**, may be used to construct a memory system. To be useful, any memory must have a mechanism enabling the state of the device to be determined, that is **read**. The two different states may be given the names 0 and 1; a single device or cell then becomes the store for a single bit.

A wide range of mechanisms have been used to build storage systems, and for any application memories should be compatible with the CPU and other system components. Modern electronic processor systems require large numbers of fast and low cost storage elements; consequently most storage devices are based on electronic circuits or on magnetic effects. Optical storage mechanisms are being developed but, if successful, it will be several years before they are common.

8.1 Properties of storage devices

The essential features of any mechanism used for storage in a modern processor system are cost, physical size, the time to store data (write access), the time to retrieve data (read access), and power consumption. Table 8.1 summarizes some of the important features of common memory devices.

Some types of memory can retain the stored data when the power supply is removed, for example most devices based on the magnetization of ferromagnetic materials have this property. These memory devices are known as **non-volatile** types. Conversely, memory devices which lose their data on power removal, for example many electronic storage circuits, are **volatile** memories.

One group of storage devices do not even retain the data with power connected; because of imperfections there is a slow decay in the condition of the device which indicates the stored value. However, these memories have some very useful features and this fault is tolerated. Additional circuits are used with such memories to read the contents automatically before they are completely lost, and then restore the full value. This restoration process is called **refreshing** and devices of this type are **dynamic memories**. Devices which do not require refreshing are **static memories**.

The action of reading the contents of some designs of memory device destroys the contents of the memory. Devices for which this occurs have **destructive read out**; those devices for which reading the contents does not destroy the contents have **non-destructive read out**.

Table 8.1   Features of common memory devices

Storage mechanism	Typical access time	Access mode	Features
Bipolar circuits	10–50 nsec	Random	Volatile, high power consumption, relatively few memory cells on an integrated circuit
Dynamic MOS circuits	40–250 nsec	Random	Volatile, low power consumption, requires refresh, largest number of memory cells on an integrated circuit
Static MOS, CMOS circuits	50–500 nsec	Random	Volatile, moderate power required, simple to use
Ferrite core	150 nsec–1 μsec	Random	Non-volatile, destructive read out, relatively expensive to manufacture (several variants, e.g. plated wire)
Magnetic bubble	5 msec seek 10 μsec per bit	Serial (cyclic)	Non-volatile, destructive read out, built in automatic re-write
Magnetic surface recording	Depends on system	Serial (some cyclic)	Non-volatile, bulk store systems, mechanical components, wide range of speed (1 msec to 15 min seek, according to mechanism)
Optical	1–50 msec seek 0·1 μsec per bit	Serial (cyclic)	Read only (non-volatile) bulk store, mechanical components, very high density

8.2   Electronic read and write memory circuits

When power is connected to the simple transistor bistable in Fig. 8.1, it will either settle with T_1 on (conducting so $V_1 \approx 0$) and T_2 off (non-conducting so $V_2 \approx V_{cc}$), or with T_1 off ($V_1 \approx V_{cc}$) and T_2 on ($V_2 \approx 0$). If a mechanism is provided to force it into either one of these states as required by the signal at some control input, then the circuit is a storage device for one binary digit (bit). Note that in logic circuit form this bistable is just a loop of two inverters; when the write input circuit is added it is a D-type bistable (latch).

This bipolar transistor circuit has faults but is a basis for development of useful circuits. Large numbers of storage units (cells) are required by processor systems, so cells must be cheap with high speed performance. To meet such requirements, large numbers of cells are formed on a single integrated circuit and circuit designs are dominated by considerations necessary for integrated circuit manufacture.

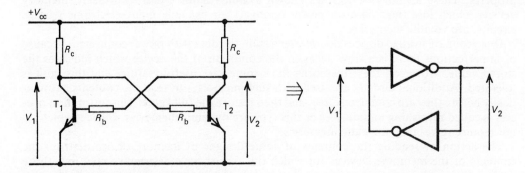

Fig. 8.1   A basic electronic bistable circuit

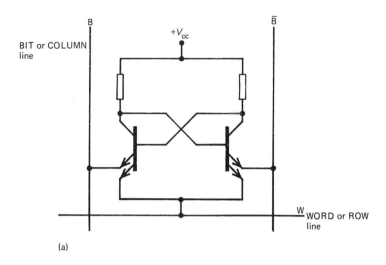

(a)

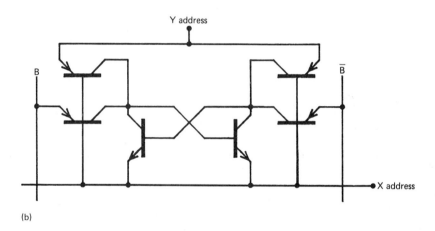

(b)

Fig. 8.2 Typical bipolar integrated circuit memory cells

Integrated circuit memories using bipolar transistors are available with several different designs of memory cell. Figure 8.2a shows one cell design used in several memory devices, while Fig. 8.2b shows another cell for devices combining I²L and ECL circuits. The lines indicated as bit line (B), word line (W), or X and Y address provide the control and signal paths for storing new data and retrieving present contents.

Although bipolar memory circuits are the fastest types available, their only advantage is high speed. Compared with other memory devices they require a large amount of power, and relatively few can be fitted onto a single integrated circuit. One reason for the difficulty of building these circuits in integrated circuit form is the need for resistors, which require a large area on integrated circuits.

With careful circuit design, the current limiting resistors, R_b, in Fig. 8.1 may be omitted (as in Fig. 8.2a). They are never required if MOS transistors are used for T_1 and T_2; no current flows into the insulated gate of the MOS transistor and hence there is no need for limiting resistors. Further, an MOS transistor with the gate correctly biased behaves as a

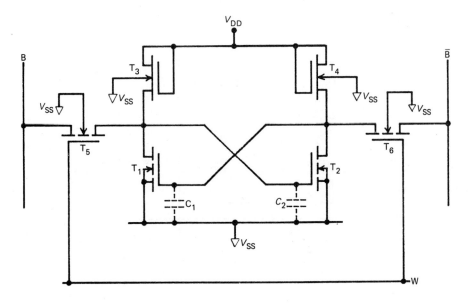

Fig. 8.3 Static NMOS memory cell

resistor but requires much less space on an integrated circuit. Consequently an MOS bistable memory cell may be designed with MOS transistors for T_1 and T_2, no limiting resistors in the gate bias circuits, and MOS transistors as loads in place of the resistors R_c. Adding the MOS transistors T_5 and T_6 to form the mechanism for writing data into the cell and reading data from it produces the basic six transistor static memory cell, Fig. 8.3, used in many integrated circuits.

A major reason for slow speed in MOS circuits is the insulated gate. The gate construction is essentially that of a capacitor, and there is an inherent capacitance between the gate and the other electrodes of the transistor. This is shown in simplified form by C_1 and C_2 in Fig. 8.3. These capacitors must be charged and discharged when the state of the cell is changed; the resulting circuit time constants slow the cell switching speed.

Early in the development of MOS memories it was realized that although the capacitors slow the circuit, they provide a means of reducing power consumption. Examining the circuit in the state with T_1 conducting, C_1 is charged, T_2 is not conducting and C_2 is not charged (since T_1 is a short circuit across it). To change state, T_1 must be turned off, but C_1 helps to keep it on by holding the gate at about V_{DD}. The transistors T_3 and T_4 may be used as switches as well as resistors by connecting their gates together to the input labelled 'clock' in Fig. 8.4. When the clock input biases T_3 and T_4 on, the circuit is the same as that in Fig. 8.3. However, if the clock is used to turn T_3 and T_4 off (non-conducting), there is no discharge path for C_1 and it remains charged with no currents flowing in the circuit (C_2 will remain uncharged). When T_3 and T_4 are turned on again, C_1 is still charged and T_1 turns on, ensuring that T_2 remains off. Hence the memory condition of the circuit may be held with the circuit essentially turned off (no currents flowing).

In a real integrated circuit, C_1 and C_2 are not perfect so C_1 slowly discharges and C_2 slowly charges. Provided that the clock is used to turn T_3 and T_4 on before the charge on C_1 has decayed by a significant amount, there will be sufficient voltage at the gate of T_1 to turn it on. Once T_1 is on, the circuit will settle in the original T_1 on, T_2 off state which fully re-charges C_1 and discharges C_2. This restores, that is refreshes, the correct state and the circuit is a dynamic memory cell. As the circuit is symmetrical, an identical argument may be used

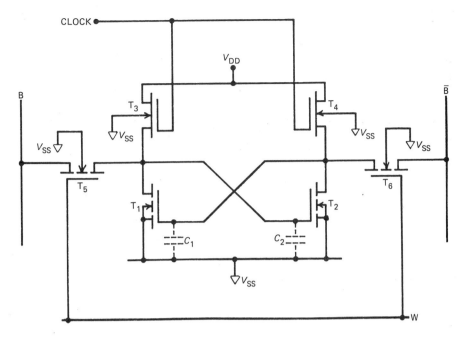

Fig. 8.4 Early dynamic NMOS memory cell

to describe the behaviour with T_1 off and T_2 on.

For reasonable performance, a simple dynamic cell requires refreshing about every millisecond. The refresh for this design consists of turning on transistors T_3 and T_4 for typically less than a tenth of a microsecond. Consequently current only flows for a small fraction of the time and average power consumption is greatly reduced. This power reduction is the only significant advantage of this simple dynamic cell; it must be balanced against the complexity of the refresh circuits required.

Examination of the cell when the refresh transistors are off indicates a somewhat different memory action than that of a bistable circuit. At refresh, the correct state is restored because one capacitor is charged and biases the gate of one transistor so that it turns on; the other transistor has its gate held at the source potential and is kept off. The state of the circuit is now controlled by the charge on a capacitor, and the stored value may be regarded as being indicated by the charged or uncharged state of one of the capacitors (the state of the other capacitor is always the inverse). The bistable section of the circuit is now simply acting as a mechanism which detects the charge state; it is a **sense amplifier**.

If the value stored in a memory cell is indicated by charge on a capacitor, then a cell may be devised with only a storage capacitor plus one MOS transistor to route charge into or out of the capacitor, as in Fig. 8.5. With careful organization, all the circuits required to load the cell (write) and determine its contents (read) may be shared by many cells (512 for the latest devices). The original six transistor static cell is reduced to a one capacitor and one transistor dynamic cell. This gives a great reduction in cell size and power consumption, allowing a large increase in the number of memory cells on a single integrated circuit. The storage capacitor value may be below 10^{-13}F; consequently the amount of charge stored is very small, making design of the circuits which detect it difficult.

Another approach to memory cell design using MOS devices is to use CMOS circuit configurations. A major fault of the circuit in Fig. 8.3 is that current is always flowing down one branch, either through T_1 and T_3 or through T_2 and T_4. This leads to high power con-

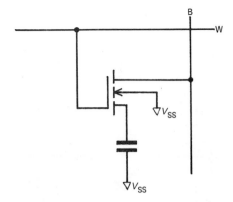

Fig. 8.5   Modern dynamic NMOS memory cell

sumption when there are many cells in a memory. CMOS designs are such that power only flows (except for leakage currents) when the circuit switches from one state to the other. Returning to Fig. 8.1, the logic for the simple bistable is shown as a loop of two inverters; these may be CMOS inverters and addition of the read and write circuits produces the CMOS static memory cell in Fig. 8.6.

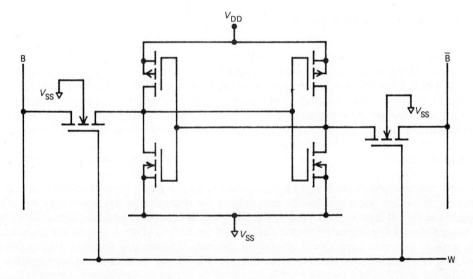

Fig. 8.6   Static CMOS memory cell

A wide range of integrated circuit read and write memory devices are available; common types and properties are summarized in Table 8.2. The maximum size (number of cells on one integrated circuit) of memory device of all types has approximately doubled every two to three years, and it is probable that this will continue for many years; maximum size is still limited by manufacturing difficulties and not by fundamental physical properties.

8.3   Organization of semiconductor memory devices

A modern integrated circuit memory contains many storage cells organized to appear as an

Table 8.2 Available integrated circuit memory devices

Circuit form	Typical access time	Max. cells on an ic (density)	Features
ECL (static)	10 nsec	4 k	Very high speed, high power, low density, fast mainframe use
TTL (static)	25 nsec	16 k	High speed, high power, for special applications
NMOS (dynamic)	100 nsec	1 M	High density, used in most mainframes and many minicomputers
NMOS (static)	100 nsec	256 k	Used in small to medium systems when DRAM refresh overheads too high in cost or speed
CMOS (static)	150 nsec	256 k	Almost as fast as NMOS, lower power, now used instead of NMOS for many applications

array of a specified number of words, all the same length, at contiguous locations (addresses). For example, a readily available size of memory is one containing 16384 cells: a 16k-bit memory. These 16k-bit memories are available organized as units of 16k × 1-bit, 4k × 4-bits and 2k × 8-bits. All units contain the same memory array; only internal sections of the integrated circuit between the array and the external connection pins are different.

Semiconductor devices are generally arranged as random access memories (Chapter 2). Random access memories built with static cells are known as **SRAMs**, and those with dynamic cells are **DRAMs**. Figure 8.7 illustrates the typical organization of an integrated circuit RAM arranged in words of 1 bit. The area labelled store matrix contains the memory cells in a rectangular array. There is one cell at every crossing point of p row lines and q column lines. The row lines are usually called **word lines** and the column lines are **bit lines**. Normally $p = q$ so the matrix is square, but some SRAMs have $p = a \times q$ where a is typically 4, 2, 1/2 or 1/4. When $p = q$ there are p^2 memory cells. The internal row and column selection circuits of the integrated circuit have M inputs each, and all 2^M input values are allowed; each value corresponds to the selection of a different row or column by the decoder, hence $p = 2^M$.

Summarizing, an integrated circuit with n memory cells usually has a square matrix of cells. The matrix has p rows and p columns with $p = \sqrt{n} = 2^M$. There are $2M$ external address inputs, although most DRAMs have a multiplexed address bus with only M external connections.

There are many different internal arrangements of connections to the cell matrix and, although the design of these may affect the memory performance, the system designer need not know the arrangement used. To use memory devices, only the complete specification is required. Modern DRAM devices have extremely complex internal organization involving internally generated timing signals. Introductory descriptions of their detailed design may be found in some of the references.

8.4 Storage using magnetic effects

Ferromagnetic materials have the property that when placed in a magnetic field they become permanently magnetized in the direction of the field. If a coil is wound around or placed close to a piece of such material, then a current flowing in the coil magnetizes the material in a particular direction; a reverse current magnetizes it in the opposite direction. The directions of magnetization may be used as the states of a memory system. To operate

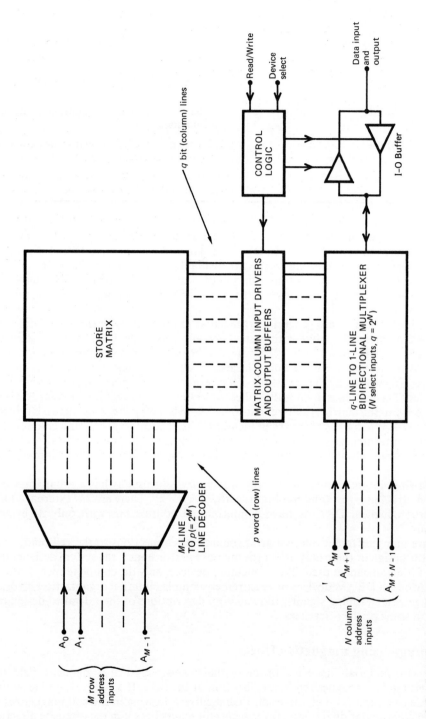

Fig. 8.7 Organisation of an integrated circuit RAM device

at the high speeds required by electronic processor systems any magnetic material used for a memory device must be non-conducting (the eddy currents which arise in a conducting material limit speed). Consequently the materials are selected from the oxides of iron, chromium and nickel; or from a group of complex materials called ferrites.

Before the advent of cheap large scale integrated circuit memories, most processor system memories consisted of magnetic core store. (The main memory of large computers is still sometimes called the core.) Only a brief description is given here, because these are rarely used now, although they have the advantage of being non-volatile and physically robust; useful properties in extreme environments.

The core element is a very small ring (bead) of ferrite; outside diameters as small as 0·5 mm (0·02 in) have been used. When operated as a store the ring is magnetized in the direction of its circular axis. For the most simple memories, magnetization is by currents in two coils wound on the core. Normally the coils are reduced to a half turn each; they simply consist of a wire threaded through the bead. Figure 8.8a shows the construction and Fig. 8.8b shows the required magnetic characteristic of the ferrite. To write a 1 to a core element a current of $+\frac{1}{2}I_b$ is passed through both wires simultaneously (currents of $+\frac{1}{2}I_b$ in one wire only are insufficient to change the direction of magnetization; equal but opposite direction currents cancel one another). If both wires carry currents of $-\frac{1}{2}I_b$ (that is the current is in the opposite direction to that required to write a 1) then a 0 is written. To read the stored value, one wire becomes the select line and the other the sense line. A current of $-I_b$ is passed through the select wire, forcing the core to the 0 state (destructive read out). If the core was already in the 0 state it does not change and no signal is produced in the sense wire; if the core was in the 1 state the magnetization is reversed and this change induces a current (signal) in the sense wire. Hence detection of a signal or no signal in the sense wire indicates that the stored value was 1 or 0 respectively. In practice, rather more complex systems involving several wires through each core are used and details may be found in the literature.

At present a more important form of magnetic storage is magnetic surface recording; the process is similar to that used in audio and video tape recorders. A miniature electromagnet, a **head**, is placed very close to, or touching, a flat surface which is uniformly coated with ferromagnetic material; usually a very fine powder of iron oxide or chromic oxide bonded to some base material. The head and coated surface are moved relative to one another (normally the surface moves) and the passage of currents through the coil magnetizes small

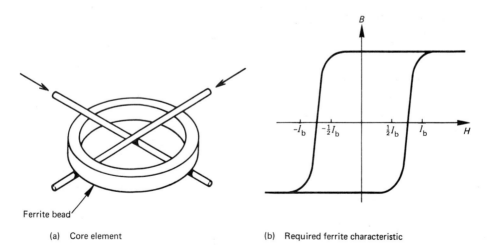

Ferrite bead

(a)   Core element   (b)   Required ferrite characteristic

Fig. 8.8   Ferrite core memory cell

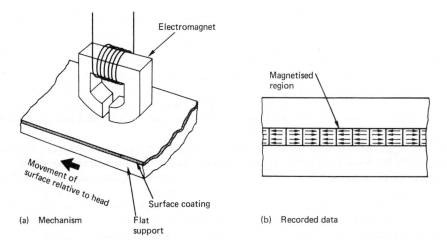

Electromagnet

Magnetised region

Movement of surface relative to head

Surface coating

(a) Mechanism   Flat support

(b) Recorded data

Fig. 8.9 Magnetic surface recording principles

regions of the surface in either of two directions. Figure 8.9a illustrates the mechanical system while Fig. 8.9b indicates how a track of magnetized regions is produced in the magnetic material. The direction of magnetization is usually parallel to the direction of motion, although systems are under development with the magnetization perpendicular to the surface. This *vertical* magnetization reduces the size of magnetized regions, increasing available storage space and speed of operation.

To retrieve the data, the surface and head are again moved relative to one another but this time no current is applied to the coil. The magnetized regions moving past the head induce currents in the coil; when amplified these currents allow the original data to be reproduced. Most systems use one head for both read and write, although some have separate read and write heads. This type of memory is not a random access one; the access time depends upon the distance from the head to the required data item. The data is stored in a sequential form and can only be accessed in the order in which it was written onto the surface. The memory is a **sequential** or a **serial access** one. If the recording track is circular, so that any data item repeatedly passes the head, it is also known as a **cyclic access memory**. Magnetic surface recording is of major importance in systems requiring a large amount of low cost storage; a detailed description is given in Chapter 9.

Another magnetic system is the magnetic bubble memory, which utilizes complex magnetic effects that occur in thin crystals or thin amorphous layers of some materials (e.g. rare-earth iron garnets). When the thin sample of material is placed in a strong magnetic field from a permanent magnet, very small cylindrical zones with magnetization in the opposite direction to the field may be selectively created or destroyed. These are the magnetic bubbles, and they may be moved around in the material by an additional varying magnetic field. Presence or absence of a bubble is used to indicate 1 or 0. The complete bubble memory unit is a cyclic access system which is small and robust with no mechanical parts to wear out. It is non-volatile and at present is more expensive than magnetic surface recording systems. Bubble memories are usually used instead of magnetic surface recording when the environment is too harsh for systems with mechanical components.

8.5 Read only memories

Nearly all of the memory in processor systems intended for general purpose applications is read and write random access memory, RAM. A very small section of the memory of such systems is of a read only form; the contents have been permanently fixed in some way. This small read only memory holds a very short program which is used to start the system correctly when power is switched on.

With the development of cheap microprocessor systems, it is economical to use a processor system for a single task that is never changed. That is, processor systems are mass produced at low cost but different units are fitted with different fixed programs to perform specific tasks; these programs are known as **firmware** (software which is fixed in a hardware device). This requires a section of the memory to be random access but with permanently fixed contents; a read only memory, **ROM**.

A number of techniques exist for producing ROMs; one of the earliest is the diode matrix shown in Fig. 8.10. The organization is similar to that of a semiconductor RAM but,

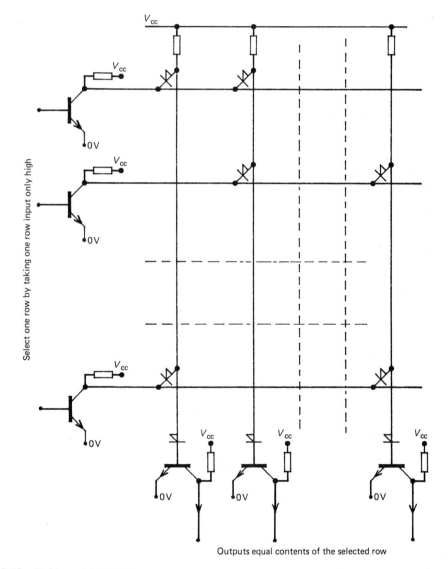

Outputs equal contents of the selected row

Fig. 8.10 Doide matrix ROM

instead of memory cells, diodes are connected or omitted at crossing points of the matrix. When the input address decoder selects a row, the contents of that row appear at the outputs. For the version shown, a diode present indicates a 1 while a diode absent indicates 0. This system is simple to create using discrete components, and one form frequently used is the plug-board controller. The matrix is constructed with two-pin sockets at each crossing point and diodes are fitted into mating plugs. Any required pattern of ones and zeros can be created by putting the plugs containing diodes into the appropriate sockets. This is a common method of providing the control program for industrial machines which follow a short sequence of operations; the technique is suitable only when occasional program modification is required.

Many read only forms of integrated circuit memory exist. As in the case of the plug-board controller, their structure is similar to that of a RAM. They have a set of word lines and a set of bit lines, with single semiconductor devices at the crossing points instead of the memory cells used in RAMs. The devices may be diodes, bipolar transistors or MOS transistors (even resistors or capacitors have been used). Manufacturing a ROM with a unique pattern as an integrated circuit is only economical when many thousands of identical units are required. Normally devices are made at every crossing point of the matrix so that most manufacturing steps are identical for all ROMs regardless of the pattern stored. Only the devices required to form the pattern are connected to both the row and column lines. The connections are usually made by the final step in manufacture; this forms the required interconnection pattern by a photographic process in which a mask (essentially a negative) determines the required connections. This form of memory is known as a **mask programmed read only memory** (a masked ROM) and is used in mass production units. Although the initial setting up costs to create the mask and the necessary unique test schedules are high, the production costs for large quantities, typically more than a thousand, are lower than those of any other type of ROM.

Several other types of ROM are available. **Programmable read only memories**, **PROMs**, allow the user to enter the pattern by a special programming operation after manufacture. The ROM is manufactured with a semiconductor device, usually a bipolar transistor, connected in place at every crossing point in the matrix. Part of the circuit connecting each device in place includes a special link, and there are additional circuits so that any link may be selectively destroyed by a high current generated in the programming process. The user can permanently write any required pattern into the memory. Consequently small quantities of memories with permanently written contents may be produced economically. Most available PROMs are bipolar devices of relatively small size; they have fast access and fairly high power consumption.

A disadvantage of a PROM is that once links have been destroyed during programming they cannot be restored, and only limited program changes are possible. Provided that the highest read access times are not required, MOS devices based on the FAMOS structure overcome this limitation. The device is an MOS transistor manufactured with the gate totally isolated in an insulating oxide layer; the floating gate structure in Fig. 8.11. Provided that the device is built with very thin insulating layers, it is possible to force charge onto the floating gate under special bias conditions. Once on the gate, the charge will remain present for many years of normal operation. When FAMOS devices are used as the elements at the crossing points of a memory matrix, each transistor will be biased on or off according to the presence or absence of charge on its gate. A programming process is devised to force charge selectively onto the gates of transistors in the matrix, and once programmed the unit behaves as a ROM. The charge can be removed from the gate by exposing the device to a strong source of ultraviolet light; the light provides sufficient energy for the charge to escape from the gate. An obvious feature of these devices is that the integrated circuit package has a quartz window for erasure. The erasure is total restoring all elements of the device to their original unprogrammed state; the device is an **eraseable programmable**

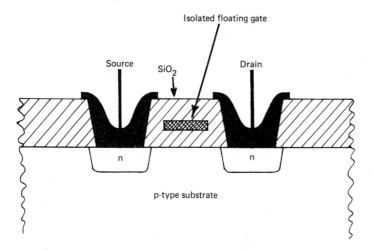

Fig. 8.11   Cross section of the FAMOS device structure used in EPROMs

read only memory, an **EPROM**. The EPROM is now a common device, and integrated circuits containing up to 1024k individual memory transistors are readily available.

In addition to the EPROM, erased by exposure to UV light, devices are available which can be erased by applying an electrical signal; these are **electrically eraseable**, or **alterable**, programmable read only memories, **EEPROMs** or **EAROMs**. There are several designs of EEPROM but most are based on a modification of the FAMOS structure. The erasure process for early designs of EEPROM erases all memory cells, as for UV EPROMs; newer designs allow selective erasure and reprogramming of a single word. These should not be regarded as read and write memories (RAMs), because the write process is slow and requires about 10 msec; the read access time is typically 200 nsec.

A totally different form of read only memory can be constructed using optical recording techniques (a simple photograph is a form of ROM and contains a large amount of data). The video discs now available for television picture and for sound reproduction (compact discs) hold the information in digital form as a series of reflecting and transparent zones on the disc. The pattern is read by a laser beam and photo-detector system. A single disc can hold over 10^{11} bits, and some computer manufacturers are adapting these disc systems to hold binary information to be used by their computer systems.

8.6   Summary

Memory devices are available with a wide range of properties, and new or improved devices are continually being introduced. In many applications, the memory design for a processor system is straightforward and standard solutions may be used. In cases with specifications near the limit of processor or memory performance, the design of memory systems requires great care and knowledge of the component behaviour and limitations.

9 Magnetic surface recording

As indicated in Chapter 8, binary data may be stored as a pattern of magnetized zones created in a thin coating on the surface of a non-magnetic support. Such systems provide low cost non-volatile read and write memories with very large capacities. Many different surface recording systems exist with wide ranges of speed, capacity, and cost.

9.1 Properties of surface recording systems

Magnetic surface recording systems are serial access ones, many are cyclic access. Data is recorded by forming a sequence of magnetized zones in the coating on a support which is moved past the record (write) and replay (read) head or heads. Although these systems are similar in concept to audio and video tape recorders, the recording method is less complex. The zones are fully magnetized, **saturated**, in either of the selected directions, whereas audio systems do not allow magnetic saturation to occur. Non-saturating systems record a high frequency signal, **bias**, which is modulated by the signal being recorded.

In many data systems the magnetic zones do not directly represent zeros and ones. However, for any system the quantity of data stored depends directly on the number of zones, capacity is limited by how closely together differently magnetized zones can be created. This is a function of several features including the properties of the magnetic material and the size and position of the heads. Improvements are continually being made, and for any device the limit may be expressed as the **maximum recording density**. In principle this is the maximum number of distinct magnetized zones which can be created on a unit area of the surface. However, technical requirements cause the distance between adjacent recording tracks to be much greater than the distance between adjacent zones along a track. Consequently recording density may be given as the product of the number of zones in a unit length of track and the number of parallel tracks in a unit distance. More frequently, the number of **flux reversals** (zone changes) possible in a unit length of track is used to specify storage density for surface recording systems.

Storage by magnetic surface systems is organized with data stored and retrieved in large groups of bits referred to as **blocks** or **records**. Blocks are stored with additional information to indicate what is stored and to provide a check of recording and retrieval accuracy. Note that complete blocks must be written and read, individual bits of data cannot be stored or retrieved.

When access to a particular block is required, the mechanical system must first move the area of surface holding the required block to the head. This movement takes a time which is relatively long compared with the time to read or write an individual bit once the surface and head are correctly positioned. Surface recording systems have two access times: the time to find a required area of the surface, and the time taken to transfer a bit once that area is found. The time to find the area required is often called the access time. To avoid confusion with semiconductor memory devices a better term is the **seek access time**. Depending upon the application, either the mean seek access time or the worst case, maximum seek access time, is important. As mean values are less than maximum ones, the mean seek access time is usually given in manufacturers' specifications. Once the area containing the required data is found, complete data blocks may be transferred to or from the surface rapidly. Hence a data **transfer rate**, not an individual bit or word access time, is specified. Transfer rate is just the number of bits per second that can be written or read in a continuous stream. Both the seek access time and transfer rate are functions of the mechanical design of the system. Some systems may have features which give slightly more comlex access times. Retrieval of data from a storage system may also be described in terms of **latency**. This usually refers to complex systems and is the time for the storage system to accept or return data in response to a request.

There are many ways of representing binary data as magnetized conditions of the surface. Before storage, a number of data items are organized as a block and encoded to form a binary sequence. This sequence is used to generate the current to the record head. For some systems, the method of representing individual 0 and 1 data bits allows the zones corresponding to individual bits to be identified. In other systems the encoding is such that individual data bits cannot be associated with specific magnetic zones. Block format and encoding affect reliability of storage and retrieval, the bit transfer rate, and the data capacity of a fixed size system.

9.2 Mechanical systems

9.2.1 Tape stores

Although some very early computers had small magnetic drum stores, these were the main store. The first magnetic surface stores for bulk data were tape systems, and improved versions are important elements of modern computer systems. As in a domestic audio tape recorder, the magnetic material is coated onto a strong thin flexible polyester tape. A single head may be used with one track along the length of the tape, but most tape systems designed for data storage have several heads. These are in a row at right angles to the direction of motion of the tape forming parallel data tracks. Common numbers of tracks are seven and nine, although other numbers are used. Some systems use the same head for read and write, others have separate heads.

Many mechanical systems have been developed to move the tape past the fixed heads; Fig. 9.1 is a schematic diagram of a large tape system for mainframe computers. The tape is normally about 0·5 in (12·5 mm) wide, and the reels may hold nearly a kilometre of tape. High tape speeds are used with rapid acceleration (up to about 30g) from rest to running speed. The snatch on starting would stretch or break the tape if it was pulled directly from the reel; the buffer loops overcome this problem. They also even out speed fluctuations because both spools and the capstan are driven using separate motors (unlike domestic recorders where one motor may drive all components through belt or gear systems).

Data is recorded at a fixed density on the tape, common values are in the range 600 to 2400 bits per inch (**bpi**) although higher densities are being introduced. Typical tape speeds are in the range 20 to 250 inches per second (0·5 to 5 metres per second). These figures indicate that a large 9-track tape can store over 10^9 data bits with retrieval at up to 10^7 bits per second if all tracks are used simultaneously. Allowing for formatting and various check mechanisms, more realistic values are significantly lower.

A reel of tape holds a very large amount of data and is a cheap form of non-volatile read and write memory; consequently it is used for bulk data storage (e.g. for holding large commercial data files in accounting, stock control, etc.). It is compact, allowing large permanent records to be stored in a small space, and transport from one computer to another is simple. The main disadvantage for many applications is the long access time; if the tape is near one end of its travel and the next required data block is near the other end, the access can take over ten minutes. Although this may be reduced by good data management systems, average access times are still several minutes. Once the data is found the transfer rate is high at around 10^7 bits per second.

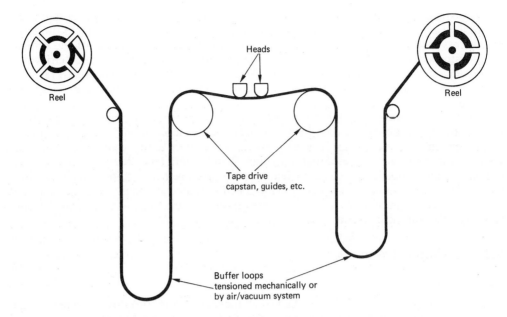

Fig. 9.1   Schematic form of a high performance magnetic tape system

There are other tape systems in addition to large reel to reel tapes, for example data cartridge systems. Cartridges hold less data than reel to reel tapes, and have lower data transfer rates. Their main use is in small to medium size systems where they provide a convenient and reliable long term data storage mechanism.

Domestic tape recorders, usually cassette machines, are used for data storage in very low cost applications (e.g. home computers). Single bits cannot be reliably represented by small magnetized zones; instead, the normal recording of audio frequencies with a modulated bias is used. A technique known as frequency shift keying (**FSK**), described in Section 9.4, is adopted with two different audio frequency tones representing the binary data. The recording is a pattern of tones from which the original binary values may be derived on replay. The system requires much larger areas of tape for each bit (however mass produced domestic cassettes are very cheap), utilizes only a single track, and is inherently slow. Typical data transfer rates are around 300 bits per second (baud) using standard tape speeds of 1·875 inches per second (equivalent to about 150 bpi). Each side of a standard one hour cassette holds about 10^6 bits of data (at less than 10^{-4} pence per bit). Seek access time is very long but is improved using manual operation of fast wind and rewind controls.

9.2.2   Drum stores

Drum stores consist of a rigid cylinder coated with magnetic material and rotated at very high speed, typically about 5000 rpm. The multiple read and write heads are usually fixed just above the drum surface, so recording tracks are circular giving cyclic access with short seek access time. Surface recording systems usually operate at the maximum possible density at the time when they are designed, hence high rotation speed produces a high transfer rate.

Seek times are below 10 msec and data transfer rates may be in excess of 10^7 bits per second. The main disadvantages of drum stores is their limited storage capacity, typically 10^6 to 10^7 bits (the drums are fixed in place and cannot be changed by the user), and the need for carefully controlled temperature, humidity and dust free environment to maintain the high mechanical tolerances required. Their main use is in the complex memory structures of very large computers, although other developments have reduced this application.

9.2.3   Rigid disc stores

While drums provide one mechanism with a rotating surface, an alternative is to use a disc. The tracks are circular ones, not spiral, on the disc surface with a single head used for both read and write to all the tracks on one side of a disc. This mechanism is more compact than a drum although not capable of quite such high speeds, so the access time and transfer rates are slightly lower. Disc stores exist in a wide variety of forms but the major divisions are between rigid *hard* disc systems and flexible *floppy* disc ones. Disc stores are the major area of current surface storage development, so a wide and continually changing range of systems is available.

Rigid disc systems have one or more discs fitted on a common axle and rotated at high speed. Large computers use discs up to 14 in diameter but 8 in, 5·25 in and 3·5 in diameter discs are now common in other systems. The discs are usually aluminium and their surfaces are accurately machined flat; one or both sides are coated with magnetic material. There is usually a single head for each surface, with the head moved radially across the disc; some systems use two or four heads per surface to reduce the distance and time for head movements. Generally the heads for all the disc surfaces in a multiple disc pack are fitted to a single positioning mechanism as shown in Fig. 9.2, a photograph of a medium size disc

Fig. 9.2   A Winchester disc system (covers removed)

unit. Note that even with several heads only a single serial data stream on one surface is used at any time; alignment and other problems make simultaneous use of several heads unreliable.

In rigid disc systems the heads do not touch the disc surfaces, they are designed aerodynamically to *fly* on the thin boundary layer of air dragged along by the moving disc. Flying height is around 20 microinches (0·5 μm). In some systems the complete head assembly must be drawn clear of the discs before the system is allowed to slow down and stop, in others there is an unused area of the disc on which the heads land when the disc is stopped. The very low flying height requires extremely clean conditions, a particle of dust can cause a head to crash into the disc damaging both the surface and head. Smaller systems with non-retracting heads are built into a factory sealed box (these are often called Winchester drives), whereas larger systems with retracting heads are used in computer rooms which are dust free, with regulated temperature and humidity conditions. The retracting head systems can have removable disc assemblies, allowing large data changes to be made manually very quickly; this has several advantages including reliable back-up in the event of damage to a disc surface.

There is a wide range of disc systems with capacities from below 10^8 bits to over 10^{11} bits. Access times are longer than those for drum stores, because the head must move to the track required in addition to the delay while the disc rotates to the data start. Times range from about 0·02 sec to 0·5 sec according to design. Typical data rates are in the range 10^5 to 10^7 bits per second.

9.2.4   Flexible disc stores

The flexible or *floppy* disc system has many of the advantages of both tape and rigid disc systems although it has limited capabilities. A plastic disc, thicker than the material used for a tape but still flexible, is coated with the magnetic material. The disc is permanently fitted into a cardboard or plastic envelope with precise dimensions. When the envelope is inserted into the drive a central hole in the disc and envelope enables the drive mechanism to rotate the disc within the envelope. There is a slot in the envelope through which the head makes direct contact with the disc surface once the disc is rotating.

The range of floppy disc systems is large, and changing quickly as improvements are still being made in all aspects of design. Disc diameters are 8 in, 5·25 in, and two sizes around 3 in. One or both sides are used with disc capacities from 10^6 to 10^8 bits. Rotation speeds are in the region of 200 to 400 rpm with access times from 0·1 to 1·0 sec and data transfer rates around 10^5 to 10^6 bits per second.

9.3   Recording and retrieval

Data is recorded as a pattern of magnetized zones created by passing currents through the head coil. Two directions of magnetization are produced by two directions of current flow. The size of a zone is determined by the duration of current flow and the relative velocity of the surface and head. Recording density is limited by the physical size of head, head to surface distance, system speed, and magnetic properties of the surface coating. These define the distance on the surface over which the direction of magnetization can be reversed. That is, these features give a finite width transition between zones rather than the ideal sudden change.

Retrieval relies on magnetic induction; as the surface passes the head any change in magnetic field from the magnetized surface induces a current in the head coil. Because detection is by induction, only zone boundaries produce a signal; there is no signal from a succession of zones with the same direction of magnetization. Figure 9.3a is an oscilloscope trace of a typical detected waveform for a modern hard disc system with an arbitrary data

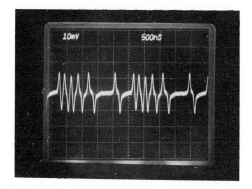 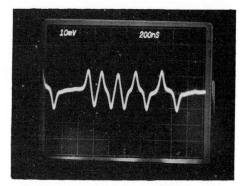

Fig. 9.3 CRO trace of a typical read signal from a Winchester disc system, a) 500nsec/ cm. b) 200nsec/ cm

pattern; Fig. 9.3b is a section with an expanded time scale. Features apparent include small variations in pulse height and peak position. These arise because the data, information, is stored by having zones of different size, and when zone boundaries are close together complex effects arise. With suitable electronic systems the actual magnetization, and hence the original data, may be determined from the signal.

9.4   Representation of data

A recording is a pattern of magnetized zones which form a code representing the original data. As the surface moves rapidly past the head, it is necessary to know the exact time at which to magnetize the surface when writing and when to examine the signal while reading. There are several timing methods: in one an extra track of alternate direction magnetized zones is written simultaneously with the data track (or pre-recorded and read during the write process). This extra **clock track** supplies a synchronization (clock) signal to indicate the data position. A second method is to devise a data recording pattern which includes its own synchronizing clock signal; such recordngs are **self-clocking**. Other methods use constant speed drives with optical or mechan   ʼosition indicators.

For those methods with direct correspondence between magnetization and individual data bits, common recording schemes are easily demonstrated. Figure 9.4 illustrates a number of recording patterns for the same arbitrary data sequence. These show the ideal current waveform required to magnetize the surface and the corresponding ideal signal received on the same scale. When appropriate, the separate clock track is shown. Early systems used **return to zero** in which 0 is recorded as one direction of magnetization, 1 as the other direction, with a non-magnetized zone separating each recorded bit. This system can be self-clocking because the read signal includes a component at twice the data frequency. The method is reliable, although it is expensive and slow. The non-magnetized zones require an additional erase mechanism to ensure that previous data is completely removed, space is wasted by the blank zones, and two changes in magnetization occur in every bit interval. For a given speed and recording density this leads to a low data capacity, hence to high cost per bit and low transfer rate.

A simple step is to omit the non-magnetized zones to produce a **non-return to zero** system (**NRZ**). The disadvantage is that long sequences of either 1 or 0 can occur and produce no change in magnetization. Read signals are generated by magnetic induction, that is a change in magnetic field is required to produce a signal. Any long continuous regions with no change in magnetization produce no signals and, even with a separate clock track, reliability is reduced.

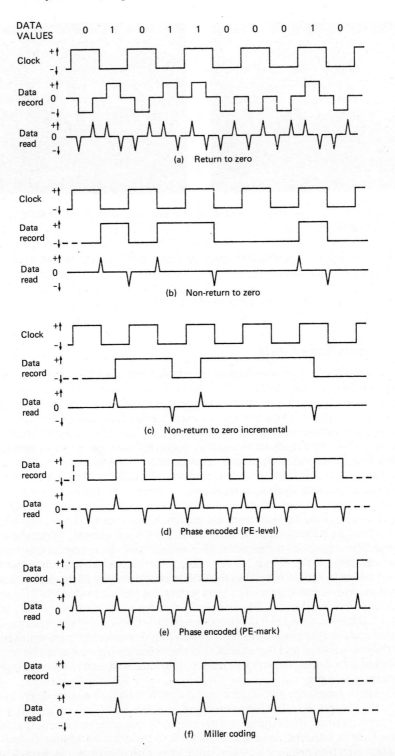

Fig. 9.4   Recording patterns and the corresponding read signals for common data representations

A modification of NRZ is **non-return to zero incremental (NRZI)**, also called non-return to zero inverted. In this system the data value is not given by the direction of magnetization. Instead, when the direction of magnetization changes at the position used to store a bit, the change represents a 1 regardless of initial or final directions of magnetization. When there is no change in magnetization the data bit stored is a 0. Provided that NRZI is used with a data format designed so that long sequences of zeros cannot occur, there are no long periods without change in magnetization. NRZI is a commonly used format, although it is not self-clocking in its general form.

The two forms in Figs 9.4d and 9.4e are both **phase encoded** schemes and are self-clocking. In one format there is always a change in magnetization at the data position, a change in one direction (upward illustrated) indicates a 1 while a change in the opposite direction indicates a 0. When necessary there is an additional change at the data boundary to produce the correct magnetization state in advance of the data change. The other phase encoded form always has a change at the data boundary, but there is only a change at the data position when the data stored is 1. The direction of the change does not matter, either at the boundary or at the data position. Both phase encoding forms are self-clocking, because at least one signal is produced in each data bit interval. A filter (e.g. a phase locked loop) can isolate a component from the detected signal with a frequency equal to the data rate, and this may be used as the clock signal. The format has half the data density of NRZI; it must allow two changes in magnetization, two zones, for every bit, whereas NRZI requires only one change or zone. However, the system is more tolerant of small fluctuations in drive speed. Phase encoding also provides a method of detecting drop-outs, small faulty areas of recording surface which cannot be magnetized. As there must be at least one change in magnetization in every bit space, a drop-out is easily detected. Many methods of data encoding include error correction mechanisms, and small numbers of drop-outs can be overcome.

The final form illustrated, Fig. 9.4f, is known as **delay modulation** or **Miller code**. It may be regarded as a modification of the second phase encoded form (Fig. 9.4e) which always has a change at the boundary. The change at the boundary is removed except in those cases when the boundary is between two bits which are both 0. Instead of there being up to two zones per bit, there is never more than one. The length of zones is different, and there is no longer a component in the signal at the data frequency. However, a component exists at a sub-harmonic which can be isolated, and the fundamental may be generated by frequency multiplication. This is one example of a **run length limited code**; for such codes the pattern of zones is no longer determined by individual bits but is influenced by the data sequence. Many other codes of this nature, **group codes**, are used but are not considered in detail here.

Modifications and developments of all recording schemes are used. Group code forms are often much more elaborate than any examined. Also different names are adopted, for example some floppy disc systems are stated to use **frequency modulation (fm)**, while others use **modified frequency modulation (mfm)**. These are phase encoded and Miller code respectively, they meet a general definition of frequency modulation but are extreme cases. The names are inappropriate but commonly used.

For low quality systems (e.g. home computers using domestic recorders) **frequency shift keying (FSK)** is adopted. There are many different forms but all rely on recording short tone bursts of two distinct frequencies. Some FSK techniques require the frequencies to be unrelated harmonically, while others require a specific harmonic relation.

9.5 Specific systems

Data recordings are made in blocks, the data for a block is formatted and the complete sequence encoded as a pattern of magnetic zones. There are many systems and they vary with device type. Most systems include some form of error detection and correction, that is the data retrieved can be examined for errors and in many cases any errors found can be corrected. These techniques greatly increase the reliability of memory systems, they are also adopted for data transmission systems and in some main core memories. Error detection and correction when data is retrieved from a store or received on a transmission link is a major topic in communication theory; Chapter 11 has a brief introduction and the suggested reading includes more detailed treatments.

The following are brief outlines of two particular data formats to demonstrate typical features.

9.5.1   IBM 3740 floppy disc format

It is often difficult to transfer data from one computer system to a different type using floppy discs because of format and hardware differences (including disc size). Although 5·25 in discs are the most common, data transfer is most often possible from one make of computer to another using single density 8 in discs with IBM 3740 format. This is an early format, and is common although it is inefficient (low density).

Floppy disc systems record data on about 40 to 80 concentric tracks, track numbering starts with 0 for the outer track. Track 0 is a special one, and the head movement system adjusts for minor imperfections by finding its exact position. The 3740 format uses phase encoding and 77 tracks with each track divided into 26 sectors. The start of the first sector is identified by an index hole in the disc.

A special track 0 format stores information describing the data stored on the other tracks; this special format is ignored here. On the remaining tracks (except 74, 75 and 76 which are reserved), 128 data bytes are recorded in each sector, as illustrated by Fig. 9.5. As indicated in Fig. 9.5, each sector has 188 bytes recorded but gaps (areas of all FF_H or all 00_H) and 13 bytes of identification information reduce this to 137 bytes. Further formatting, including error detecting CRC (cyclic redundancy check) characters, reduces the amount of user's data stored to 128 bytes in a sector.

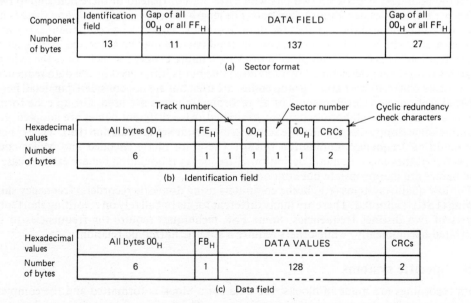

Fig. 9.5   Sector data format for a floppy-disc (IBM 3740 format)

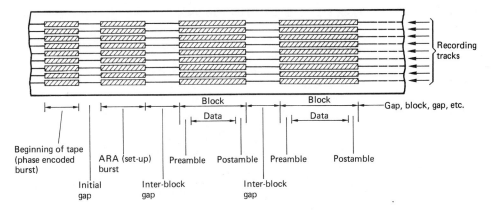

Fig. 9.6 Overall GCR recording pattern for tape systems

9.5.2 Group code recording (GCR)

This format is complex and is used with NRZI encoding on 9-track tape. It enables density to be increased from the common value, 1600 bpi, used with phase encoded tape systems, to 6250 bpi. This saves tape, reduces storage space and requires fewer tape changes when manipulating large amounts of data. GCR also provides better inherent error correcting facilities than earlier phase encoding systems.

The format is too complex to describe in full, but the overall recording scheme is shown in Fig. 9.6. The essential part of the system is the method of preparing the data for recording. A cyclic code is used so that no more than two zeros can occur in succession on any track, this allows NRZI encoding to be made self-clocking. Data to be recorded in GCR form is first broken into groups of seven bytes. An error correcting code is calculated, and forms an eighth byte, also all eight bytes are converted to 9-bit words by the addition of parity bits (usually to form 9-bit words with even parity). The group, codeword, is illustrated in Fig. 9.7. Before recording, each group of 4 bits along a track is replaced by a 5-bit cyclic code group, using the conversion in Table 9.1, the final codeword is ten characters, each of

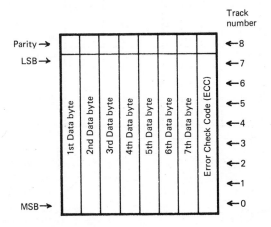

Fig. 9.7 Block of 7-bytes of data before GCR encoding

Table 9.1 Conversion table to form
5-bit GCR groups

4-bit initial data	5-bit group recorded
0 0 0 0	1 1 0 0 1
0 0 0 1	1 1 0 1 1
0 0 1 0	1 0 0 1 0
0 0 1 1	1 0 0 1 1
0 1 0 0	1 1 1 0 1
0 1 0 1	1 0 1 0 1
0 1 1 0	1 0 1 1 0
0 1 1 1	1 0 1 1 1
1 0 0 0	1 1 0 1 0
1 0 0 1	0 1 0 0 1
1 0 1 0	0 1 0 1 0
1 0 1 1	0 1 0 1 1
1 1 0 0	1 1 1 1 0
1 1 0 1	0 1 1 0 1
1 1 1 0	0 1 1 1 0
1 1 1 1	0 1 1 1 1

9 bits as shown in Fig. 9.8. This encoding allows detection and identification of any single error in a codeword when it is read; such errors can be corrected. Double errors are also detected and many can be corrected.

The full format, outlined in Fig. 9.6, includes extra block formatting and check characters. GCR offers many improvements over earlier recording formats, but requires complex encoding and decoding circuits. LSI circuits are now inexpensive and such requirements are not a major disadvantage.

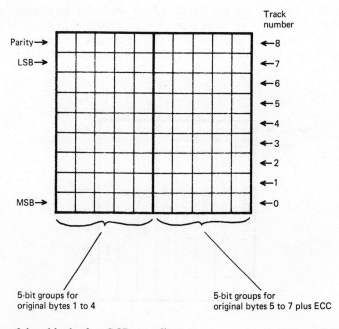

Fig. 9.8 Form of data block after GCR encoding

9.6 Summary

A wide range of magnetic surface recording systems are available. Developments in all aspects — materials, heads, mechanical systems, encoding and formatting — are occurring rapidly and are supported by large investment. Present systems do not approach the fundamental physical limits of surface recording, and it is probable that large increases in speed and density will be achieved.

9.7 Problems

1 Give timing diagrams showing how the binary sequence 1100101011101 would be written to a magnetic surface recording system (i.e. give the write current). Where necessary, assume magnetization or data values before and after the given sequence.

a) Using return to zero.
b) Using NRZI.
c) Using any specified phase encoding scheme.

In each case, also show the read signal when the data is retrieved. Use a common time scale for both signals.

2 A magnetic disc store has 256 concentric tracks and the following features.

a) One track holds system information and is not available for data.
b) Six tracks are unused (spares for fault tolerance).
c) Each track is divided into 24 sectors separated by gaps equal to the space to record 16 bits.
d) All tracks store the same amount of data (i.e. density varies with radius).
e) Maximum recording density is 200 flux changes in 1 mm.
f) Phase encoded recording is used.

If the innermost track is 80 mm diameter, what is the maximum number of bits, N_{max}, that may be stored on the disc? (Round down to a sensible value.)

The data is formatted so that each sector starts with a preamble of ten bytes and ends with two check bytes (for error detection) then ten further bytes (postamble). How many useful (actual) data bytes can be stored in a sector? How many useful data bytes may be stored on the disc? Comment on the difference between eight times this last answer and the result for N_{max}.

3 Show the data pattern (10 × 9 codeword) which would be generated in a GCR system to record the seven byte data sequence 93_H, $2C_H$, 67_H, 32_H, EF_H, 23_H, $D8_H$. (The error check word before coding is 58_H and even parity is used.)

10 Memory systems and hierarchy

Most of the memory devices used in modern processor systems have been described in Chapters 8 and 9. Design of complete processor systems includes determining memory requirements, selecting suitable components and devising their connection. In general the **main (core, primary) memory** directly connected to the CPU bus system will consist of semiconductor memory devices. Except for the fastest systems, these will be NMOS or CMOS components; use of bipolar memories is restricted to applications for which their speed is essential. For small systems cost is the main design consideration; as system size increases requirements of speed and absence of programming restrictions also influence design.

10.1   Memory for small systems

Much of the design of small system memories has already been outlined in descriptions of decode schemes (Chapter 4). Until recently, memory costs were such that for many systems a significant part of the design effort was minimization of memory requirements. Advances in semiconductor manufacture have reduced memory costs, and now it is rarely necessary to design hardware and software to operate with absolute minimum size memory.

Initial development work for small systems is usually undertaken with experimental systems having larger memories than will be required in the final design. Development systems often have RAM for sections which will eventually contain programs and data to be fixed in ROM. After development to a functioning state, the necessary amounts of RAM and ROM should be apparent and the memory design may be completed.

Most small systems have an MOS microprocessor as their CPU, hence highest speed memory is not required; for these systems MOS memory is selected. It is often uneconomic to provide refresh circuits, and NMOS or CMOS static RAM is chosen. NMOS devices are cheaper, slightly faster and more readily available. However, the differences are decreasing and, with their low power consumption, CMOS devices are chosen for many new designs. The ROM requirements will depend on system function and manufacturing quantities, with selection made from mask ROM, EPROM or EEPROM. Again NMOS devices are cheaper and more readily available, but CMOS components are becoming competitive.

Once type is chosen, the selection of an actual ROM device is usually simple because the designer has a limited choice of size. Almost all MOS types of ROM are organized with word lengths of 8 bits, and versions with 2k, 4k, 8k, 16k, 32k and 64k words are available. Design choice is little more than checking timing specifications and determining the size of unit; this is usually straightforward because the device which just exceeds the required size is selected. There are other considerations set by the choice of RAM devices as both ROM and RAM affect decode circuit design, some cases lead to difficult choices. For example, if 17k words are required should a single 32k device be used? Usually the large device is chosen, but alternatives include a mixture of device sizes giving more complicated decode design; or the use of several smaller devices, for example five 4k ones giving 20k words. Possibly the best solution is to attempt to reduce the material in ROM to below 16k words. This is another design situation where experience is required to make good choices.

When the word length exceeds 8 bits several devices are used; all their address and selection inputs are connected in parallel. Their data lines are separate, to produce the required word length or one slightly larger.

Examination of integrated circuit RAM components shows that, for a given number of bits, several devices are available. For example, many 16k-bit SRAMs are available organized as 16k words of 1 bit, 4k words of 4 bits, or 2k words of 8 bits. The 4-bit and 8-bit versions are useful when designing small or special purpose memory systems, but for larger systems the 1-bit versions are usually chosen. Choice of RAM units for small systems is complicated. The memory of such systems often has a significant proportion of ROM, selection of ROM components influences decoder design and hence RAM choice. When the total amount of RAM required in an 8-bit system is less than or equal to the unit size chosen for the ROM components, a single 8-bit word RAM device is chosen. This assumes that a device of sufficient size is available, several such devices are parallel connected for larger word lengths. For cases with more RAM than the ROM unit size, or where sufficiently large RAM devices are unavailable, several devices must be used. The designer has to choose between using devices of short or long word length, in nearly all cases the short word length is chosen.

Example

A system requires 32k words of RAM, each of 8 bits; 16k-bit devices are the largest suitable ones available. These are manufactured with 16k words of 1 bit, 4k words of 4 bits and 2k words of 8 bits. Unless the decode circuits for the ROM already provide selection signals for units of 2k or 4k words, the 1-bit word devices are chosen. Figure 10.1 illustrates the three arrangements that could be made and indicates that selection of the 1-bit word version results in a more simple decode circuit. Hence when many components are used to construct a memory, a *long-thin* arrangement is used rather than a *short-wide* one. As with most design rules, this is not a rigid rule and there are cases when it does not apply.

While selecting ROM and RAM components, the designer must consider the decode circuit to be built. Such circuits were examined in Chapter 4, and small systems are those for which incomplete decodes are sometimes used. If restrictions make a complete decode essential, memory component choice will be influenced by attempts to form simple decode circuits. Any memory system must also be compatible with total system timing requirements.

10.2   Standard semiconductor memory designs

In medium size processor systems, the complete main memory is similar to the fully buffered and fully decoded unit outlined earlier in Fig. 4.14. When the complete processor system, including I–O, is only of moderate size, the buffers may be omitted and one memory unit will probably occupy the whole memory address space. Larger systems contain several units with this structure; any selection links or switches are set so that the units form one continuous large memory. As already indicated, most RAM devices are available in versions of different word size; however, once memory units require many integrated circuits the 1-bit word version is almost always chosen. The principal reason for this choice is that it leads to the most simple decode circuits, because maximum use is made of the internal decode circuits of the memory device. There is also a reduction in data bus loading: loading of a few address lines is increased, but only to the level that occurs on the lower lines regardless of device choice. Further, in memory systems with error correction the failure of one integrated circuit will often be tolerated.

As well as selecting 1-bit word devices to reduce decode complexity, the largest size of memory device available in the required technology is normally chosen. This maximum size is steadily rising, doubling every two to three years; this will continue for some time. At the

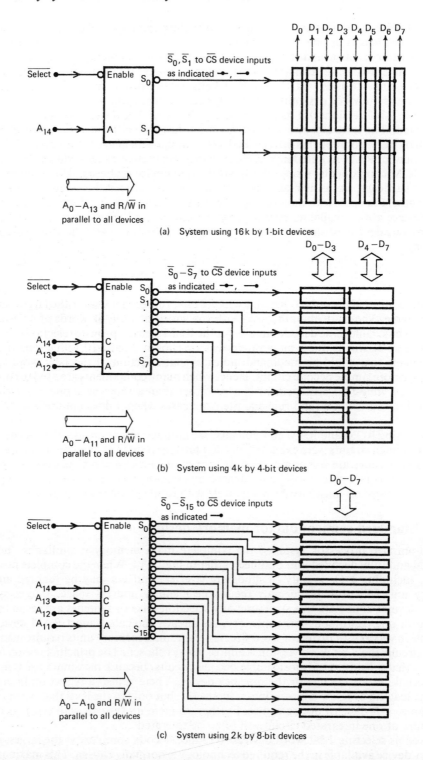

(a)   System using 16k by 1-bit devices

(b)   System using 4k by 4-bit devices

(c)   System using 2k by 8-bit devices

Fig. 10.1   Possible arrangements of a 32k x 8-bit memory constructed with 16k-bit SRAMs

time of writing the maximum available devices (larger ones exist in development laboratories) are 4k bits for ECL and other bipolar devices, 256k bits for NMOS and CMOS static RAM, and 1 M bits for DRAM (mainly NMOS but some CMOS). Thus, before determining device size the designer must select device type; bipolar devices are only used in exceptional cases and the usual choice is one of static or dynamic MOS components. Dynamic memories are generally slightly slower than static ones, require refresh, are unavailable during refresh, but are significantly cheaper. The refresh costs are almost independent of memory size, and in large systems the unavailability in refresh may be avoided, consequently dynamic devices are used for most large memories. The point when economic considerations indicate that dynamic rather than static memory should be used is difficult to define; it is continually rising with increases in device size. At present, selection of DRAM rather than SRAM seems reasonable when memory size exceeds a value in the region 64k to 256k words. This choice assumes that DRAM speed is adequate for the system; if not, SRAM must be used. Whichever type of RAM is chosen, specifications of the complete memory unit speed must be checked against required performance set by the bus specifications.

A final feature of large memory units is that they may include **error detection** or error detection and correcting mechanisms (**EDAC**). When memories become very large, the chance of an error in reading or writing becomes significant, the cause is either random interference effects (e.g. background radioactivity) or a device fault. The actual chance of an error is very low, but even moderate size processor systems access over 10^9 bits per second; an error rate as low as 1 in 10^{12} will lead to an error about every twenty minutes. EDAC schemes involve using more bits to represent a word than there are digits in the number; the schemes use techniques similar to those outlined in Chapter 11 for serial data transmission. Thus if EDAC schemes are in use, the memory will have N-bit words where the data word is n bits and $N > n$. The final form of each memory unit is a number of sets of memory components, each set containing N devices to form an N-bit word. Figure 10.2 is a block diagram illustrating the organization of a memory unit using SRAM devices. Extra circuits for an EDAC scheme are included as part of the data buffer system, they are absent in cases when $N = n$ because there can be no EDAC mechanism. A similar memory unit using DRAM components is shown in Fig. 10.3. The block marked 'controller', often a single integrated circuit, provides the circuits automatically refreshing memory and connecting the processor address bus to the multiplexed one used by DRAM devices. The controller also includes the internal address decoding circuits for the unit.

When constructing large assemblies of memory devices, the circuit board layout of devices and connecting tracks requires careful design; most manufacturers provide detailed notes describing the necessary techniques.

In describing larger memory systems ROM has been ignored. It is unusual for large systems to contain significant amounts of ROM in the normal memory address space. When a large amount of ROM is present, it is usually a complete memory unit replacing one RAM unit. However, most processor systems require a small ROM as the memory holding an initial start-up program for the system. There are several connection methods for this ROM; one is to place it in parallel with RAM and use additional circuits to select the ROM instead of the RAM during the start-up sequence.

10.3 Complex systems

Even small processor systems often include some memory in addition to the main semiconductor memory. Usually this employs some form of magnetic surface recording.

In small processor systems this additional *back-up* memory, **backing store**, is provided for two main purposes. It is a non-volatile store for programs and data, they are always available and do not have to be input from a keyboard or other manual device whenever

162 *Memory systems and hierarchy*

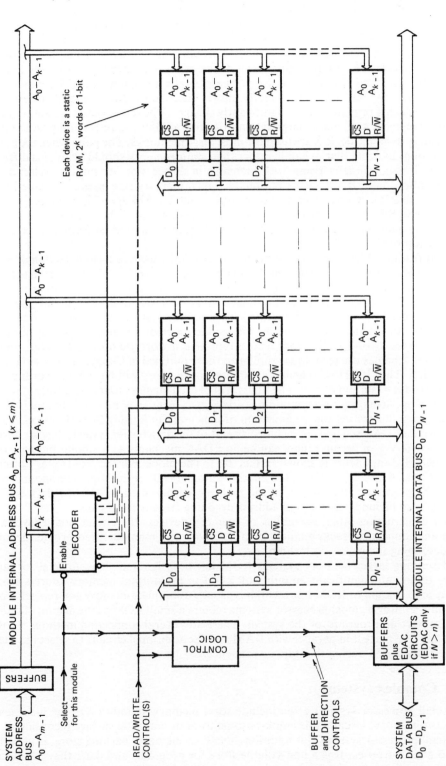

Fig. 10.2 Large memory unit using SRAM devices

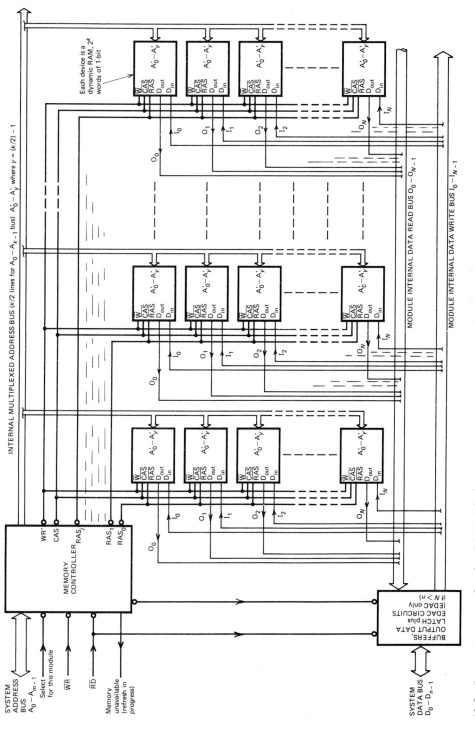

Fig. 10.3 Large memory unit using DRAM devices

required. The backing store also extends the size of memory available to a program by allowing material temporarily not required to be transferred out of the main memory and the locations freed used for material required; this is a form of **overlay**. Early systems required the user to make all choices and to control the transfers between main and back-up memories at the time when they were required. Modern systems have features enabling programs to run and make transfers to and from backing systems automatically. This automation affects both hardware and software design of the processor system.

A simple system with main memory and some form of back-up has **two levels of storage**; the structure overcomes volatility and size limitations although overall speed is reduced. More complex structures with several levels of storage provide other advantages as well as non-volatility and increased size. Although systems with back-up have been classed as having two memory levels, most are strictly three level, the CPU registers are one word memories placed in special locations and accessed directly without using the main bus structure. Consequently registers function as frequently used very fast memory locations. (There are some CPU designs which use part of the main memory as the CPU registers; such an architecture has useful features but the memory access time limits CPU speed.)

A two or three level memory structure has improved performance when compared with that of a simple system; more complicated structures give further improvements. With the exception of simple microprocessors, the CPUs of most processor designs operate faster than those memory components which can be economically used for main memory. Therefore if simple memory structures are used, a large proportion of running time for many processor systems consists of pauses while memory transfers are completed. The system speed is severely limited, being almost entirely set by the memory access time. Some improvement could be obtained by increasing the number of registers, but there are problems if the number of registers becomes large. One technique described when CPU architectures were examined was a pipeline for instructions, this forms a small, fast memory between the main memory and the CPU. Provided that the required instruction is in the pipeline, the instruction fetch (memory read) is reduced from the normal read access time by a factor of between ten and a hundred.

Larger CPU register sets and pipelines are common methods of supplying additional fast memory which is more closely associated with the CPU than the main memory. This additional fast memory concept may be developed much further, a technique adopted in many computers is to incorporate a **buffer** or **cache memory**. The name cache (hidden) memory is used because, to the programmer, the system just appears to be the CPU with normal main memory. The cache memory is a unit of very fast access RAM which is small compared to the main memory but much larger than a register array or a pipeline. There may be a single cache memory, or separate caches may be used for different items such as program, data, etc. Cache memories are not in the normal main memory address space. They have relatively few locations compared with main memory and are built using devices which are typically ten to fifty times faster than those in main memory.

The purpose of a cache is to hold copies of values in those main memory locations most likely to be accessed. When there is a CPU access, it is redirected from main memory to cache at cache access speed if the location is one currently duplicated by the cache. Examinations of running processor systems show that most memory accesses by the CPU are to locations near those previously used. If a CPU access is to a memory location not currently in the cache, a small block of main memory locations around the required location is copied to the cache. This results in a high probability that future accesses will be to cache, the operation using the location not in cache is at the normal main memory access speed. Organization and control of the cache is extremely complicated, and detailed consideration is beyond this text. A first requirement is that, in addition to the cache itself, there must be a memory holding system status data. This indicates areas of main memory duplicated in cache and relates addresses in main memory to positions in cache. Control must be by hardware because extremely fast operation is essential. For each memory access by the CPU, either cache or main memory must be correctly selected; if cache is used, the necessary main memory address to cache location translation is required. The control circuit decides which main memory locations to copy to cache, and must provide space in cache for such transfers by deciding which cache contents to overwrite. Finally the control circuits must ensure that when the CPU writes to cache locations, a correct copy is placed in main memory before a cache location is overwritten. One parameter used to measure the performance of the control circuits is the **hit ratio**, this is the ratio of the number of memory accesses for which the required data is in cache to the total number of accesses. The hit ratio is a function of many system design features, not just the control circuit, values as high as 0·95 can be achieved.

Optimum size of cache memory depends on the CPU architecture; the relative speeds of the CPU, cache memory and main memory; and the decision processes used for transfers in both directions between cache and main memory. Cache memory sizes range from below 1k to about 16k words, generally the larger the main memory, the larger the cache. Use of a cache memory decreases the effective memory access time, t_{eff}, to a value between that of the main memory components and that of the cache components. Typical speed improvements are by factors of three to ten, with cache speeds ten to fifty times those of main memory and hit ratios above 0·9. The exact speed achieved depends on many factors, a greatly simplified approximate value is given by

$$t_{eff} = t_{ctl} + H \times t_{ch} + (1 - H) \times t_{mn}$$

where t_{ctl} is the control circuit propagation delay, H is the hit ratio, t_{ch} is the access time of the cache memory, and t_{mn} is the access time of the main memory.

Example

For a particular system, $t_{ctl} = 20$ nsec, $t_{ch} = 50$ nsec and $t_{mn} = 500$ nsec. Determine the effective access time for hit ratios of 0·5, 0·75, 0·9, and 0·95.
Substituting for the system speeds gives

$$t_{eff} = 520 - 450 \times H \text{ nsec}$$

Evaluating for the specified values for the hit ratio gives

H	t_{eff} (nsec)
0·5	295
0·75	182·5
0·9	115
0·95	92·5

In the example a hit ratio of 0·5 gave $t_{eff} = 295$ nsec, only a 40% improvement in speed. However, if $H = 0·9$ then $t_{eff} = 115$ nsec which is an improvement by nearly a factor of five. The extra cost of providing a cache is much less than the cost increase when faster main memory is used without a cache to obtain the same effective speed. A cache memory produces an effective memory speed higher than that of the main memory components without reducing effective memory size.

Another feature restricting system performance is the memory size. It is uneconomical to have a very large main memory; when memory size exceeds some optimum for a particular system, there are long periods during which many locations are not used. The areas of unused locations change, but at a slow rate compared with CPU speeds. Additionally the hardware and interconnection costs of a wide address bus are high. There is a point above which increasing memory size produces little improvement in system performance. It has already been indicated that some form of back-up memory, backing store, can be used to overcome limitations of memory size in small systems. The penalty is a slowing of system performance while transfers are made to and from the backing store. This loss of speed will occur for any form of processor system running a single simple program. However, if multi-programming techniques can be adopted, the speed need not decrease; in addition, the programmer can be given an apparently infinite size memory.

Multi-programming requires a number of additional hardware features, and the application using the processor must require more than one program or task to be run with few restrictions on running order. All items of every program (instructions, data, etc.,) are divided into equal size units, **pages**. The main and backing stores are also organized in pages of the same size, typically set between 256 words and 16k words with values around 1k common. All software is independent of the actual page of real memory which is used. For example, the instruction code sequence is divided into pages so that all the instructions within a page are only stored at locations fixed with respect to the address of the start of the page, the code is **relocatable** to the extent that it may be placed in any real page in memory. The support software must include methods of connecting pages together, and the hardware has additional addressing features. Some aspects of addressing are similar to those when using cache; a control store is required to enable the correct complete address of required locations to be determined. Addresses have two components: a within page address, formed by the lower address bits, and a page address, with the address of a real hardware page formed by the high address bits.

There are different page addresses, and each program has its own page sequence 0, 1, 2, 3, etc; this is the order of pages in some imaginary memory as seen by that program, and forms a **virtual memory system**. The processor system has addresses giving the real address of pages in memory. When a program is run, a few pages of real memory are allocated to it, for instructions, data, working variables, etc. The first few pages of program are copied from the backing store, usually a drum or disc store, into the allocated main memory. The program is then run either until it requires material not currently in main memory or until some preset time interval is complete. At this point, the CPU moves to another program which already has pages present in store. While the CPU runs this second program, the control system stores some pages of the program just halted and replaces them by other pages of the program. After running part of the second program the CPU moves onto part of a third, then a fourth, and so on. When all current programs have been given some CPU time the system returns to the first program and continues running it from the point at which it stopped.

If the system was perfect, the CPU would run programs all the time with no waste of processor time while material is transferred between main and backing memories. In practice the system is imperfect, but performance is much better than when backing store is only used in a simple manner, also there are other advantages. There is no need to hold all the code or data of a running program in main memory, and a program page may correspond to any real memory page. Therefore a program may be much larger than one which has to reside totally in the real memory. Such large programs require a control system which can utilize virtual memory addresses larger than real ones. Also the system runs several programs apparently simultaneously, because switching from one program to another is so rapid that it is not seen by the user. Several users appear to have simultaneous use of the system; each user sees an almost infinite memory and the CPU with its full computing ability but a reduced running speed.

Only an outline can be given here of the features necessary to support a virtual memory system and multi-programming. Hardware must be present to translate program page addresses into real memory page addresses. The control hardware must correctly transfer pages to and from backing store as required, and transfers must occur at the same time as the CPU is using other pages of memory. Two (or more) units are simultaneously using the bus system; the system architecture is more complex than any examined in detail; it must allow at least two sections of the memory to be accessed separately, yet simultaneously, by two control units. Software must be prepared so that it runs in paged mode, and mechanisms must be devised to prevent one program from interfering with another.

The system is so complex that in nearly all cases much of the control, particular for page transfer decisions, is decided by a program. This is part of a general supervisory program, an **operating system**. In small multi-programmed systems, the operating system runs on the main processor as one of the programs sharing the system. Pages of memory are permanently reserved for its use and it is given priority over all other programs. For larger systems, a separate smaller processor system may undertake the control function; it runs the operating system, organizes which programs are run on the main processor, and initiates the necessary page transfer operations.

There are similarities between the page system just described and segmentation described in Chapter 5 as a method of improving CPU performance. However, paging and segmentation are different, and each has good and bad features; it is possible to use a combination of both in a system. Usually paging is better for systems running in a multi-programmed mode, especially with many simultaneous users. However, for real time control of equipment when different sections have to be controlled separately but simultaneously, often called **multi-tasking**, there are some advantages in segmentation.

10.4 Memory structures, hierarchy

A number of techniques have been introduced for improving processor system performance by incorporating additional features in memory structures. A large processor system will have several levels of memory; the highest and fastest level is the set of CPU registers and the lowest is the section used for archiving material to be stored for long periods. These levels produce a **hierarchical system** as outlined in Fig. 10.4. Control circuits and control software are required to ensure that values are correctly copied from one level to another, and these must be designed so that delays during which the CPU is waiting for a transfer to be completed are minimal. Thus when there is conflict involving several transfers, the one involving the highest level (the one nearest the CPU) normally has highest priority. Not all levels need be present, for a simple system only some CPU registers and main memory are essential.

Multiple level memory systems greatly improve processor performance but require a number of support features. When intermediate memory units (e.g. pipelines, caches) are placed between the CPU and the main memory, additional hardware control circuits are required. These connect the CPU so that it can use the intermediate memories and organize the transfer of values between the intermediate and main memories. If worthwhile performance improvements are to be achieved, these control circuits will be complex and require considerable design effort. Large increases in effective memory speed can be achieved at costs compatible with overall system cost.

Using a back-up memory to extend the main memory also requires control systems. These differ from those for systems between the CPU and main memory because the transfer decisions and speeds are different. Back-up devices are generally serial access ones, usually cyclic, with both a seek access time and a transfer rate. Relatively large blocks of data are transferred, and the choice of blocks is initiated by unpredictable decisions within programs to a much greater extent than for transfers between cache and main memory. Hardware and software features are included in the system to assist in transfers between backing store and main memory. These additions enable the CPU to continue with other tasks while transfers

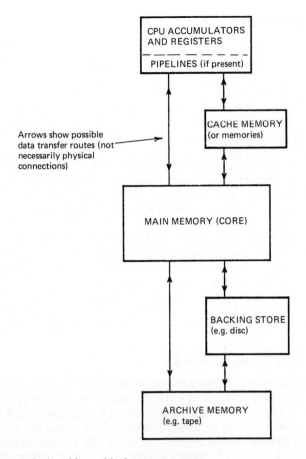

Fig. 10.4   Data flow paths in a hierarchical memory system

take place, and the processor runs several tasks in some time sharing mode. The tasks may all be parts of one running program or sections of separate programs. In large systems, a separate smaller processor system may be used to manage the memory system, and the backing store itself may have more than one level. For some of the more recent large microprocessors, single VLSI components are available to control memory systems; these are **memory management units, MMUs**. Whatever hardware method is used a supervisory program, an operating system, is required to organize the system control.

Systems handling large amounts of data, especially when the data is in the form of records to be retained for a considerable time, include as their lowest level of storage some form of **archive** system. This allows infrequently used data that is to be kept to be stored in an economical manner. Usually the storage is on magnetic tape with transfers made from the backing store, probably disc, at times decided by the operating system.

Overall design of a complete memory system with a hierarchy of levels is difficult. Decisions regarding the size and speed of each level, the number of levels, and the rules for transfer between levels are not simple. The optimum values based on cost, performance and application are continually changing as the costs of various components fall at different rates.

10.5 Other memory techniques

Descriptions of processor memory connection and systems have indicated some frequently used techniques. There are many other techniques each with advantages for specific applications.

One such technique is **memory bank switching**. There are several forms of bank switching which is also, sometimes confusingly, called paging. Paged virtual memory systems and more simple memories with a bank switch have some common features. A simple switched system has its total memory address space divided into equal units of relatively large size, typically four to sixteen divisions. More than one memory unit is allowed to occupy the same physical, real, address space, but no two units may do so simultaneously. All that is required for implementation is a latched output port and simple decoding logic to form the bank selection circuit, as shown in Fig. 10.5. By loading a specified value to the latched port, one particular memory unit is placed in the common bank address space.

In small systems with limited address bus width the maximum memory size is increased, although there are programming restrictions; only one unit of a group in the same address space will be connected to the CPU at any time. There is only limited communication between units switched into the same address space unless complicated and slow software is used. However, if the memory unit is large enough to hold all the code for a useful program, switching units allows rapid change from one program to another. This is particularly useful for small systems with programs held in ROM. With several ROMs in the same address space, a program may be run by giving a simple command; there is no load time and no risk of error in loading. One example is the Acorn BBC computer which allows up to sixteen ROMs to occupy the same 16k word address space. The machine has a 6502 CPU with memory in 16k word blocks; one block is a ROM holding the operating system, there are two adjacent 16k RAM blocks, and the remaining 16k block has the bank switching facility. ROMs in the bank are called sideways ROMs by Acorn, and the contents of their first few locations must follow a set format. The operating system operates the bank switch automatically. When a system command is issued, the operating system searches the formatted section of each ROM in turn for a present or absent response to the command name. Any ROM giving a command present response is left connected, and the operating system then finds the address for the code implementing the command and executes this code. A wide range of software for this machine is available in ROM; examples include word processing, database systems, and high level language interpreters.

To some extent, large computer paged memory systems involve memory bank switching. While the CPU is accessing one area of memory, the control system simultaneously transfers data between another area of memory and backing store. Two systems are using the memory simultaneously, and one method to prevent both systems requiring the bus simultaneously is to switch some memory from the main CPU to the control system, itself probably a processor system. This control processor will be given different pages of the main system memory during operation. If these different pages are connected into the same fixed address space of the control processor, it is using a form of bank switching.

Another important technique is **direct memory access, DMA**. Simple loading of a large amount of data into memory from some input device would use a loop reading data into an accumulator and copying the accumulator contents to memory. This requires execution of several instructions, and the CPU is unable to undertake other tasks during the data collection period. For data arriving slowly, this may occupy the CPU for a considerable time, alternatively, if data arrives rapidly there may not be time to execute the required number of instructions between arrivals of successive items. A similar problem arises for fast output of data. Many processors include DMA facilities allowing data values to be transferred directly between the memory and other devices.

For simple DMA schemes the CPU has two additional control lines, one input and the

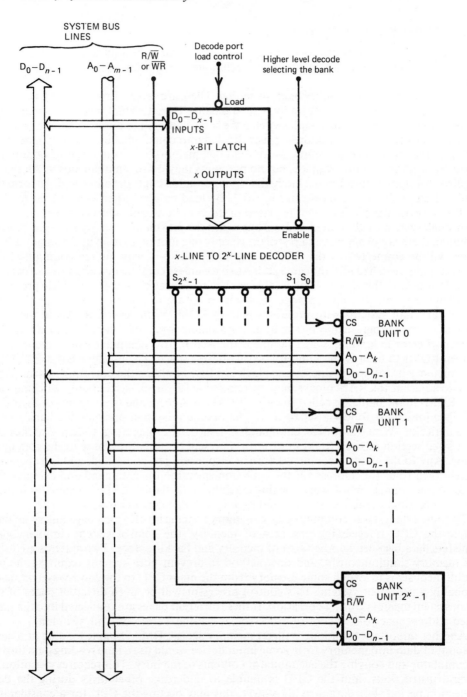

Fig. 10.5   Simple memory bank switch

other output. When an external device requires direct access to the memory it must hold the DMA request line of the CPU at a specified level. At a suitable time, usually the end of an instruction cycle, the CPU enters a wait condition with its connections to the data bus, address bus, and most control lines tri-stated (the CPU is disconnected from the buses). This state is signalled on the DMA acknowledge line. The device requesting memory access must now take over use of the bus system, perform the read or write operation, then remove the DMA request signal. Once the signal is removed, the CPU continues running from the point at which it stopped. Some effects of DMA are similar to those of an interrupt because the CPU sequence is stopped, however, there is no program branch or change of register contents. The memory contents change if the DMA access is a write one, and this could change subsequent CPU actions. As when using interrupts some form of arbitration, for example a priority system, is necessary if more than one DMA device is connected to a bus system. Implementation of DMA for direct input of data to memory, or to output data from memory, is straightforward, but requires a significant amount of hardware. For common microprocessors this hardware is available as special purpose integrated circuits.

DMA is used for I-O transfers in simple systems, and is often used for backing store transfers in medium size systems. It also allows two or more CPUs to share memory. Complex systems with several CPUs may be devised; each CPU has some memory reserved for itself but also shares some with other CPUs. Such multi-processor systems are very powerful, but there are many hardware and software design problems.

10.6 Summary

Design of small memory systems consists of choice of the most suitable semiconductor devices and production of suitable selection (decode) circuits. For larger systems, the main memory is normally semiconductor RAM and design is a choice of device type based on required speed and acceptable cost. The largest currently available devices of the selected type are assembled into complete units using 1-bit word devices.

In many systems the main memory is part of a complex system with multiple levels; such systems can be extremely complicated. The purpose of large, multiple level systems is to provide an apparently infinite size memory, with access times compatible with a fast CPU but without requiring an infinite address bus width or unreasonable cost. The memory system also provides long term non-volatile storage facilities.

Development of memory components and systems is an area of large scale investment. However, many advances will only change the point at which design decisions are reached for economic reasons; the techniques which have been outlined will remain in use for some considerable time.

Part 4
External Connections (I–O)

11 Digital input–output (I–O) connections

The wide range of applications of processor systems results in processors being connected to many different external devices. Consequently designs of processor system input and output (I–O) connections show a large degree of variation.

11.1 Simple I–O ports

Generally, the connection of input and output devices to processor bus system is similar to that of memory devices. A complete connection requires some form of combinational decode circuit to identify the particular I–O device (port) to be used with synchronizing signals provided by the appropriate control lines. Figure 11.1 illustrates an input connection using tri-state buffers, while Fig. 11.2 is an output port with D-type latches used to maintain the output signal after the processor operation has been completed. For I–O mapped input and output, appropriate control lines, typically $\overline{\text{IN}}$ and $\overline{\text{OUT}}$, are used to synchronize the transfer of data. Alternatively, memory read and memory write control lines may be used to give memory mapped I–O. For memory mapped designs an input port appears as a single word of read only memory (ROM), and an output port as a single word of write only memory. Input and output structures may be combined to form bi-directional ports; a simple form uses an additional 1-bit latched output port to control the direction of all port lines, as in Fig. 11.3. A more elaborate structure which allows individual control of

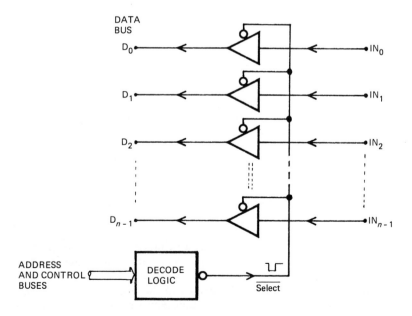

Fig. 11.1 Simple input port using tri-state buffers

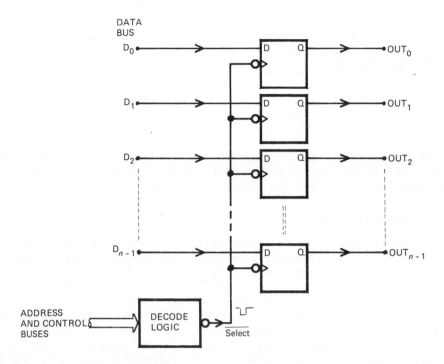

Fig. 11.2 Simple latched output port

the direction of each port line is shown in Fig. 11.4. This circuit outlines part of the 'quasi bi-directional' structure used in the Intel 8048 microcontroller.

These simple ports are adequate for many applications, but more elaborate alternatives are required to improve the performance of processor systems or to synchronize actions of the processor with the actions of external devices.

11.2 Accuracy and speed

Many output devices connected to processor systems are incapable of reacting at the high speed of electronic devices. For example, printers are usually electro-mechanical devices; common low cost printers print between 10 and 300 characters per second (**cps**) while more expensive devices may have print rates up to 10000 cps. Even the fastest printing devices use data more slowly than processor systems can supply it. Further, the rate at which data is used by a printer often varies; for example the time for simple printers to move the print head to the start of a line is often much longer than the time to print a character. Both these printer actions require the processor system to output a single code number. As the user normally requires all output by the processor to be correctly received, allowance must be made for the speed of the receiving system; successive values must not be output more rapidly than they can be reliably received.

Simple forms of output to a device such as a printer rely on knowing the worst case (slowest) response of the receiving device, after every output the program enters a simple wait loop. The length of the wait must exceed the worst case time; the device receiving the output runs below its maximum possible speed and the availability of the processor for other tasks is reduced. Performance may be improved with a more complicated output structure; a common form is the Centronics parallel interface (developed originally by

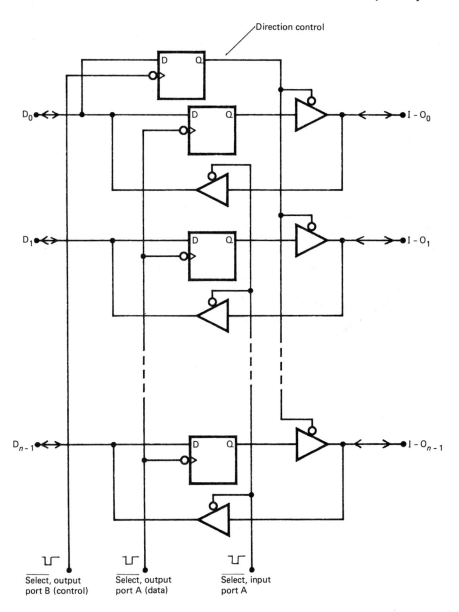

Fig. 11.3 One form of bi-directional port

Centronics Data Computer Corporation). This incorporates an elementary form of **handshake** as illustrated in the timing diagram, Fig. 11.5. In addition to the data lines which are used to output the code for the character to be printed (or control the printer, for example new line code), there is an additional output line, $\overline{\text{STROBE}}$. There are also two input lines, $\overline{\text{ACK}}$ (acknowledge) and BUSY. Several other signal lines are used in connections built to full specification but are ignored in this description (and in many implementations).

To output, the processor system (the output device) sets the $\overline{\text{STROBE}}$ line high and

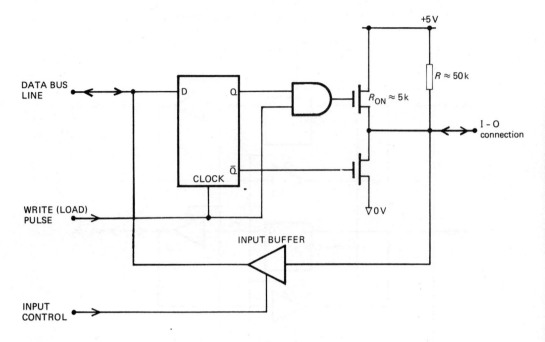

Fig. 11.4   Detail of a structure allowing direction control of individual port bits

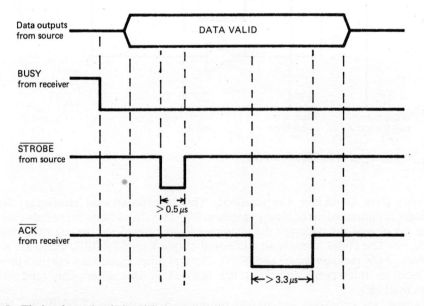

Fig. 11.5   Timing for a simple handshake connection

checks that the BUSY line is low; if BUSY is high, the processor must wait until it is low or abandon the transfer. Once the BUSY line is low the processor sets the data lines to the correct code value, allows time for the lines to settle, then pulses the $\overline{\text{STROBE}}$ line low for period exceeding 0·5 μsec. The high to low transition signals to the printer that the data is valid and in many schemes the printer responds by taking its BUSY output line high. The printer reads the data while $\overline{\text{STROBE}}$ is low, and once it has internally stored the data it responds by pulsing the $\overline{\text{ACK}}$ line low for a time exceeding 3·3 μsec. This $\overline{\text{ACK}}$ pulse must be detected by the processor before it makes any attempt to transmit more data. The BUSY line operates in a more independent manner; after the $\overline{\text{STROBE}}$ pulse it may remain low, or may go high returning low later. Changes in the BUSY line may be before or after the low $\overline{\text{ACK}}$ pulse, depending on the internal printer design. BUSY indicates when the printer is incapable of receiving data, for example while moving the print head to the start of a new line. Figure 11.6 illustrates typical processor connections for this interface.

This connection scheme with $\overline{\text{STROBE}}$ and $\overline{\text{ACK}}$ signal lines is a simple form of handshake connection, and is not restricted to printer connections. For a handshake connection a transmitting device indicates its actions to the receiving device, which then signals to

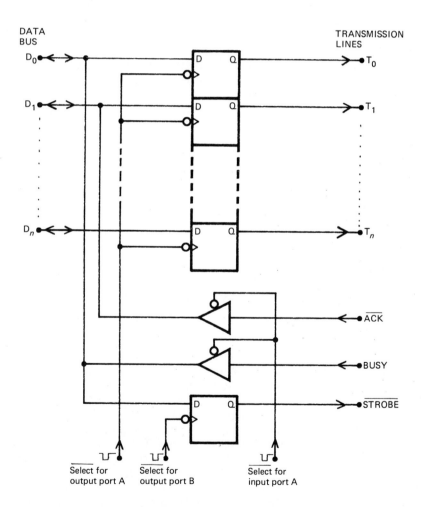

Fig. 11.6   Implementation of a simple handshake port

acknowledge reception. Several more elaborate features can be incorporated in this type of connection. In extreme cases handshake designs are such that before using the data, the receiving unit echoes the data back to the source on a separate set of connections. The source then checks that the echoed data is the same as the original value output, and an additional line provides a correct or error signal to the receiver which then takes the appropriate action. In the case of an error occurring, both processor and receiver must be designed to perform compatible preset actions.

Although handshake connections operate at the maximum speed of the receiving device, their speed is often below the maximum output rate of the processor system (source). Such situations occur in many cases, not just output to printers. Many receiving devices incorporate a small FIFO memory, typically 128 to 2k bytes, so that data can be sent to this **buffer memory** at high speed and used as required. If a large quantity of data is being output, this gives only a limited improvement because the buffer is rapidly filled and buffer space only arises at the rate of operation of the receiving device. (Using a Centronics type of interface the BUSY line can be used to prevent transmission of data when the buffer is full.) In cases when printing, or other output, is in short intermittent bursts, the buffer greatly speeds up the operation of the processor system. After sending some output to the buffer the processor can proceed with another task without waiting for the printer to complete its operations.

The handshake technique allows a fast device to output to one which operates more slowly and overcomes many of the problems that might arise. It enables two independent devices whose internal actions occur at unrelated times to be synchronized. The receiving device can only accept data from the signal lines when the data is valid, and the output device is restricted to transmitting at a rate acceptable to the receiver. Addition of a buffer memory allows the output device to run at maximum speed in many, but not all, situations.

Slow input devices can be connected to processors without difficulty provided that the most recent value from the source is always available at the input port. For such inputs a simple buffer of the form in Fig. 11.1 is adequate. However, if it is necessary to read input values only when there is no risk of them changing during reading, or at times set by the data source, then a more elaborate connection is necessary. A handshake form of connection, now inward to the processor, is often suitable. Often a partial implementation using a synchronizing signal from the source (e.g. $\overline{\text{STROBE}}$), but without the acknowledge signal, is adequate. In some cases the $\overline{\text{STROBE}}$, or equivalent signal, may be connected as an interrupt request.

When an input must be accepted as soon as available, some form of interrupt connection (Chapter 5) is usually essential. For high speed input or output of moderate to large quantities of data, direct memory access, DMA (Chapter 10), is often the only suitable method.

11.3 Serial techniques

A disadvantage of input and output connections considered so far is that they are parallel ones. Binary values are transmitted by sending all the bits simultaneously on separate, parallel, connecting circuits. This has the advantage of high speed because many bits are transmitted simultaneously, but it is expensive, particularly for long distances, as separate links are required for all bits. Links are not only two wires; they include the connectors, drive circuits and receiver circuits. Long links may also require repeater units to prevent signal loss. Provided that very high speeds are not required, an economical alternative is to transmit data one bit at a time on a single link; such systems are **serial transmission** ones.

Many serial transmission techniques exist; a common one for all but the highest speed systems is to send groups of 8 bits of data whenever required, provided that the previous transmission has been completed. Such transmission is **asynchronous**, successive data transmissions are unrelated in time. The 8-bit data word is formed into a larger word by

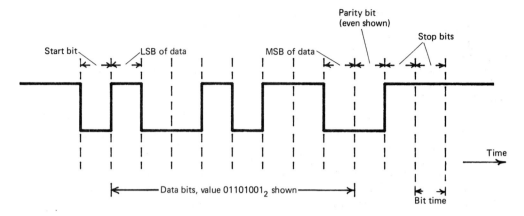

Fig. 11.7 Serial transmission signal: data value 01101001_2 illustrated

adding extra formatting bits. Each bit of the formatted word is transmitted in sequence for the same fixed *bit-time*, as indicated in Fig. 11.7 for a data word of 01101001_2.

Often the signals which represent the logic states 1 and 0 are simply a specified voltage present indicating 1 and no voltage for 0. Alternative schemes use positive and negative voltages, or two values of current, or bursts of different frequencies (tones) to represent the two states. The state of the link when no transmission is taking place is a continuous 1 level (reception of a continuous 0 state, no signal, indicates a break or other fault). The format requires addition of a start bit of 0 to precede the data bits, and the data bits are transmitted LSB first. The last data bit (MSB) is followed by several end bits; the end bits may include a parity bit which provides a method of checking transmission accuracy. Simple links often do not use a parity bit; alternatively, one is included within the data giving seven data bits plus a parity bit as the MSB of the 8-bit word. The end group is completed by one, or one and a half, or two stop bits of 1.

Serial link speed is the number of bits transmitted per second. This is the rate for all bits, including formatting bits, and is the reciprocal of the bit-time of Fig. 11.7. The actual rate of transmission of useful data is less than the bit rate, because the extra format bits do not constitute data but are necessary for reliable transmission. Data rates are often given in terms of **baud** or **baud rate** (after the telegraphy engineer Baudot). For simple links the baud rate is the reciprocal of the bit-time, that is the number of bits per second. There are links for which baud rate is not the number of bits per second; a strict definition of baud rate is the rate of transfer of binary values. It is possible to devise single transmission links which carry more than one bit simultaneously, and for these the baud rate is greater than the reciprocal of the bit-time. Common serial link speeds range from 110 baud to 9600 baud; lower and higher speeds are also used.

The use of a parity bit in serial transmission provides a simple error detection mechanism (it is also frequently used in data storage and retrieval systems; see Part 3). Addition of a suitably chosen extra bit, a parity bit, to a data word allows the new, longer, word to be forced to have a specified fixed parity (Chapter 3). On reception, the parity of a word is checked; if it does not have the specified value, a single bit, or an odd number of bits, of the received value must be incorrect. This simple parity system will not detect even numbers of errors. For any system with small probabilities of errors occurring in transmission and reception, the chance of more than one error in a word is extremely small, hence with a parity bit most errors will be detected. Parity is a simple technique which detects an error in a binary pattern but does not indicate which bit is in error.

It is possible to encode binary data using additional bits so that multiple errors, not just

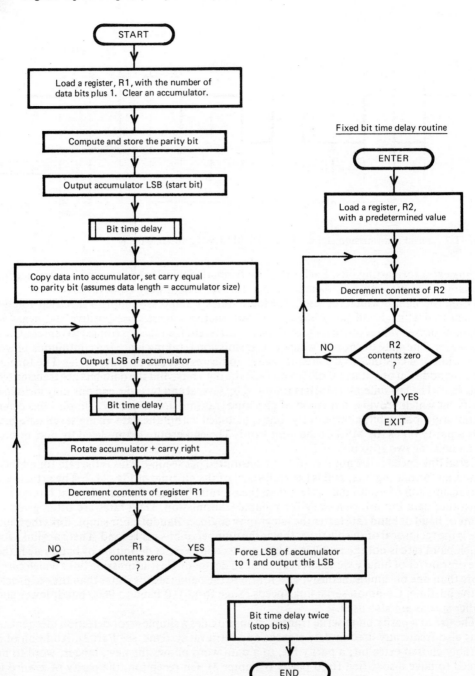

Fig. 11.8   Flowchart for a serial transmission output routine

odd numbers of bits in error, are always detected. Further, some forms of encoding provide sufficient information to indicate which bits are in error, allowing them to be corrected. Generally a sophisticated code used for the transmission of n bits of data will have the capability of detecting up to p bits in error, it is a p-bit **error detecting code, EDC**. Some codes allow up to q bits in error to be corrected, such a code is a q-bit **error correcting code, ECC**. Obviously an ECC scheme is also an EDC one, most ECC systems will detect more bits in error than they are able to correct.

Reliable transmission of binary data, or its storage and subsequent retrieval from a memory system, is a major subject. Much of the early work was by Hamming and the codes used by many ECC systems are known as Hamming codes. There is a large amount of literature devoted to this subject, and a few references are included in the suggested further reading.

The serial transmission of 8 bits of data by a processor system may be performed using a 1-bit latched output port and an output routine of the form outlined for an 8-bit CPU in Fig. 11.8. Reception requires a 1-bit input port and the appropriate routine. However, sending and receiving 8 bits of data in a serial mode is so common that single integrated circuits are available to perform many of the necessary operations. These circuits are known as **UARTs** (universal asynchronous receiver-transmitters) or **ACIAs** (asynchronous communications interface adaptors); many different versions exist providing capabilities from simple basic forms to sophisticated data transmission systems. A relatively simple form is the Motorola type 6850, outlined in Fig. 11.9; it is usually interfaced to a processor to appear as two 8-bit bi-directional ports. The UART may be used for a link in a single direction, but it contains both transmission and reception components. This enables

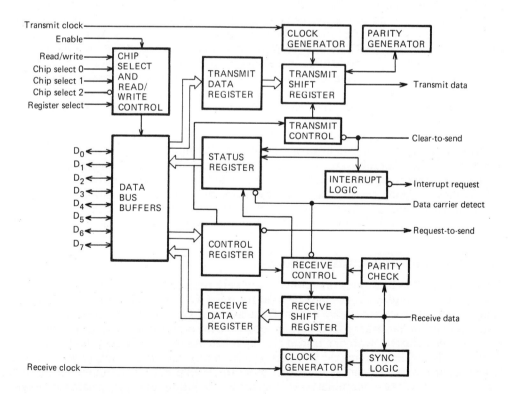

Fig. 11.9 Structured of a 6850 UART

separate transmission and reception links to be built with only a single component added to the processor system.

The first 8-bit bi-directional port of the 6850 is connected to two internal 8-bit registers in the UART. One is the output register (transmit data register, TDR) which is loaded by writing from the processor to this port, the other is the input register (receiver data register, RDR) and its contents are determined by reading from the port. The second 8-bit port is also connected to two 8-bit registers; an output to this port loads a control register, while reading from the port provides data regarding the status of the UART. Before a UART is first used, by any program running on the processor system to which it is connected, data must be written to the control register; this defines features such as the form of parity, number of stop bits, etc. Once these have been set, no further writing to the control register is necessary unless changes in format are required.

To transmit a data byte, the processor reads the contents of the status register and examines bit number 1 (next to LSB). Provided this bit is at logic 1, indicating that the TDR is empty, the processor writes the data for transmission to the TDR. Transmission is then automatic; the UART adds all the formatting bits, controls the transmission speed, etc. Most UARTS, including the 6850, are **double buffered**. That is, the TDR is not connected directly to the transmission output line but is connected so that its contents are transferred in parallel to a second register, the transmit shift register. This register is shifted to produce the output; the TDR may be loaded with new data while the previous data is still being output from the transmit shift register.

Reception is the inverse of transmission with the receiver also double buffered. Incoming data enters the receiver shift register and is only transferred to the RDR when a complete word has been received. The transfer to the RDR is indicated by either of two signals; one is an output connection from the UART which may be used as a processor interrupt, the second is a bit in the status register. When data is received some bits in the status register indicate any errors, for example no stop bit (over run) or incorrect parity. When a processor system interfaced to a UART detects reception of a full word, it must check the status word for errors and if there are none it reads the data from the RDR. The action of reading the RDR clears all status bits relevant to reception; only after data has been read will the UART control circuits allow new data to be transferred from the receiver shift register into the RDR. Thus reading from the RDR has the effect of clearing the UART for reception of more data.

Note that the serial input and output signals of UARTs are usually at the common TTL voltage levels. Most serial data links operate with higher signal levels; greater drive current and better noise immunity are required because serial links are normally longer than internal processor component connections. Driver and receiver integrated circuits are available to convert signal levels to and from those commonly used; for example the RS232C standard (EIA). Full specification links include control connections, although these are sometimes omitted; examples include RTS (request to send) and CTS (clear to send) signals.

11.4   Software and hardware choices

Serial transmission illustrates that either a software routine and a simple I–O system, or alternatively a complex circuit, may be used for this I–O task. Similar situations occur in many aspects of processor system design, frequently in I–O sections. Designers may choose either software or hardware for some function; often the proportions of software and hardware may be adjusted, with one traded for the other. As in most design situations, good design consists of determining the best compromise in each case. In general, solutions with a large proportion of software tend to cost more to develop but less to manufacture than those where hardware predominates. Hence software solutions are appropriate for designs for large scale production when design costs may be spread over many systems.

A disadvantage of software solutions is that they often operate more slowly or use more processor system resources than hardware solutions. Therefore when software is increased to reduce the amount of hardware, there is usually a decrease in processor availability for other tasks. Another feature of software designs is that it is sometimes difficult to test performance fully and to certify behaviour for all possible conditions. In situations requiring high reliability, for example safety and alarm systems, hardware solutions are frequently preferred because they are more easily tested.

The reduction of processor availability when a software solution is used rather than hardware is apparent for the example of serial data transmission. Assuming that with formatting bits the data is in 11-bit groups, and that the selected transfer rate is 110 baud, it will require 0·1 seconds to transmit each group. If this is performed in software, the processor is unavailable for the transmission period; using a UART the data is loaded and transmission initiated by instructions executed in a few microseconds. Thereafter the processor is available to perform other tasks while transmission takes place; in this case almost 0·1 seconds is available and even simple CPUs can execute several thousand instructions in this time.

When designing a processor system for some specific task, many of the choices to be made become those of deciding which I-O functions to execute in hardware and which in software. As in many design situations there are no simple rules; experience is one requirement for the production of good designs. Many integrated circuit I-O devices are available and their use often simplifies hardware design.

11.5 Complex I-O devices

A UART is one example of a special purpose device which contains hardware to perform a commonly required I-O function. Integrated circuit I-O devices may be roughly classified as special function or as multifunction devices.

Integrated circuit manufacture requires large quantity production of any single device if its cost is to be acceptable to users; therefore any device to perform I-O operations must be one which will be widely used. When an I-O function is frequently required, a special device capable of performing only this task is economical; UARTs are one such device. Among other common special purpose I-O components are devices for keyboard connection, display control, and interfaces for disc stores.

Connection of a keyboard to a processor system is another I-O system allowing a choice of hardware or software designs. The hardware design illustrates another special purpose I-O device. Keyboards are used for entry of commands and other information into many processor systems, for example by computer terminals with typewriter style keyboards. The keys are just single pole push-button switches which close when pressed and spring open when released. Each key could be wired to its own individual line of an input port; however the required port size and extent of wiring make this expensive, because most keyboards have large numbers of keys. A more common method is to use a matrix connection; this is outlined in Fig. 11.10 and is similar to a diode matrix ROM (Chapter 8).

All columns are normally driven to logic 1 by circuit outputs and all rows are pulled up to logic 1 by resistors. Each column is taken in turn to logic 0 for a short interval (the matrix is scanned), and if a switch in a column at 0 is closed, a key pressed, then the row which also contains that switch will be forced to 0. Detection of 0 on any row indicates that a key is pressed; identification of the row at 0 in conjunction with the known column at 0 uniquely identifies the key pressed. A matrix keyboard can be operated using software, the columns are driven from latched output ports and the rows read through simple input ports. Suitable software performs the column scan and detects the row signal, this software normally includes *de-bounce* features to overcome apparent multiple key strikes which arise on key closure and release. Many processor systems use software routines with matrix keyboards, for example they are adopted by many popular home computers. Software control is

COLUMN INPUTS, held normally at logic 1, each taken to logic 0 in turn

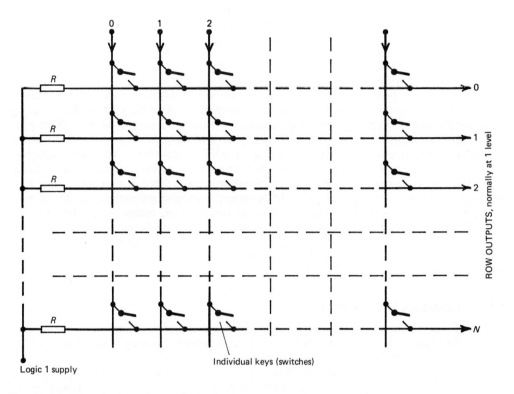

Individual keys (switches)

Logic 1 supply

ROW OUTPUTS, normally at 1 level

Fig. 11.10   Organisation of a matrix keyboard

economical for this task and is also flexible, for example particular keys may be redefined to perform different functions or to be ignored. However, the keyboard scan occupies processor time and some key operations may not be seen if they occur while the processor is undertaking another task. Special keyboard interface circuits exist, they include their own oscillators to perform the scan and de-bounce functions automatically. Such circuits only indicate key closure to the processor after a valid key press has been detected and a code for the key generated. Figure 11.11 outlines a small integrated circuit system for a 4-by-4 matrix of sixteen keys, devices for larger keyboards are readily available.

When there is no special purpose I–O device for a particular application, the necessary circuit may be built using individual logic elements and discrete components. Circuit board manufacture and assembly costs depend upon the number of components, therefore designers attempt to minimize numbers of components. Overall system costs are often lower with reduced component numbers, even when total component costs are increased; reliability is also greater. To allow designers to produce individual I–O systems, integrated circuit manufacturers have developed multifunction devices which may be configured by the user for a particular task. In many cases the processor itself may change the function during program execution, allowing a single device to perform several different I–O tasks in turn. The range of multifunction devices and their capabilities is very great; an indication of their flexibility is given by examining a few features of one device, the Rockwell 6522 versatile interface adaptor (VIA).

The 6522 is a complex device which is outlined in Fig. 11.12; a full description is too long

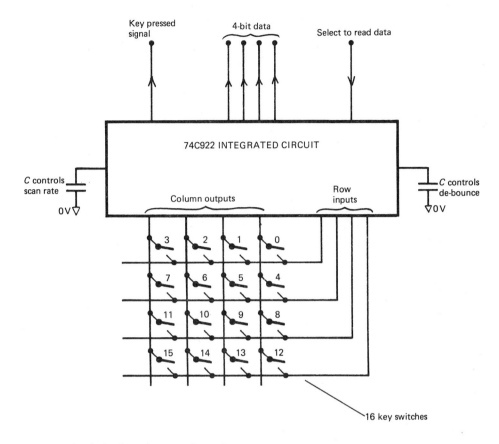

Fig. 11.11 Matrix keyboard connection using a special purpose device

to reproduce but may be found in the published data. The device includes two 8-bit bidirectional ports with several modes of operation, two 16-bit timer-counters, an 8-bit shift register and an interrupt control system. When it is connected to a processor it appears as sixteen registers, each is available for read and write access. Normally the interface is designed so that the registers appear at consecutive locations. The flexibility of the device is apparent when possible methods of using port A, one of the 8-bit ports, are considered.

Port A consists of an output register, ORA, and an input register, IRA, at the same address. Additional registers — data direction register A (DDRA), peripheral control register (PCR), and auxiliary control register (ACR) — control the operations of the port. The direction of each bit of port A is controlled by setting the corresponding bit of DDRA to 0 if the port bit is to act as an input, or to 1 if it is an output. Writing to Port A loads ORA with data, and if the control bit in DDRA is 1, the value written to the bit of ORA appears at the appropriate output pin. There are alternative handshake output modes using control lines CA1 and CA2; the output, strobe, signal is on CA2 and the acknowledge reply is received on CA1. Selection of the output mode is by data previously loaded into PCR and ACR.

Reading from IRA always provides 8 bits of data, the value depends on the port configuration. If the control bit of the DDRA is set for input, then data applied to the input pin is read; if the bit is output, then the value from ORA is read provided that the device pin is not forced by incorrect connection of an input signal. There are several ways to input

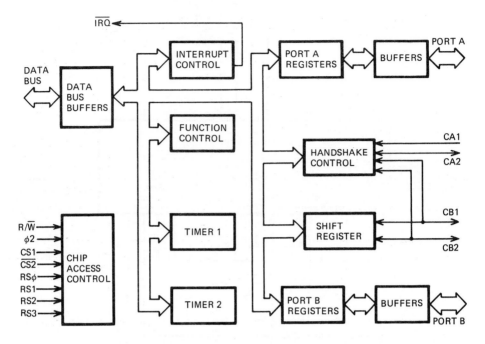

Fig. 11.12 Organisation of a 6522 VIA

through port A; again these are set by data loaded into PCR and ACR. In one mode the IRA is transparent and reading its contents simply provides the values present at the port input pins. A second mode involves IRA operating as a latch loaded by a synchronizing, strobe, signal applied to CA1. A third mode is a handshake one, with CA1 and CA2 again used as the control lines.

Full descriptions of 6522 operations are given in the published data. The device has many functions, so it may be adapted to suit many I–O requirements. The ability to change the mode of operation of part or all of the device by writing values to its control registers can give significant hardware savings. Many available I–O devices include such programmable features; the processor system must write code values to the I–O device control registers to force it to operate as required. Although this is flexible, and allows changes to be made in I–O structure by program decisions, additional programming is required; also testing for correct hardware operation is more difficult than for systems with non-programmable I–O. Some multifunction devices reduce testing and programming difficulties by having hardware control inputs rather than internal control registers; application of fixed logic values at the control inputs sets the operating mode.

The range of special function and multifunction I–O devices available is now great, making the choice of components for I–O systems difficult. Table 11.1 lists a small selection of I–O devices to illustrate the variety. Some devices even include other system components, for example the 8155 contains 256 bytes of RAM as well as 22 I–O lines and a timer-counter.

11.6 Networks

The I–O connections examined have considered a single CPU directly connected to another single unit, this may be a simple device such as a printer or keyboard, but it could be another processor system. If many units are connected by direct links a haphazard arrangement is created. Also, it is difficult to form links enabling one unit to be reliably connected on

Table 11.1 A few examples of typical multifunction I-O devices

Device	Function	Control method
6522	VIA. Flexible input output connection system includes ports, timer-counters and interrupt control	Internal registers loaded by CPU
6845	CRT controller; performs functions to create a video signal to show text etc. on a CRT monitor	Internal registers loaded by CPU
6850	ACIA (UART) for serial data transmission and reception	Internal registers loaded by CPU plus clock input signals
8155	Input–output ports, timer counter and 256-byte RAM	Internal registers loaded by CPU
8255	Flexible I-O port system	One internal register loaded by CPU
8279	Small system peripheral control for matrix keyboard plus LED display	Internal registers loaded by CPU plus a clock input signal

demand to different units (at different times). An example is a connection allowing several processor systems to share a printer.

Just as processor systems require systematic internal organization, so large assemblies also require a well ordered connection system. One approach is a bus system in which all units are connected in parallel to multiple links, in a similar manner to the internal buses of processor systems. A common scheme is the GPIB (general purpose interface bus) also known as the IEEE-488 standard bus. This operates in the same manner as a processor bus system, although more slowly, also more than one unit may initiate transfer operations. Contention mechanisms and protocols are specified to resolve conflicts if simultaneous requests arise to use the bus. While general in nature, GPIB systems are primarily used to connect measuring instruments to processors in automatic control and measurement systems.

When a more loosely connected system is needed, but with a greater range of communication requirements, a single serial link joining all units is more appropriate. Local area networks, LANs, are one group of such systems and are briefly described in Chapter 16. Typically they transfer data at 1 to 10 Mbits per second, and any device connected to the network may transmit data to any other device. The network design ensures reliable transmission with verification of receipt; also all units share the network equally, so that no unit can monopolize the common link.

11.7 Summary

The connections of a processor system to other systems are often unique for a particular application. Frequently this is the only area of microprocessor system design which requires detailed original effort, as the designs suggested by CPU manufacturers are normally suitable for basic CPU and memory systems. So far, consideration has only been of processor system connections to external systems which involve electronic logic signals. In many applications the processor is used with systems that are either not electronic or are analogue electronic ones with continuously variable signals, not two state logic ones. The signals to or from such systems must be converted for connection to processor systems; some conversion methods are examined next.

11.8   Problems

1 A processor system requires five output ports, three input ports, and one bi-directional port. Design the circuits to connect the ports of the bus system for two cases.

   a) The processor has three control lines $IO/\overline{M}$, $\overline{RD}$, and $\overline{WR}$; eight address lines define port locations. Output ports are at consecutive locations, starting at output port 0; input ports are also consecutive, starting at input port 0.

   b) The processor has two control lines, $R/\overline{W}$ and ϕ (transfer while $\phi = 1$), and a 16-bit address bus. Ports are memory mapped, with output ports at consecutive addresses starting $FFE0_H$; input ports are also consecutive from address $FFE0_H$.

2 For any processor with which you are familiar, write a subroutine to output a block of data which is already loaded into consecutive memory locations. The data is in correct form to be sent directly to the output lines (i.e. word length and number of data lines are equal), and the output device is connected by a simple handshake using $\overline{STROBE}$, $\overline{ACK}$, and BUSY signals. Specify addresses used and allocation of port bits for control connections.

3 Design I–O connections for an 8-by-5 matrix keyboard using minimum size simple I–O ports. For any processor, write a subroutine to find which key is pressed. The routine should include *de-bounce* features and produce as a code value 0 to 39_D uniquely identifying the key pressed.

4 Develop a complete specification for a software routine to receive serial data at a 1-bit input port. The format is start bit, 8-bits of data (LSB first), even parity bit and two stop bits. Each bit must be read twice, at times at least 0·2 of the bit time apart, and transmission timing tolerance may be up to ±5%. If an error is found at any point, there should be an immediate return with an error code.

12 Other input–output (I–O) systems

Many external devices used with processor systems are not electronic systems; connections between such devices and processors require transducers to convert signals into suitable forms. Further, the signals from transducers, and from many external electrical devices, are often analogue rather than digital in nature. That is variable quantities may take any value within defined limits, not just the finite set of 2^n different values allowed by an n-bit binary number. An analogue input signal to a processor system must be converted into logic signals representing a binary number related to the analogue quantity. Similarly an output to an analogue system from a processor must be derived from a binary number produced by the processor.

12.1 Transducers

To transmit information, a signal, from one point to another requires expenditure of energy. A **transducer** is any device which converts a signal utilizing one form of energy into a related signal using another form. Transducers supplying inputs to processor systems convert non-electrical signals into electrical ones, while output transducers perform reverse conversions. It is convenient to classify transducers as input or output types.

Input transducers convert the value of some physical quantity into electrical signals related to that value. A switch is a simple digital form of transducer; the position of a moving component is converted into an open or closed, 1 or 0, signal. Other common input transducers include those used to determine linear position, angular position, temperature, pressure and velocity. For each function many different mechanisms have been devised, for example several types of angular position transducer are available. The most simple is a potentiometer similar to those used as volume controls for radio or television receivers. A resistive track is formed into the arc of a circle and a wiper runs on the track. The track is fixed and the wiper is attached to the shaft whose rotation is to be measured. When a constant voltage is applied between the ends of the track the potential of the wiper is proportional to its angular position. Using high quality servo-mechanism potentiometers, accuracies of $\pm 0 \cdot 5\%$ over a 340° angular range may be achieved; total 360° measurement is difficult with this form of transducer. There are other angular measurement transducers, some cover the full 360° range, and several are digital devices. One form has a code plate attached to the rotating component; this plate has circular tracks with transparent and opaque regions. A four track version is illustrated in Fig. 12.1 and identifies twelve regions, each 30° wide. The plate is illuminated and photosensitive detectors are set behind it on a fixed radial line; hence the angle of the code plate relative to the fixed radius can be determined from the detector outputs. Many other position determination techniques exist.

Output transducers convert electrical signals into some alternative physical quantity. A solenoid actuator is a simple digital output transducer; supplying a current or no current to its coil using a logic 1 or 0 signal to control an electronic switch sets the moving armature of the solenoid into one of its two positions. There are many different output transducers, but the range is not as wide as that of input types. A large proportion involve electromagnetic effects to produce motion; most others use the heating effect of an electrical current or some form of electrical energy to light conversion.

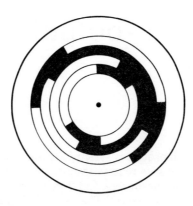

Fig. 12.1 Code plate for an angular position transducer

The problem of producing some form of visible output by actions of a processor system is a major one whenever human interaction with the system is necessary. There are many types of output transducer, **displays**, which produce visible results. Displays can be as simple as an on–off indicator lamp, or as complex as a visual display unit (VDU) allowing several thousand characters (letters, numerals, etc.) to be shown at any time.

Selection of a transducer for some task is usually straightforward, and it is unusual for transducers of similar specification to differ greatly in cost. A more common problem is that transducers are often relatively expensive and impose an economic limit on applications of processor systems. Many transducers require analogue electrical connections, even totally electrical systems without transducers often include analogue sections. Signal conversion is necessary for analogue device to processor system connections.

12.2 Analogue signal conversion

Conversions between analogue and digital systems are performed by **analogue to digital converters (ADCs)** and **digital to analogue converters (DACs)**. As no conversion can be instant, or exact, both the speed and accuracy of conversion systems are important parameters.

12.2.1 Digital to analogue conversion accuracy

A DAC produces a voltage or current related to the n-bit number represented by logic levels at its n inputs. The converter is **linear** if the output is directly proportional to the input number. Figure 12.2 is the ideal characteristic for a 4-bit (4 input) linear DAC; the actual characteristic is discontinuous and represented by the points. The maximum output, V_{max}, is usually related to an accurate reference supplied to the DAC. In Fig. 12.2 the straight line is to indicate that the points should lie on it; conversion accuracy is a measure of how closely the linear relation holds. While several different errors are quoted for DACs, the most useful measure is the largest amount by which any one of the 2^n possible outputs deviates from the ideal value. It is given either as a proportion of the maximum (full-scale) output, or in terms of the fractional change required in the value of the least significant input bit to produce the allowed error. For example, an 8-bit DAC may have input values ranging from 0 to 255 decimal. If the greatest deviation between any output and its corresponding ideal output is the amount the output should change if it were possible to change the input value by $\pm\frac{1}{4}$ of the least significant bit (LSB), then such a DAC is stated to have an accuracy of $\pm\frac{1}{4}$ bit. Alternatively its accuracy is $\pm0\cdot25$ in 255, that is $\pm0\cdot1\%$ of full scale.

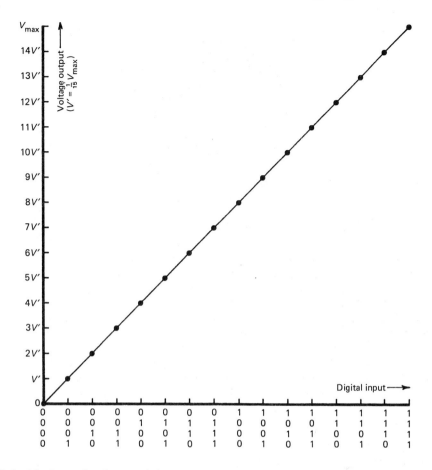

Fig. 12.2 Ideal transfer characteristic for a 4-bit DAC

Differential non-linearity is important in some applications, it is the difference between the actual change in output and the change expected when the input value changes. For example, if a DAC has an accuracy of $\pm\frac{1}{4}$ LSB it is possible that the output for one input value, N, could correspond to the ideal value less $\frac{1}{4}$ LSB and the output for an input value of $N + M$ could be the ideal value plus $\frac{1}{4}$ LSB. Both outputs are within specification, but when the input changes from one value to the other the output change for this particular case is equivalent to an input change of $M + \frac{1}{2}$ LSB. That is the error in the change, the differential error, is $\frac{1}{2}$ LSB, although the device error is only half this. Differential non-linearity cannot exceed twice the DAC accuracy, but it may be less than this for some devices.

12.2.2 *Analogue to digital conversion accuracy*

A voltage, or current, is input to the ADC circuit which outputs an n-bit unsigned binary integer (signed versions also exist). The output number is proportional to the input signal within the device accuracy; this accuracy is often presented in a confusing manner by ADC manufacturers.

The binary output value can only be proportional to the input voltage within the limitations allowed by integer binary numbers. Any ADC producing an n-bit output has to select

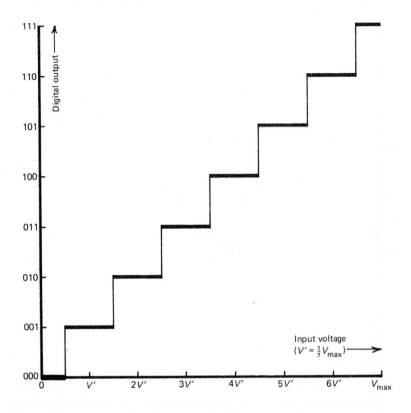

Fig. 12.3   Ideal transfer characteristic for a 3-bit ADC

the value of the input at which the output number changes from one value to the one immediately above or below. Ideally this change should be half way between the analogue inputs which exactly correspond to adjacent binary values; that is Fig. 12.3 is the ideal transfer characteristic for a 3-bit output linear ADC. A binary value, N, output by an ideal ADC corresponds to any analogue input in the range from a value infinitesimally above $N - \frac{1}{2}$ to one just below $N + \frac{1}{2}$. Therefore a particular output from a perfect ADC represents a range of input values; using the output value the input may only be deduced within a range corresponding to the digital value $\pm \frac{1}{2}$LSB. Most manufacturers ignore this inherent **quantization error**; their specifications only state how close the actual point of output change is to the ideal one. Accuracy is often given in terms of separate individual sources of error, whereas the concern of users is usually the overall accuracy with which the output represents the original input. Hence the accuracy of the output from any ADC is $\pm (\frac{1}{2} \text{ LSB}$ plus the worst case combination of all other inaccuracies).

12.2.3   Conversion speeds

No circuit can operate without some delay between a change at an input and the corresponding output response. This applies to both ADCs and to DACs; the DAC is the more simple case and the circuit delay is usually called the **settling time**. This is the maximum time between applying a new digital input value and the output reaching a steady new value; the settling time is the worst case (longest) delay that can occur for all possible changes in input values (2^{2n-2} different cases for an n-bit DAC).

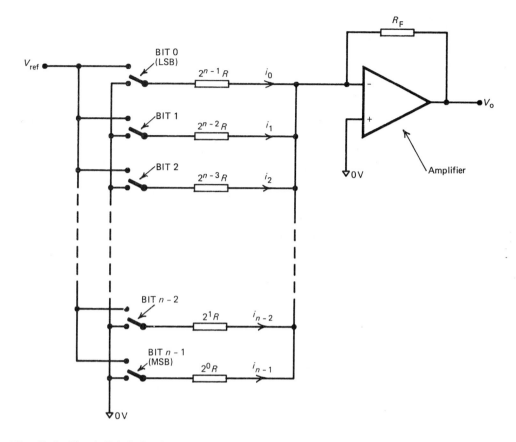

Fig. 12.4 Simple DAC circuit

For ADCs the circuit speed is sometimes just the delay between applying a new analogue input and the corresponding digital output appearing. However, most ADCs operate by performing a sequence of actions, and for such devices **conversion time**, the time to produce the output value after a start signal, is more appropriate. Many ADCs also have a **reset** or **dead time**, a period following a conversion during which further conversions cannot be initiated.

When considering converter designs it is convenient to examine DACs first as some forms of ADC incorporate DACs.

12.3 DAC designs

There are only a few basic DAC designs; most rely on controlled switching of voltage or current sources into a summation circuit. In Fig. 12.4 a differential amplifier, a resistor network, and a reference voltage source of V_{ref} connected by switches form a DAC. If the amplifier gain is very large, typically over 10^5, and its input resistance is high it can be shown that the difference in voltage between the input terminals is so small that it may be regarded as zero. Elementary theory then gives

$$V_o = -R_F \times (i_0 + i_1 + i_2 + \ldots + i_{n-1})$$

For any resistor R_k, the current through it is $i_k = V_{ref}/R_k$ when the switch is set to V_{ref} and the current is zero when the switch is set to 0 V. Hence if B_k indicates the switch position by being 1 or 0 for the two cases then

$$i_k = B_k \times \frac{V_{ref}}{R_k}$$

Substituting in the equation for V_o having selected $R_{n-1} = 2^0 \times R$, $R_{n-2} = 2^1 \times R$, ..., $R_k = 2^{n-k-1} \times R$, ..., $R_1 = 2^{n-2} \times R$, $R_0 = 2^{n-1} \times R$ produces

$$V_o = K \times \left(\frac{B_{n-1}}{1} + \frac{B_{n-2}}{2} + \frac{B_{n-3}}{4} + \ldots + \frac{B_k}{2^{n-k-1}} + \ldots + \frac{B_1}{2^{n-2}} + \frac{B_0}{2^{n-1}} \right)$$

where K is a constant. If the switches are controlled by the bits of an n-bit binary number with B_{n-1} the MSB and B_0 the LSB then V_o is proportional to the binary number.

A fault of this design is that it requires n resistors ranging in value from R to $2^{n-1} \times R$. An error of 1 part in 2^{n-1} in the lowest value resistor, R, has the same effect as an error of a factor of 2 in the largest resistor. Production of a wide range of resistors with the high relative precision required for the lowest values is dificult except for small numbers of bits.

Figure 12.5 shows an alternative circuit using an R—$2R$ ladder network. Analysis of the network shows that as for the previous circuit the output voltage, V_o, is proportional to the binary number whose bit values control the switches. The resistors still have to be precise if high overall accuracy is to be achieved but only two values are required (one if the value $2R$ is made from two resistors R). Only the relative values of resistors, not their absolute values, are important, and resistors close to the MSB switch must be the most accurate. High relative accuracy is most easily achieved if all resistors are of similar value and formed simultaneously in a single process, as in integrated circuit or thick film device manufacture. Most modern integrated circuit or hybrid module DACs use an R—$2R$ ladder.

Precision DACs are readily available with $\pm\frac{1}{2}$ LSB accuracy up to about 12-bits and are based on R—$2R$ networks. Many are known as multiplying DACs as examination of the constant, K, in the equation

$$V_o = K \times \left(\frac{B_{n-1}}{1} + \frac{B_{n-2}}{2} + \frac{B_{n-3}}{4} + \ldots + \frac{B_k}{2^{n-k-1}} + \ldots + \frac{B_1}{2^{n-2}} + \frac{B_0}{2^{n-1}} \right)$$

shows it to be of the form $K' \times V_{ref}$. If V_{ref} is supplied by the user, then V_o is proportional to V_{ref} multiplied by the binary input.

Inaccuracies in DACs arise from imperfections in the resistor network. Additional errors are caused by the switches, these are electronic devices and are not perfect; they do not have

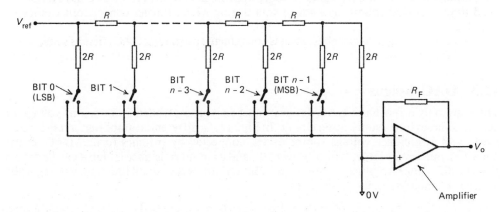

Fig. 12.5   R-2R ladder DAC

zero resistance when closed and infinite resistance when open. It is possible to design circuits reducing such effects, but there are limits to the extent of reduction possible. DAC settling time is mainly limited by the amplifier performance, a small additional delay arises from the switching devices.

12.4 ADC designs

ADCs are usually electronic circuits, although mechanical devices such as code plates and Moiré fringe counters are used in machine tools. Most electronic ADC designs include one or more **analogue comparators**, which make the change from a linear (continuously variable) signal to a logic one. An analogue comparator is a high gain differential amplifier with its output restricted to values between the upper limit for logic 1 and the lower limit for logic 0. When the voltage at the non-inverting ($+$) input exceeds that at the inverting ($-$) input by a very small amount, the output rapidly rises to the upper limit, logic 1. Similarly a small difference in the reverse sense produces the lower limit, logic 0. These circuits exhibit **hysterysis**, the input voltage difference causing the output to change is slightly positive when the differential input voltage is rising and is slightly negative when the voltage is falling, as indicated in Fig. 12.6. Careful design is required to produce low hysterysis comparators ($V_U - V_D$ small) with hysterysis characteristics independent of any common offset on both inputs. Another problem is that the circuit is driven hard to the output limits, and when required to change output it may respond slowly.

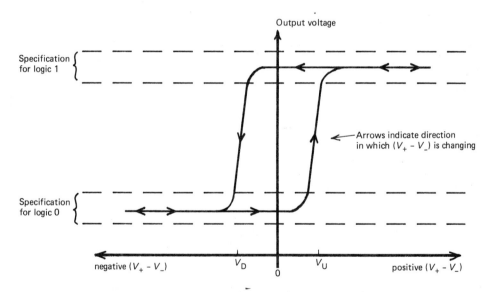

Fig. 12.6 Analogue comparator behaviour

ADCs may be **direct** or **indirect** types, an obvious feature of indirect designs is the inclusion of a DAC. Only a selection from the wide range of designs is presented here. The most simple design for an ADC with an n-bit output has 2^n resistors connected in series with a constant reference voltage applied across the complete resistor chain. Using a multiway switch, the voltage at each junction on the chain is compared with the input voltage (Fig. 12.7). Starting at the lower end, the switch is connected to each junction along the chain until the comparator output changes to indicate that the voltage from the chain

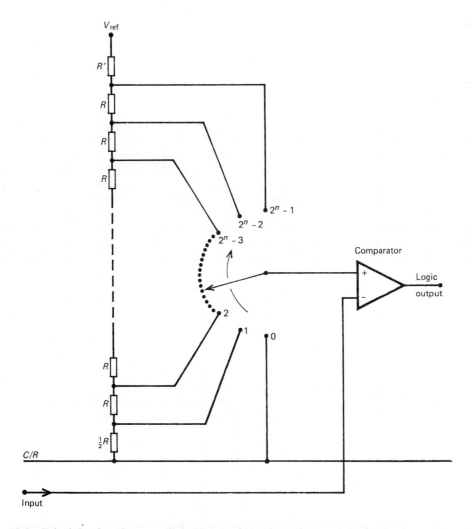

Fig. 12.7 Principle of analogue to digital conversion using voltage comparison

exceeds that from the input. At this point the numeric position of the switch is proportional to the input signal voltage.

The switch mechanism is not ideal for an electronic circuit, but the concept is the basis of the **flash converter**. For an n-bit converter the 2^n position switch is replaced by $2^n - 1$ comparators ($2^n - 1$ because the zero case can be inferred). All the comparators have one of their inputs connected to the signal; often the signal is first amplified. The other inputs of the comparators are connected to the junction points on the resistor chain, as in Fig. 12.8. When the input signal is proportional to some conversion result with numeric value N, the first N comparators will indicate that their inputs from the resistor chain are below the input while the remaining comparators indicate the opposite. The comparator outputs are logic signals, so a combinational encoding circuit converts the comparator output pattern into the appropriate binary number to be output. Table 12.1 is the encoding circuit truth table for an $n = 3$ example; note that impossible codes are not regarded as don't care conditions because they may arise as transients.

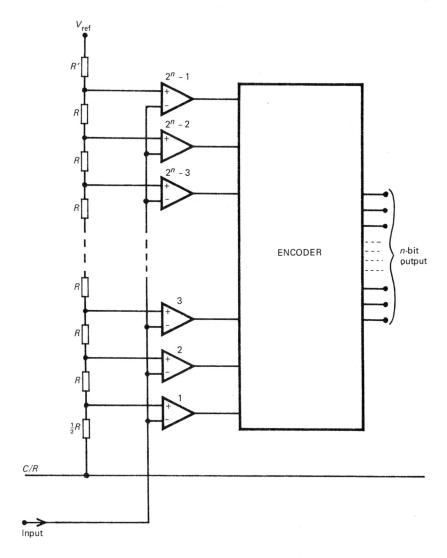

Fig. 12.8 Flash Converter

Flash converters are very fast (capable of conversions in under 0·05 μsec), but the manufacture of $2^n - 1$ matched fast comparators is difficult; also the resistor chain requires a large space on an integrated circuit. Few commercial devices have more than 8-bit outputs. Accuracy depends on the degree to which the resistors are matched and the quality of the comparators. Speed is limited by comparator switching time with small additions caused by other circuit delays; there is no dead time.

Many ADC designs avoid the use of multiple resistors and comparators; **single slope converters** form one group. A direct version is shown in Fig. 12.9; this one has the feature that it produces an output proportional to the amplitude of the input regardless of input polarity. In Fig. 12.9, several features have been selected; a negative slope is shown but positive ones work equally well. The reference point has been set at zero volts, although an offset may be used. Operation is simple: initially the ramp exceeds both input and reference

Table 12.1   Truth table for flash converter encoding circuit

Outputs of comparators							Binary result		
7	6	5	4	3	2	1	C	B	A
0	0	0	0	0	0	0	0	0	0
0	0	0	0	0	0	1	0	0	1
0	0	0	0	0	1	X	0	1	0
0	0	0	0	1	X	X	0	1	1
0	0	0	1	X	X	X	1	0	0
0	0	1	X	X	X	X	1	0	1
0	1	X	X	X	X	X	1	1	0
1	X	X	X	X	X	X	1	1	1

(X = either 1 or 0, both input values give same output)

so both comparator outputs are 1. With a positive input, the ramp eventually falls below the input; comparator 1 output becomes 0 with comparator 2 output still 1. Finally both comparator outputs become 0. The output of the exclusive-OR gate is a pulse of width proportional to the amplitude of the input voltage (the pulse has the same width but is at a different time for a negative input). A timer-counter circuit counts oscillations from a constant frequency clock during this pulse, and the total count is proportional to the input voltage.

Inaccuracies with this form of ADC usually arise from non-linearities in the ramp generator and hysterysis effects in the comparators. Conversion time and dead time depend on the ramp gradient and the design of the reset circuits.

The most accurate ADC designs are usually **dual slope converters**; a simple form is outlined in Fig. 12.10. The input is applied to an integrating circuit for a fixed time, and its output reaches a voltage proportional to the input. A constant reference voltage of opposite polarity is then applied to the integrator, causing its output to fall until the comparator indicates that the integrator output has returned to zero; this fall time is proportional to the input voltage and may be measured by a counter-timer as in the single slope converter.

Several features of this design give high accuracy. As the same integrator is used on both slopes, most imperfections in the integrator cancel. The comparator only operates at a single point with input changes in one direction, consequently hysterysis is not a problem. If the initial integrating period is exactly the period of any unwanted frequency that is probably present (typically the local a.c. power frequency), high rejection of this is achieved. With careful design accuracies of 1 part in 10^6, or better, may be obtained. The main disadvantage of this design is that conversion is relatively slow.

One ADC for which a comparator is not required is based on a voltage controlled oscillator, **VCO**. Several designs of circuit produce an oscillatory output at a frequency directly proportional to an input voltage, or an input voltage plus some constant. If oscillations are counted for a fixed time, the total count is proportional to the input voltage. These designs tend to be slow and relatively inaccurate, but can be employed in low cost applications, particularly if software is used for the timer-counter function.

Many low cost ADCs are indirect designs, because medium speed and accuracy circuits are easily built. The single slope converter is easily adapted as illustrated in Fig. 12.11. Outputs of a simple up-counter are the data inputs to a DAC whose output is compared with the input. Starting with the counter at zero, pulses are input to it until the DAC output just exceeds the input signal; at this point the count value is the required digital value (a small offset overcomes the slight error in the conversion).

The accuracy is limited by the comparator characteristics as for other single slope designs; it is also limited by the accuracy of the DAC. Conversion is relatively slow and depends on the pulse rate with the conversion time proportional to the input value. A simple

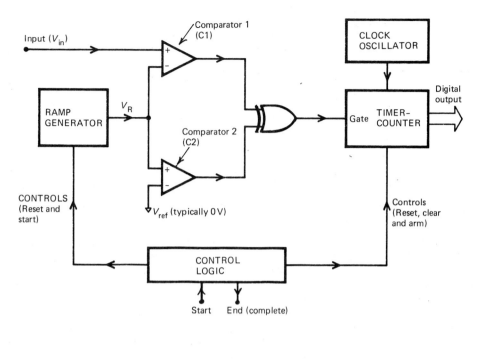

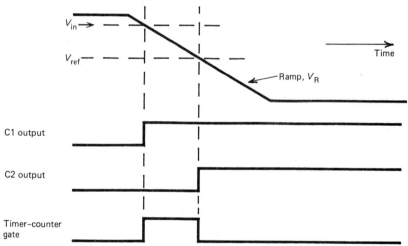

Fig. 12.9 Single slope ADC

modification to the counter design produces the **tracking converter** shown in Fig. 12.12. The up-counter is replaced by an up-down counter with the count direction controlled by a single input. When the DAC output is less than the input signal the count is upward, and when the DAC output exceeds the input the count is downward.

Initially the converter behaves as a counter type, but after the DAC output exceeds the input signal for the first time the value of the count will always be within ± 1LSB of the correct result. This assumes that the rate of change of the input is less than the maximum

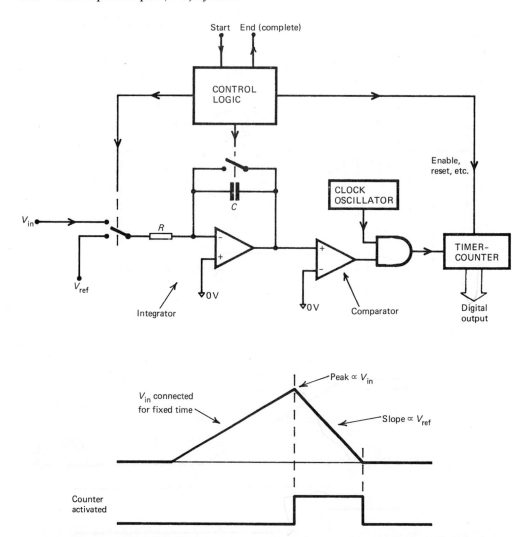

Fig. 12.10 Dual slope ADC

possible rate of change in DAC output. Conversion is initially slow, however once the counter reaches the input level it provides a conversion value without delay, provided that the input does not change too rapidly.

The **successive approximation converter** is another counter design and operates with a special counter, the successive approximation register (SAR), as illustrated in Fig. 12.13. The conversion starts by setting the most significant bit (MSB) in the SAR to 1 with all other bits zero. The DAC converts the value from the SAR to an analogue equivalent; this is compared with the input. If the SAR value is too large the MSB is reset to 0, otherwise it is kept at 1. The next most significant bit in the SAR is then set to 1, and the test is repeated for this bit which is kept or reset according to the result. This process continues until all bits have been tested. For an n-bit converter a fixed number, n, tests are required, whereas the counter and tracking designs have variable conversion times which may require 2^n tests. As

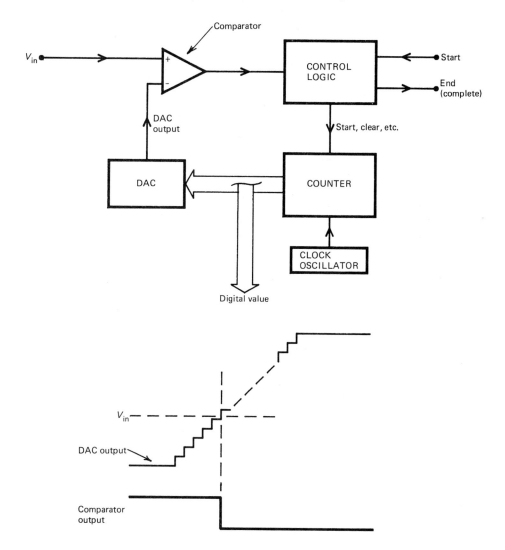

Fig. 12.11 Indirect ADC using a simple counter

for all counter type ADCs, accuracy is limited by the comparator and the DAC. A feature of this design is that an approximate result is available after each test and progressively becomes more accurate each time a test is made.

12.5 Device selection and processor connections

Normally the user selects a DAC or ADC to have the minimum specification meeting the requirements of the application. Devices are usually integrated circuits or hybrid modules, and the internal mechanism is not important provided that the device meets the required specification. However, there will be cases when some feature of a particular design could cause problems or be of benefit. In very low cost, mass production situations it is possible to imitate some designs in software; for example many indirect ADC designs may be created

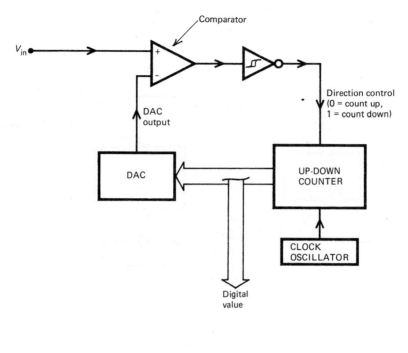

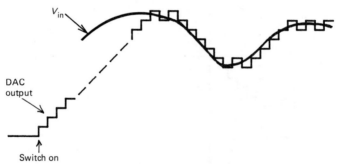

Fig. 12.12   Tracking converter

with a DAC, a comparator, and a program performing the required sequence of actions.

The device descriptions have all assumed linear conversion characteristics. There are applications, especially in communication systems transmitting digitized speech signals, for which converters with **non-linear characteristics** have advantages. Devices with suitable characteristics are available; a simplified version of a typical ADC characteristic using linear segments to approximate a logarithmic characteristic is illustrated in Fig. 12.14. The original signal may be restored using a DAC with an inverse characteristic.

The final feature of concern is the ease of connection of the converter to a processor system. Many newer devices are designed for connection to processor bus systems; some are suitable for most processors, while others are designed for use with a particular type of processor. DACs for direct bus connection incorporate an n-bit latch so that they may be used as simple output ports. Figure 12.15 illustrates one such DAC, a Ferranti ZN428 device, connected to a 6502 system.

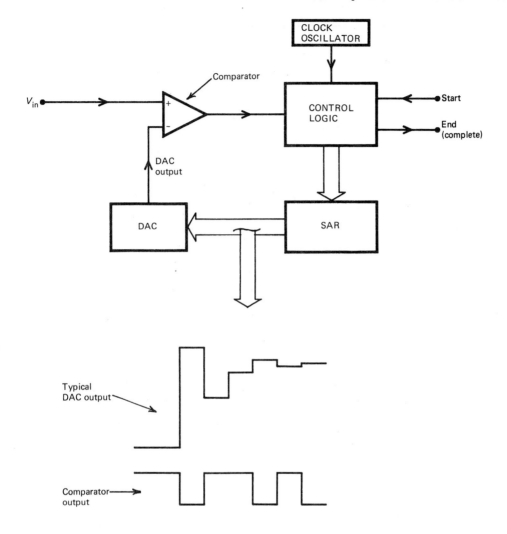

Fig. 12.13   Successive approximation ADC

Connection of ADCs is usually more complex; most types require a start conversion signal after which the system must wait until the conversion is complete before the digital value is available. Figure 12.16 illustrates a National Semiconductor ADC0801 device used in a 8085 system. The device is designed for use with 8-bit microprocessors; it is connected as a one word RAM, or as combined input and output ports. Writing any value to the device starts a conversion, and the end of conversion produces an interrupt signal; reading from the device gives the result of the last completed conversion and clears the interrupt signal if it is active.

Additional analogue circuits, **signal conditioning circuits,** are often necessary with ADCs and DACs. Frequently the analogue signals to or from external devices do not match the requirements of an ADC or DAC, and the signals must be suitably modified. Analogue connections to ADCs, DACs and any signal conditioning circuits require care and expert circuit design. The logic circuits of the processor system create a large amount of electrical interfer-

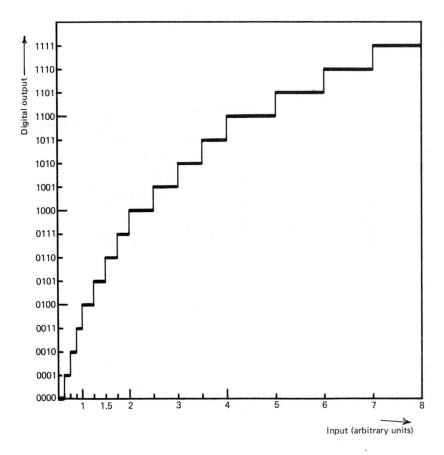

Fig. 12.14   Logarithmic conversion characteristic

ence (noise), and unless the analogue circuits, particularly power supply connection and signal line layout, are well designed great inaccuracy results regardless of actual device accuracy.

12.6   Problems

1 A flash converter is built using comparators whose maximum hysterysis is $\pm 0\cdot 01$ V. Assuming that the reference voltage and the maximum input voltage are both approximately 4 V, and that the resistor chain is perfect, what is the maximum size (number of bits) converter it is worthwhile constructing?

  The comparators are guaranteed to switch output state within $0\cdot 1$ μsec of the difference in their inputs exceeding the hysterysis limit. The converter is used to digitize a sine wave of 1 V peak to peak amplitude offset by $+2$ V; this is later reproduced by feeding the digital values to a perfect DAC. If no point on the restored waveform must be in error by more than 5%, what is the maximum permitted frequency of the original sine wave?

2 A processor latched output port is used as the input to a DAC. The DAC output is compared with an incoming analogue signal, the result 'greater than' or 'less than' is a logic signal supplied to an input port of the processor. For any particular processor, develop a program to act as an ADC. On entry the program behaves as successive approximation converter. Once this conversion is complete the program behaves as a tracking converter.

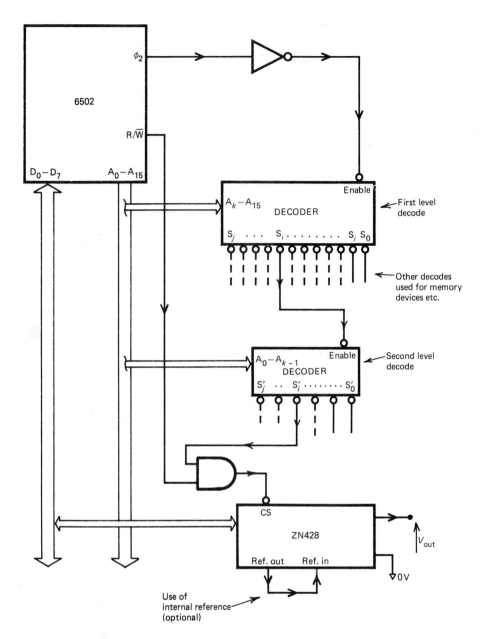

Fig. 12.15 Interface of a DAC to a processor system

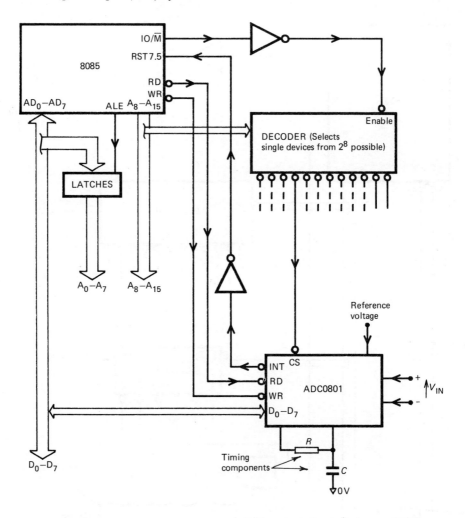

Fig. 12.16   An ADC to processor interface

Part 5
Software

13 Program preparation

The primary concern of this book is processor hardware; however hardware and software are so interdependent that it is often possible to replace one by the other. Also, to understand many common hardware features some examination of software is required. Ultimately the purpose of software design is to produce a sequence of binary numbers which, when run as the code sequence forming a program, cause a processor to perform some required task. For small tasks requiring only tens of instructions, it is possible to prepare the binary sequence directly. However, programs with large numbers of instructions are common, and alternative methods are essential for their preparation.

13.1 Code production

There are three common methods of generating a sequence of instruction codes to form a binary program. Direct manual preparation of binary code sequences is possible; a reliable method is the tabular one briefly described in Chapter 3. Such tabular methods are closely related to assembly language programming; they become difficult and uneconomic when programs of a significant size are required.

In tabular programming the instructions are written as mnemonics in the order of execution; each mnemonic is associated with the appropriate addresses at which the corresponding instruction code numbers will be placed in memory. For simple processors these are the true addresses at which the code will be placed, while for more elaborate systems it is the address relative to a starting value which may still have to be determined. Preparation of the code sequence requires determination of the code corresponding to each mnemonic, essentially a look-up process, and its association with the correct address. It is also necessary to evaluate the addresses for destinations of branch (jump and call) instructions when forming their complete binary codes.

Once the programmer has decided the sequence of mnemonics and the starting address of a program, the preparation of the code sequence is straightforward; it is ideally suited to automation. **Assemblers** are computer programs which convert a sequence of mnemonics into the correct binary code sequence. Additional features are included to simplify the programming task and to reduce the risk of human error. The initial mnemonic list becomes an **assembly language** or *low level language* program.

The third common method of preparing code for some task is to use a *high level language*. These languages are methods of defining operations to be performed by a processor system. Normal human languages are inadequate, because they lack precision; statements made are often ambiguous, being capable of several interpretations. Such statements are not suitable for a processor which executes instructions one at a time with each instruction having a single exact meaning.

Artificial languages for computer programming are defined so that any statement made in the language has a single precise meaning. The languages are similar in concept to mathematical notation; such notation consists of a set of definitions and manipulation rules. The definitions and rules have single meanings which must be maintained if the notation is to achieve the objective of reliable communication of ideas and results. Programming languages are similar, except that they must define different concepts and rules. Although the languages often exhibit features of mathematical notation, frequently using mathematical symbols, the user must be aware of their correct *but different meaning*. Once such a language is available, a program is written as set of statements in that language; the program statements define the task to be performed by a computer. In general, the language incorporates no features of any particular computer; it must be translated in some way to produce the instruction code sequence for the computer on which the program is to run. This translation could be performed manually, but this would generally take too long; it is usually undertaken by running a program on a computer. The data input to the program is the high level language program; the output is a binary number sequence which, when loaded and run as a program, will perform the task described by the high level program.

Table 13.1   Example of an 8080 assembly language program

```
;  Simple 8080 assembly language program example.
;  An 8-bit number obtained by IN 10H (input port 10H) is the value
;  from a transducer. A mechanical system affects the transducer,
;  increasing the value while 01H is output, decreasing it while 81H
;  is output, and there is no change when 00H is output. All outputs
;  are to port 20H. The value required is read from 8 switches used
;  as memory location 8000H and is to be maintained within ± 1 bit.

                ORG 1000H    ; Set address of first instruction.
SWIT            EQU 8000H    ; Define address of switches.
TRAN            EQU 10H      ; Define transducer input port address.
DRIV            EQU 20H      ; Define output drive port address.
                LXI SP,4000H ; Set up a stack.
                LXI H,SWIT   ; Set pointer to switches.
STAT:           XRA A        ; Zero value for no change.
                OUT DRIV     ; Prevent any change until required.
READ:           IN TRAN      ; Find present transducer value.
                SUB M        ; Subtract the value required.
                JZ READ      ; Jump if exactly correct.
                JNC POSV     ; Jump if difference is positive
                             ; (might be too large).
                INR A        ; Add 1 in case difference was − 1.
                JZ READ      ; Jump if it was − 1 (within limits).
                MVI A,01H    ; Set so drive increases transducer value.
                JMP COMM     ; Jump to common end of sequence.
POSV:           DCR A        ; Subtract 1 in case difference was 1.
                JZ READ      ; Jump if it was 1 (within limits).
                MVI A,81H    ; Set so drive decreases transducer value.
COMM:           OUT 20H      ; Turn drive on.
                CALL WAIT    ; Drive on (mechanical system) for set time.
                JMP STAT     ; Jump to turn drive off and test again.
;  Subroutine used to set the time the drive is on.
;  Corrupts A, B, C and FLAGS.
WAIT:           LXI B,5000H  ; Load a delay loop counter (must be set
                             ; for the response of system used).
WAIT05:         DCX B        ; Count down.
                MOV A,B      ; Part of present count to A.
                ORA C        ; Mask to find any 1 in B or C.
                JNZ WAIT05   ; Jump if not counted down to zero.
                RET

                END
```

13.2 Assemblers and assembler features

The fundamental requirement of an assembler is that it must convert a sequence of mnemonic names into the correct sequence of binary instruction codes, and associate them with specific memory addresses. It must also correctly determine all destination addresses for branch instructions, and insert these at the correct positions in the code.

Each different CPU has its own instruction set, hence assemblers are unique to a particular CPU. An assembly language, low level language, program is a sequence of mnemonics in the order in which the programmer wishes the instructions they represent to be executed. In addition, positions in the program may be defined by names, **labels**; when reference is made to a particular position, the appropriate name may be used instead of the address. Many other facilities are included to assist the programmer and reduce errors. Once prepared, the assembly language program is used as the data for the assembler, itself a

Table 13.2 Example of a 6502 assembly language program

```
; Simple 6502 assembly language program example.
; A push button switch is connected to appear as the value of the
; LSB read from memory location $2000 (2000 hexadecimal). It gives 0
; when held down and 1 if not pressed. On each press the value output
; to a DAC memory mapped to location $3000 is incremented.

               * = $8000  ; Set address of first instruction.
          SWIT = $2000  ; Define address of push button.
           DAC = $3000  ; Define DAC address.

          LDA #0      ; Set initial output.
          STA DAC     ; Initialise DAC.
          STA $80     ; Copy DAC value to zero page.
PRESS     LDA SWIT    ; Get push button condition.
          AND #1      ; Mask out all but required bit.
          BEQ PRESS   ; Jump if not pressed.
          JSR BOUN    ; Wait to de-bounce switch.
          LDA SWIT    ; Read switch again.
          AND #1      ; Mask to find switch.
          BEQ PRESS   ; Jump if initial find was spurious.
          INC $80     ; Set memory to next DAC value.
          LDA $80     ; Get updated value.
          STA DAC     ; Set DAC to new value.
RELS      LDA SWIT    ; Read switch again.
          AND #1      ; Mask to get switch.
          BNE RELS    ; Jump if still pressed.
          JSR BOUN    ; Wait to allow de-bounce.
          JMP PRESS   ; Loop back to wait for next press.

; Subroutine used to set the de-bounce wait.
; Corrupts A, memory $0081 and FLAGS.
BOUN      LDA #$FF    ; Set a delay count (must be set
                      ; for the response of system used).
          STA $81     ; Load delay counter.
BOUN05    DEC $81     ; Count down.
          BNE BOUN05  ; Jump if not counted down to zero.
          RTS

          .END
```

program. Assuming that no errors are indicated, for example an attempt to branch to a label which does not exist (typically caused by a typing error during input), the assembler output is the code sequence which will perform as required. Most assemblers also produce a listing showing the whole program combined with the code and addresses. Assemblers include many other useful facilities; for example, frequently used numeric values may be given names, and reference made to a name each time the value it defines is required. Although assemblers are unique to the processor for which the code is produced, most have common features; experienced programmers rarely have problems when changing from the assembler for one processor to that for another.

Because an assembler is unique to a particular processor, general descriptions are not particularly helpful; the manuals supplied with assemblers usually provide full details of their capability and use. Table 13.1 is an example of a simple assembly language program for an 8080 CPU and Table 13.2 is another for a 6502. While there are detail differences in representing certain items, for example the 8080 version uses a colon after a label whereas that for the 6502 does not, the general forms are similar. These programs are **source programs** written in assembly language; they are the data input to a processor system running an assembler. For most systems, source programs are entered by typing on a keyboard and are then stored in the backing store as a file of data. Once input is complete, the assembler program is run with this file as its input data; usually two sets of results are output and left in further data files in the backing store. One file holds a listing of the binary code program, an **object code file**, and the other holds a listing showing the source program as well as the code generated and the addresses used. Table 13.3 is the listing produced when the 8080 source program in Table 13.1 is assembled by one particular assembler.

The program which is run to generate the object code is called an assembler when it produces code to run on the same type of CPU as that running the assembler itself. If the assembler runs on a CPU which is not the same type as the one for which the code is generated, it is a **cross-assembler**.

13.3   High level languages

To create an artificial computer language, two problems must be solved. First, the language must provide a convenient method of expressing the operations to be performed; so far no single language has been devised that is ideal for all the different applications of processors. The second problem is that the high level language has to be translated into the binary code for the processor system on which the program is to run. If the language is designed primarily for ease of describing the task to be performed, it will probably be difficult to translate it into code; alternatively, languages designed for ease of translation to code are often poor at describing tasks to be performed.

As a result of these problems there are many computer languages, each providing a different degree of compromise in meeting the conflicting requirements of problem description and language translation. Even when high level languages are designed to make translation to code simple, the definition of the language does not depend on any features of a particular processor system design.

There are two conventional methods of generating code from high level language source programs; the most efficient method is **compilation**. As when using an assembler the source program, now written in the selected high level language, is input and stored as a data file. This file is the data for a program called a **compiler**; the output is an object code program for a processor system. The original high level language is not unique to any particular CPU design; however, the compiler is unique to a CPU type because it translates the high level language into code for a particular processor. Hence a source program written in high level language may be run on any system for which a compiler is available, that is the same program can be run on CPUs of totally different designs and should give the same results.

Table 13.3 Assembler output listing for the source program of Table 13.1

ISIS-II 8080/8085 MACRO ASSEMBLER, V4.0   MODULE   PAGE   1

LOC	OBJ	LINE	SOURCE STATEMENT	
		1	;	Simple 8080 assembly language program example.
		2	;	An 8-bit number obtained by IN 10H (input port 10H) is the value
		3	;	from a transducer. A mechanical system affects the transducer,
		4	;	increasing the value while 01H is output, decreasing it while 81H
		5	;	is output, and there is no change when 00H is output. All outputs
		6	;	are to port 20H. The value required is read from 8 switches used
		7	;	as memory location 8000H and is to be maintained within ± 1-bit.
		8		
1000		9	ORG 1000H	; Set address of first instruction.
8000		10 SWIT	EQU 8000H	; Define address of switches.
0010		11 TRAN	EQU 10H	; Define transducer input port address.
0020		12 DRIV	EQU 20H	; Define output drive port address.
1000	310040	13	LXI SP,4000H	; Set up a stack.
1003	210080	14	LXI H,SWIT	; Set pointer to switches.
1006	AF	15 STAT:	XRA A	; Zero value for no change.
1007	D320	16	OUT DRIV	; Prevent any change until required.
1009	DB10	17 READ:	IN TRAN	; Find present transducer value.
100B	96	18	SUB M	; Subtract the value required.
100C	CA0910	19	JZ READ	; Jump if exactly correct.
100F	D21B10	20	JNC POSV	; Jump if difference is positive,
		21		; (might be too large).
1012	3C	22	INR A	; Add 1 in case difference was − 1.
1013	CA0910	23	JZ READ	; Jump if it was − 1 (within limits).
1016	3E01	24	MVI A,01H	; Set so drive increases transducer value.
1018	C32110	25	JMP COMM	; Jump to common end of sequence.
101B	3D	26 POSV:	DCR A	; Subtract 1 in case difference was 1.
101C	CA0910	27	JZ READ	; Jump if it was 1 (within limits).
101F	3E81	28	MVI A,81H	; Set so drive decreases transducer value.
1021	D320	29 COMM:	OUT 20H	; Turn drive on.
1023	CD2910	30	CALL WAIT	; Drive on (mechanical system) for set time.
1026	C30610	31	JMP STAT	; Jump to turn drive off and test again.
		32	;	Subroutine used to set the time the drive is on.
		33	;	Corrupts A, B, C and FLAGS.
1029	010080	34 WAIT:	LXI B,8000H	; Load a delay loop counter (must be set
		35		; for the response of system used).
102C	0B	36 WAIT05:	DCX B	; Count down.
102D	78	37	MOV A,B	; Part of present count to A.
102E	B1	38	ORA C	; Mask to find any 1 in B or C.
102F	C22C10	39	JNZ WAIT05	; Jump if not counted down to zero.
1032	C9	40	RET	
		41		
		42	END	

USER SYMBOLS
COMM A 1021 DRIV A 0020 POSV   A 101B READ A 1009 STAT A 1006 SWIT A 8000
TRAN   A 0010 WAIT A 1029 WAIT05 A 102C

ASSEMBLY COMPLETE,   NO ERRORS

Table 13.4   Example of a simple PASCAL source program

```
MODULE example;
(* PASCAL procedure compiled for 8086. Finds the sum and mean of N
   integers. Uses integer arithmetic to keep short code. Value N and
   the integers, array a, are passed to the routine. Returns sum as
   tot, mean as mean, ER = 0 or 1 (error flag) *)

TYPE defn = ARRAY [1..100] of integer;
PROCEDURE sumn(var a : defn; var N,tot,mean,ER:integer);PUBLIC;
         VAR I:integer;
         LABEL 1;
            BEGIN
                    ER: = 0;
                    tot: = 0;
                    IF N < 1 THEN
                       BEGIN
                          ER: = 1;
                          GOTO 1;
                       END;
                    FOR I: = 1 TO N DO tot: = tot + a[I];
                    mean: = tot DIV N; (*  Warning: truncated result  *)
         1:    END; (*sumn*)
   END.
```

Like assemblers the name compiler implies that the CPU running the compiler is the same type as that on which the code will be run; a **cross-compiler** runs on one processor but produces code for another.

An advantage of writing programs in high level languages and producing code with a compiler is the great reduction in programming time, and therefore cost, required to obtain reliable working programs. Further, these programs are less likely to contain errors that remain undiscovered for a long time, and to some extent the language is self documenting so that later program changes are more easily made. The disadvantage of a high level language is that the code is less efficient, that is it requires more memory and runs more slowly, than a well written assembly language program. With a good compiler this penalty may be less than 25% in both size and speed; the cost and reliability advantages are such that whenever possible high level language should be used.

Table 13.4 is a source program for a simple procedure (a form of subroutine) written in the language PASCAL. Table 13.5 is the output listing when one particular compiler converts this into code for an 8086 CPU. This compiler has an option which, if selected, interlaces a form of assembly language for the code program generated in the output listing (the original PASCAL statements are emphasized by bold type). That is, the code generated by the compiler can be related to the high level language; this is a common feature of compilers producing code for microprocessors. Examination of the assembly language in the example listing indicates some of the reasons why high level languages are less efficient than low level ones. For example, in high level languages the programmer uses variables to identify quantities which change; this is necessary even when the quantities are only required within a short section of the program. High level languages use memory locations to hold variable quantities, and each use of a variable requires transfers to or from memory. In assembly language the programmer would probably leave short term values in a CPU register, saving several memory transfer operations.

The alternative method of converting high level language to code is by an **interpreter**. Interpreters have been produced for several languages but are primarily associated with the

Table 13.5 Output of compiler for simple PASCAL example (Table 13.4)

MDP	Pascal	(VO1.02–040)	Example
1			MODULE example;
			global DATABASEQQ
			G2 equ DATABASEQQ
			global CODEBASEQQ
			G1 equ CODEBASEQQ
			section C.EXAMPLE,align(2),class = CONSTQQ
			G4 equ C.EXAMPLE
			section I.EXAMPLE,align(2),class = INSTRQQ
			G6 equ I.EXAMPLE
			global SUMN
			SUMN equ G6
			resume G6
			org 0
		L3:	PUSH BP
			MOV BP,SP
			SUB SP,G4-(G2)
2			(* PASCAL procedure compiled for 8086. Finds the sum and mean of N
3			integers. Uses integer arithmetic for a short listing. Value N and
4			the integers, array a, are passed to the routine. Returns sum as
5			tot, mean as mean, ER = 0 or 1 (error flag) *)
6			
7			TYPE defn = ARRAY [1..100] of integer;
8			PROCEDURE sumn(var a : defn; var N,tot,mean,ER:integer);PUBLIC;
9		−2:B	VAR I:integer;
10			LABEL 1;
11			BEGIN
12	1	7:S	ER: = 0;
			MOV BX,4[BP]
			MOV [BX],#0
13	2	14:S	tot: = 0;
			MOV SI,8[BP]
			MOV [SI],#0
14	3	21:S	IF N < 1 THEN
			MOV SI,10[BP]
			CMP [SI],#1
			MOV −4[BP],SI
			MOV −6[BP],BX
			JGE L2
15	4	35:S	BEGIN
16	5	35:S	ER: = 1;
			MOV [BX],#1
17	6	39:S	GOTO 1;
			JMP L1
		L2:	
18	6		END;

(Table 13.5 continued over)

Table 13.5   Continued

MDP	Pascal	(VOl.02–040)		Example
19	7	41:S		**For I: = 1 TO N DO tot: = tot + a[I];**
			MOV AX,#1	
			MOV BX,[SI]	
			CMP AX,BX	
			JG L4	
			MOV −8[BP],BX	
		L5:	MOV −2[BP],AX	
			MOV BX, −2[BP]	
			SHL BX	
			ADD BX,12[BP]	
			MOV AX, −2[BX]	
			MOV SI,8[BP]	
			ADD [SI],AX	
			MOV AX, −2[BP]	
			CMP AX, −8[BP]	
			JZ L4	
			INC AX	
			JMP L5	
		L4:		
20	9	83:S		**mean: = tot DIV N; (* Warning:— truncated result *)**
			MOV BX,6[BP]	
			MOV SI,8[BP]	
			MOV AX,[SI]	
			CWD	
			MOV DI,10[BP]	
			IDIV [DI]	
			MOV [BX],AX	
21	10	99:S		**1: END;(*sumn*)**
		L1:		
			MOV SP,BP	
			POP BP	
			RET 10	
			resume G4	
			org 0	
			textblock 2	
			8,0	
			end	

	0 Errors	0 Warnings		
Section Statistics		Name: C.EXAMPLE	Class: CONSTQQ	Size: 2
		Name: I.EXAMPLE	Class: INSTRQQ	Size: 105

language BASIC. This language was developed for introductory teaching of programming, and was designed to be interpreted; it is widely used by small home and personal computer systems. However, most computer manufacturers have their own versions (dialects) of BASIC; therefore programs are not readily transferred from one type of computer to another. To be interpreted, a program must be written as a sequence of self-contained statements; in BASIC this is achieved by requiring the program statements to be in sequence and numbered.

To run an interpreted program, both the program source and the interpreter are loaded into the main memory of the processor system; many small computers have a BASIC interpreter permanently present in ROM. The interpreter is the program, and the high level language is once more the input data; both are located in the main memory. Once started, the interpreter takes the first line of the source program and converts it into a code module. This module is immediately executed; on exit from the module, control returns to the interpreter which processes the next line in the same manner. The process continues as long as no errors are found in the program or until an exit point is reached. Interpretation is inherently slow; one cause is that every time a program line is reached it is converted into code. Most programs contain loops in which sections of program are executed many times. When an interpreter is used, each line of a loop is converted into code for every execution of the loop. With a compiler code conversion only occurs once, this takes place during the compilation run (code conversion and program execution are performed separately); the whole program may be run many times with only a single code conversion. In applications when speed is not important, interpreters have some advantages; for example, errors in the source program are easily associated with the line of program which probably contains the error. This is why interpreted programs are useful in initial teaching of programming.

There is rarely a single best choice of high level language for a particular application, although the choice is often restricted by available compilers, interpreters or other requirements. Where possible, both the language and use of compilation or interpretation must be selected. Further, on many large computer systems more than one compiler may be provided for the same language, the differences usually being that those producing programs which run faster give less information regarding errors in the source program. Such errors occur during compilation because of errors in writing the high level program; other errors occur while running the object code program, for example when a calculation results in too large a result (overflow) or an attempt to divide by zero.

13.4 Software design

The design of a program, or set of programs, to perform some task requires as much care as the design of the hardware. Both the problem to be solved and the programming process must be fully understood. However, many badly constructed programs will run, sometimes even if they contain errors; consequently program design is not always treated with the necessary care. Lack of programming discipline also arises because this is a relatively new and rapidly evolving profession; formal rules and methods are still being developed.

For engineering applications of processors, it is usually essential to establish that a program will operate correctly under all possible circumstances. This is particularly important if the processor is used in control systems. Often an error in operation could create a serious hazard; for example in the control of a chemical process plant or aircraft systems. Validation of program behaviour is complex and difficult; it is the subject of much research. Testing and validation problems are fewer when good programming techniques are used.

In the past, programmers used clever *tricks* to reduce memory requirements or increase running speeds. However, this often creates problems in the production of reliable programs and when later revision is required. The economics of total system design, hardware plus software, have moved from the situation of hardware constituting most of the cost to one in which software costs are significant, particularly at the design stage. There are many cases where software design costs greatly exceed the hardware design costs. As software costs are lower, and reliability is higher, a suitable high level language should be adopted for any system requiring a significant programming effort. If speed or size penalties incurred by use of a high level language result in the hardware being inadequate for the task, it is often more economical to use higher performance hardware than to write a large low level language program. The main exception is when the system is to be produced in large quantities, for example when a domestic product contains a microprocessor system. In such cases even small reductions in hardware requirements may justify large software development costs.

To design software, a systematic approach must be adopted as a complex process is being undertaken. Software is a manufactured product and will probably be used for several years; during this time it is probable that modifications and improvements will be required. These are only straightforward if the design is well documented and easily understood.

As in any design task, the initial step is development of an overall plan of the software with the total specification clearly determined. Even for small systems software usually contains a large number of instructions, therefore the full specification is divided into small sections, each clearly defined. A major requirement of such modular development is that the interconnection of units must follow rigorous rules. This is analagous to the interconnection of integrated circuit logic elements. Such components are built so that the output from one meets a specification which ensures that it will reliably drive the inputs to other elements. Modular software development can be undertaken in many ways; subroutines are one mechanism, and a common approach is to build a library of subroutines for frequently required functions. Another modular software form is that for a page organized system; software must be in units of pages with systematic links to other units.

Once modular programming is adopted, further techniques are possible. For example, **mixed language programming** may be used; the majority of a program may be in a high level language with critical sections written in assembly language. Also, modules may be written in different high level languages, enabling special features of each language to be used. Mixed language programming requires detailed information about the code produced by a high level language: typically the method of representing variable quantities and the way in which values are transferred to and from subroutines (or other units). When developing a program in modules, those produced have to be built into a complete program; most software development systems include facilities to assist in the building process.

13.5 Software development

Software is a component of any product which contains a processor system, and care in its design is as important as care in hardware design. The concept of software as a product which requires rigorous testing and validation is relatively new; techniques are still at an early stage of development. As for creation of any other product, the design and development starts with a specification giving the exact behaviour required. The method of solving the problem set by the specification is decided next and a structure, a plan, for this solution is devised. Except for the most simple designs, the complete software is divided into small modules, each capable of being individually developed and tested; some systematic method of communicating between modules must be devised. Approaching software design starting with an overall plan is a *top-down* method; there are other methods, but this one is reliable for most applications. As each module can be developed and tested separately, future changes often require only the addition or modification of a single module.

Once the basic design of the software is fully specified, the actual preparation may begin. Decisions are required as to the use of low level or high level language and, in the latter case, which. High level languages should be chosen whenever possible. Modular structure allows mixed language programming, enabling high level languages to be used even when part of a program must be in low level language.

In modular programming, some modules are required so often that **libraries** of commonly used modules may be built. Some tasks occur so frequently that a library of routines for them is often supplied with a compiler or assembler.

Developing programs now include complex software building processes. The creation of an individual module is outlined in Fig. 13.1. Once all the modules for a program have been

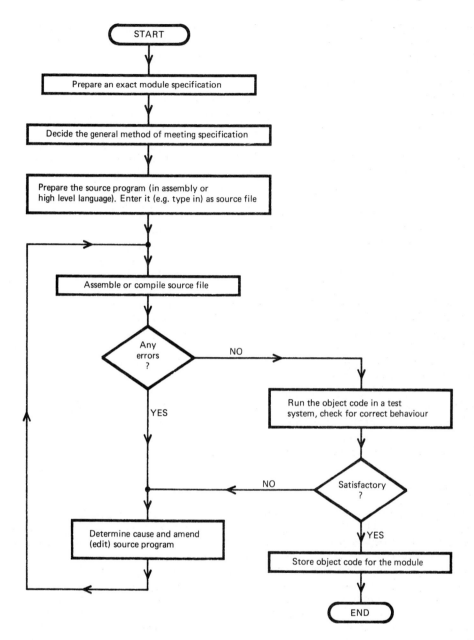

Fig. 13.1 Development cycle for a software module

prepared, they must be combined and suitably positioned in memory to form a final code program. The detailed method of combining modules varies from one software development system to another, but Fig. 13.2 outlines a typical sequence of actions. This building process requires support systems with suitable features incorporated in assemblers and compilers.

A consequence of modular structure is that the programmer writing routines, modules, etc., does not know the memory locations at which these will be placed when all the software is connected together. Therefore modules for general use must be capable of being positioned anywhere in memory. This is apparently difficult; instructions, particularly branches, often include an absolute address as part of the code. This address is related to the branch destination, usually the position another instruction code in the memory, and is an unknown value if the module position is not fixed. Most sophisticated assemblers and compilers generate **relocatable code**, that is the code they output may be positioned at any address in memory.

Relocation is another term associated with processor systems which has several different meanings. It is possible to write code for many processors in such a way that it may be loaded at any position in memory and will run correctly. This usually imposes restrictions on code preparation; it is only possible when certain compilers are used, or by choosing a carefully selected part of the instruction set when writing in assembly language. In practice, totally relocatable large programs are uncommon; usually a less general page relocatable form is adopted. As indicated in Chapter 10, programs to run apparently simultaneously are usually prepared in units of pages; a page consists of a convenient sized block of 2^n memory locations. Page relocatable code is prepared so that it must be loaded and run in a fixed position within a page, but it is independent of the actual page used to hold the code in memory. An alternative form of relocatable code, often associated with microprocessor systems, is that the code produced by the assembler or compiler is incomplete. All features which would restrict the position of the code in memory are omitted; a list is appended to the code and contains all the information necessary to complete the code when its position in memory is finally decided.

Consequently, the first requirement for the process of software building is that the assemblers and compilers used must generate a specified form of relocatable code. When all the modules have been produced, they must be connected together to form the complete code sequence. Most assembler and compiler software packages include a **linker**; this is a program run on the same processor as the assembler or compiler which makes all the necessary connections. The linker combines all the modules and inserts any library routines required. If no errors arise in the link process a complete code program, still in relocatable form, is produced.

The final stage in code preparation depends upon the form of relocatable code produced. If the code is page relocatable and intended for use in a multi-programming environment, then after production it will have been placed in the backing store. A command is given to the operating system to run the code as a program. This command causes the operating system to use a routine, a **loader**, to place pages of the code in memory as required and run it as a program. The operating system makes the necessary translations of program page to real memory page address.

If the code forms a unit to be run as a single program, often the situation for a microprocessor system, then the addresses omitted in the relocatable code must be added. Another software package, a **locater**, converts the relocatable code program into an absolute code program. The program addresses are chosen by the programmer at this stage in the preparation, the absolute code runs correctly only when positioned at selected addresses. When a program is built from several components and uses fixed locations, a **software memory map** assists in program use and in future development. The map is similar to a hardware memory map (Chapter 4) but shows the positions of software elements in memory rather than the

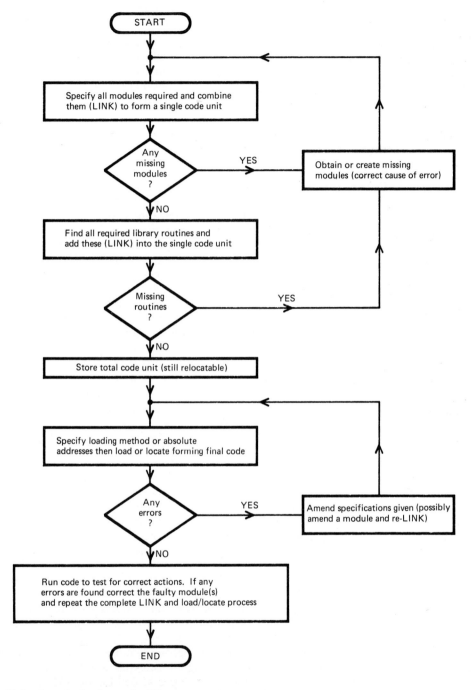

Fig. 13.2 A typical software building process

address ranges occupied by actual memory devices. Figure 13.3 is a simple example for an 8080 system with a program permanently fixed in ROM.

The complete software development process consists of preparing all necessary modules, compiling or assembling them, and testing them individually if possible. Once the code for all modules is prepared they are linked; provided that no errors are found, the complete code is then passed to an operating system to be loaded; alternatively it is located and stored in the correct memory locations. At both module and complete program level, testing can be assisted by suitable software and hardware tools.

13.6   Operating systems

Writing a program to perform a single task on a processor system with a single level of memory is straightforward; the only complications which arise are those inherent in the task. However, for systems with hierarchical memory structures, complex organization operations are required to run programs. Further organization problems arise when a processor is used to perform several tasks apparently simultaneously. The control of systems requiring significant organization effort is normally undertaken by a special program, an **operating system**. This may run on the processor itself as one of the multiple tasks; in large systems all, or part, may run on an auxiliary control processor system.

An operating system is a program which performs much of the internal organization to run programs on a processor system. This is usually extended to allow a user to give simple commands to the operating system. These commands initiate the complex sequences of actions for commonly required system tasks. A typical simple task is to compile a source program that already exists in a file, store the resulting code in another file and print the listing output by the compiler (including any error messages). Most operating systems would allow the user to perform this by giving a single command, probably of the form:

command ⟨*source file name*⟩ ⟨*code file name*⟩ ⟨*destination for listing*⟩

Such a command is an order to the operating system requiring it to undertake complex tasks with no assistance from the user. The compilation task is included in the queue of programs to be run. The operating system decides when to run a program, making the decision on many criteria; once this compilation task is selected to be run, the compiler is loaded and run. Input to the compiler is supplied from the program source file; this requires appropriate file to main memory transfers. Output is correctly routed to the output file and printer. The operating system must choose how much real memory to allocate to the program; it must also organize all the necessary transfers of program pages, input data and output data between main and backing store as required during the program run.

Although operating systems have existed in some form for more than twenty years, they vary greatly and are still far from ideal. The operating system of a large computer is much more elaborate than that for a small one, but even for systems with roughly similar specification there are large variations. No standards exist and usually each computer manufacturer implements an individual and unique system. A few operating systems are available to run on many different systems and are becoming more widely adopted. Many small 8-bit systems use the CP/M system from Digital Research, and medium size 16-bit and 32-bit systems often use UNIX which was developed at Bell Laboratories.

13.7   Comments

A brief outline of software preparation methods has been given which indicates commonly used methods and techniques. Complex software design requires expert specialist pro-

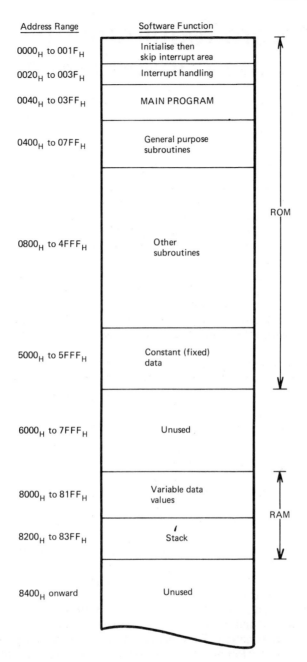

Fig. 13.3 Example of a software memory map

grammers if reliable programs are to be produced. However, hardware engineers must have knowledge of software and understand the problems encountered by software designers to develop suitable hardware. The affect of these software requirements on hardware is briefly examined in Chapter 14.

14 Software requirements and hardware consequences

The production of well designed programs is assisted by the provision of appropriate hardware features. A major hardware influence is the instruction set obeyed by the CPU being used. Instructions are usually described in terms of an action, an operation, which is performed using appropriate operands. Source operands provide values used by the operation, while destination operands define where results are placed. Some instructions do not require any operands to be specified, for others several operands must be given; two is a common maximum and instructions which require the specification of more than three operands are uncommon.

The instruction set for a processor consists of all the possible operations allowed for that processor. Each operation must be combined with its required operands; the methods of determining the operands are **operand addressing modes**. Ideally, any requirement by an instruction for an operand should allow the use of every addressing mode implemented by the processor. In practice this cannot be achieved, and each instruction is restricted with only specified addressing modes allowed for each of its operands. Generally there are few addressing mode restrictions for large processors but many for small ones, especially microprocessors; often restrictions follow no apparent pattern. Types of addressing mode available for a processor and restrictions on their use affect the ease with which software can be developed.

14.1 Addressing modes

Many addressing modes have been devised for processor systems, but only a few modes are implemented in any individual CPU design. Names for addressing modes can be confusing, because different CPU manufacturers do not use identical terminology. The following are some frequently used simple addressing modes with examples for common microprocessors.

14.1.1 Implied addressing

In this mode an operand is inherent in the instruction itself. For example both the 8080 and 6502 have arithmetic instructions with the mnemonic name CMA, complement accumulator, for which no operands are specified. (With two accumulators the 6800 has two instructions, COMA and COMB.) There are two operands, one is the data source and the other is the result destination. These are the same, the accumulator; neither is specified as an operand but both are **implied** in the instruction. Many instructions have this form of addressing; an operand is so restricted by the instruction action that it is not selected by the programmer; the operand becomes part of the definition of the operation.

14.1.2 Immediate addressing

An operand is obtained immediately when an instruction code contains its value. Typical examples are the 8080 instruction MVI r,*data*; the 6502 instruction ADC #*data*; and the 6800 instruction LDAA #*data*. These instructions have more than one operand, although some are implied operands for ADC and LDAA. The value of the immediate operand is fixed by the programmer and forms part of the instruction code. By its nature an immediate operand must be a source operand; it cannot be a destination one.

Note that many jump or call instructions use immediate addressing, although some CPU manufacturers describe them as using absolute addressing (see Section 14.1.3). An instruction of the form *JUMP TO ADDRESS* includes the value of the destination address in the code sequence; the instruction is simply one to move this address value into the program counter. *JUMP* (or *JMP*) is just a more appropriate mnemonic for the instruction *MOVE IMMEDIATE TO PROGRAM COUNTER*.

14.1.3 Direct or absolute addressing

The instruction code contains the address of the memory location whose contents form the operand. Typical examples are LDA *address* and STA *address* used by several processors. The absolute value of a memory address becomes part of the instruction code; when the operand is referenced, the processor must perform a read or write access to the memory location whose address is part of the code.

14.1.4 Register addressing

The operand is the contents of a register; for example the 8080 instruction MOV r1,r2 has two operands, and both are register addressed. The source operand is the contents of register r2 and the destination operand is register r1.

This is a common addressing mode for a CPU with many registers. It is used frequently for the 8080 with multiple registers but is not used for the 6502 with few registers. The small number of cases for the 6502 when register addressing would be appropriate use separate instructions with implied addressing. If the registers may also function as accumulators, as for the 6800 family, this mode may be known as **accumulator addressing**.

14.1.5 Indirect addressing

There are many forms of indirect addressing, often several for one CPU. Derivation of an operand involves two steps; first the source of an address is defined and then this address is used to specify the memory location for the operand. The first step is itself a form of addressing with many possibilities. For example, the 8080 instruction LDAX B is load the accumulator with the contents of the memory location whose address is the current contents of the register pair B–C. The source operand is addressed indirectly by register indirect addressing.

14.1.6 Indexed addressing

This is a powerful mechanism which requires a CPU capability to perform computations of address values, as part of a memory access. Indexing may be implemented in several ways and is often combined with other forms of addressing. An **index register**, or the ability of a general purpose register to act in an index mode, is necessary. The address of an indexed operand is determined by adding the contents of the index register to some base address value. Often the width of one value is less than that of the full address; its contents are added to the least significant bits of the full address with the missing, higher, bits assumed to be zero.

One form implemented by both the 6502 and 6800 is direct (absolute) indexed addressing; a typical 6502 instruction is LDA *addr*,X. The contents of the index register, the 8-bit X register, are added to the 16-bit direct address value in the instruction code to form the

Instruction LDA $aaaa_H$, X   with $aaaa_H$ = $2AC5_H$ and X contents of $7D_H$.

$aaaa_H$ value	0010 1010 1100 0101
Contents of X when executed	0111 1101
Address whose contents are copied to A	0010 1011 0100 0010

(a)   Example of 6502 indexed addressing

Instruction ADC (bb_H), Y   with bb_H = 25_H, Y contents of $3E_H$, also 0025_H and 0026_H contents

of 37_H and $2E_H$ respectively.

Contents of location 0025_H	0011 0111
Left shifted contents of location 0026_H	0010 1110 0000 0000
Sum = base address	0010 1110 0011 0111
Contents of Y when executed	0011 1110
Address whose contents are ADDED into A	0010 1110 0111 0101

(b)   Example of 6502 indirect indexed addressing

Instruction JMP   *disp*   with *disp* = 10010101_2 and the two instruction bytes located at

addresses 01234_H and 01235_H. (The 8086 data bus is 16 bits wide but memory is in

separately addressed bytes).

Assume (CS) = 0000   hence (IP) = 1234_H

Contents of IP (instruction pointer) after fetching both instruction bytes	0001 0010 0011 0110
Value *disp* extended to 16 bits by copying the sign bit into the added high 8 bits	1111 1111 1001 0101
Total (IP) + *disp* ·	1 0001 0001 1100 1011

Ignore the final carry, the new instruction pointer is $11CB_H$.

(c)   Example of 8086 relative addressing

Fig. 14.1   Examples of addressing modes

address from which data is obtained (Fig. 14.1a). The 6800 instruction LDAA X,#*data* is similar except that the index register, X, is 16 bits wide and the value *data* supplied immediately is only 8 bits.

The 6502 also implements some indirect indexed addressing modes; one form is shown by the instruction ADC (*addr8*),Y. For this a 16-bit address is obtained from two adjacent memory locations; the first location has the address with the high byte zero and low byte the value *addr8*. The contents of the index register, Y, are added to the 16-bit value fetched and the total is used as the address of the operand (Fig. 14.1b).

14.1.7 Relative addressing

This is usually associated with branch instructions; data manipulation forms are not common for small processors. It is similar to indexed addressing, but the value to be added is contained in the instruction code (immediate) rather than a register. The 8086 family has many forms of branch instruction; one is a short form of jump which uses relative addressing for fast execution. The instruction is JMP *disp* where *disp* is an 8-bit number in twos-complement. *disp* is added to the value of the instruction pointer (program counter) after the complete code has been fetched. This forces a jump to a location with an address within − 128 to + 127 of the instruction following the relative jump; an example is shown in Fig. 14.1c.

Although many addressing modes have been outlined, an even wider range is found in practice. Each mode enables useful program structures to be developed, but only a selection are implemented in any particular CPU design. When the CPU is more complex, for example the 8086 with a segmented structure, more elaborate addressing modes may arise. This is illustrated in Table 14.1 which lists some methods of loading the 16-bit A register (denoted by AX, because 8-bit loading of each half, AH and AL, is possible).

Table 14.1   Some 8086 addressing modes illustrated for AX register loading

Instruction	Code(Hex)	Action
MOV AX,2C31H	B8 31 2C	Load (immediate) value 2C31H into AX
MOV AX,CX	8B C1	Copy contents of CX into AX
MOV AX,*addr*	A1 *ll hh*	Copy contents of memory location into AX. Address is contents of segment register DS multiplied by 10H plus 16-bit value *hhll*
MOV AX,[BX]	8B 07	Copy contents of memory location into AX. Address is contents of segment register DS multiplied by 10H plus contents of BX
MOV AX,ES:[BX]	26 8B 07	Copy contents of memory location into AX. Address as for MOV AX,[BX] except ES is used not DS
MOV AX,[BX + *nn*]	8B 47 *nn*	Copy contents of memory location into AX. Address is contents of segment register DS multiplied by 10H plus contents of BX plus 8-bit value *nn*
MOV AX,[BX] DI	8B 01	Copy contents of memory location into AX. Address is contents of segment register DS multiplied by 10H plus contents of BX plus contents of DI

14.2   Instruction sets

Instruction sets for CPUs vary greatly; generally small versatile sets with a range of addressing modes and few restrictions on the use of addressing modes are the most useful. MOS single component CPUs, that is most of the common microprocessors, tend to have large instruction sets. One reason is that if these large sets are fully utilized they compensate for the relatively low speed of MOS devices. However it is difficult for either an assembly language programmer or a compiler to make full use of large instruction sets.

Generally all instruction sets will have data transfer, arithmetic, logic and branch instructions. Further, most also have rotate or shift (or both) instructions, and some method of implementing a subroutine call and return sequence. Provided that general forms of these instructions are available, compilers for high level languages often ignore the elaborate instructions provided in some instruction sets. Exceptions to this are arithmetic instructions, for example multiply and divide, which are not present in simple CPU instruction sets. When available, they are used by compilers because both the code generated and the execution time may be greatly reduced. Compilers often fully utilize complex addressing modes to assist in manipulating the elaborate data structures that are created in many high level languages.

A wide range of special purpose instructions exist and vary from one CPU design to another. Processors intended for control applications have instructions assisting in testing signals on input lines and supplying logic control signals to individual output lines. Similarly, processors intended for use in systems for signal transmission and signal processing have fast integer multiply and support for operations to check encoded data. Such orientation of instruction sets towards applications produces processors which are no longer general purpose but suited only for a limited range of tasks.

14.3   Software requirements

When programs are written in low level languages it is difficult for a programmer, even an expert, to make full use of a large instruction set. Examination of well written low level programs shows that programmers tend to use a subset of a large instruction set; the subset chosen will vary slightly from one programmer to another. With a few exceptions the methods used in good low level programming are similar to those used when a compiler generates code from a high level language. Low level language programming produces shorter code sequences, primarily because compilers use general methods to allow for all possibilities that could occur. In low level language less general cases can be adopted when appropriate.

To examine the influence of software requirements on instruction sets, the tasks frequently performed within programs must be determined. A current good programming practice is called **structured programming**. This requires that all programs are constructed using three elements: *sequences* (i.e. one task executed immediately after another without branches), *if-then-else* constructions, and *repetition* until a specified condition is met. Programs are built from these components; the components themselves may be built from units constructed using the same three elements. The *if* condition may be extended to allow multiway decisions rather than simple alternatives; also units used several times may be in the form of subroutines built from the three elements.

Programs operate on data items and data structures, for example arrays of data are often required. Complex data structures are developed, particularly for large commercial data handling systems. Instruction sets may assist in manipulation of such data, for example when searches are made to find all data records which contain particular features.

Implementation of programming and data manipulation requirements is assisted by suitable support in the instruction set. Sequences of tasks are themselves any sequence of

Table 14.2   Use of 8080 instruction PCHL for multi-way branch

```
; Program sequence from which multi-way branch occurs.
                . . .
                . . .
                . . .
; Determine numeric value (1 to 4 allowed here) of branch required
; and leave it in B. (Range not checked in this example).
                . . .
                . . .
                . . .
          MOV A,B      ; Branch number to A
          DCR A        ; Change so branch number is 0 to 3
          RLC          ; Double branch value (16-bit addresses)
          LXI H,TABL   ; Point to list of branch addresses
          ADD L        ; Compute low address of branch required
          MOV L,A      ; Low branch address to L
          JNC SHORT    ; Jump if no change needed in high address
          INR H        ; Increment high address if necessary
SHORT:    MOV E,M      ; Fetch iow branch address
          INX H        ; Point to high branch address
          MOV D,M      ; Fetch high branch address
          XCHG         ; Move branch address to H-L
          PCHL         ; Jump to required branch
; Table of branch addresses
TABL:     DW   BRAN1
          DW   BRAN2
          DW   BRAN3
          DW   BRAN4
; Instruction code sequence for branch 1
BRAN1:    . . .
          . . .
          JMP XYZ      ; Rejoin common sequence
; Instruction code sequence for branch 2
BRAN2:    . . .
          . . .
          JMP XYZ      ; Rejoin common sequence
; Instruction code sequence for branch 3
BRAN3:    . . .
          . . .
          JMP XYZ      ; Rejoin common sequence
; Instruction code sequence for branch 4
BRAN4:    . . .
          . . .
; Common sequence after branches
XYZ:      . . .
          . . .
          . . .
```

actions (including subroutine calls) forming a non-branching program section. No special support is necessary, such sequences are an inherent feature of any programmed sequential machine.

14.3.1   Branches and loops

A two way branch is of the form *IF condition THEN action 1 ELSE action 2*. While the stated condition may be complicated, the final result of its evaluation by a sequence of logical and arithmetic operations must be TRUE or FALSE. Simple *IF-ELSE* conditions, also *repetition loops*, may be constructed with conditional branch instructions. Multi-way branches may also be built with conditional instructions, but the program operation is slow and difficult to understand. Implementation of multi-way branches is easier if a mechanism to load a computed value into the program counter is available. Trick methods are possible for most CPUs, but many provide methods of performing branches to computed addresses. Table 14.2 is part of an 8080 program using instruction PCHL, move the contents of H–L to PC, which performs a multi-way branch in a fast, obvious, and easily modified manner.

14.3.2   Subroutines

A standard *CALL* and *RETURN* sequence with addresses stored on a stack satisfactorily handles the problems of correct sequential behaviour. However, programming effort is reduced if a subroutine is suitable for application in many situations. A typical case occurs when a subroutine is written to output to a device which requires a long sequence of control operations. The same routine should be available for output to any other devices of the same type fitted to the system. That is, if a high level language routine for output to a device exists it should be of the form *SEND TO (N)* where *N* may take any one of several allowed values and identifies the particular device to be used.

This has introduced the concept of a **parameter** for a subroutine. Detailed operation of the subroutine is influenced by a value transferred (passed) to it by the program when running; this value may vary from one call to another, making the subroutine more generally applicable. A single parameter has been introduced, but a more general form allows any number of parameters; also these may both transfer values to the routine and may receive results from it. Typically in a high level language a sequence, subroutine, could be devised to determine the two roots, *X1* and *X2*, of the equation $aX^2 + bX + c = 0$. In the program its use might appear as a statement of the form ROOTS(*X1*,*X2*,*a*,*b*,*c*), where all five terms in the brackets are variable quantities. Whenever the routine is called, the values of *a*, *b*, and *c* will only be known at the time it is executed and it will produce the results *X1* and *X2*. Obviously the high level language compiler must produce a code program which transfers the parameter values to and from the routine.

Simple CPUs provide no assistance in this task; a common method of implementing parameter transfer is to pass single parameters through a specified register. Multiple parameters are passed by storing either their values, or their addresses in memory, in a reserved area of memory and passing the address of this area in a register. More elaborate processors incorporate methods of parameter passing; the 8086 allows parameters (or their addresses) to be passed on the stack along with the return address. A more elaborate return instruction enables the stack to be correctly reset after execution of the routine. Table 14.3 is a partial program showing the use of this 8086 parameter transfer mechanism. The mechanism may also be used to return values from a routine although this is more complicated.

14.3.3   Data handling

There are several features of data handling which can be assisted by suitable instruction

Table 14.3 Simple example of 8086 parameter passing on the stack

```
; Partial program sequence which uses a procedure XYZ requiring two
; word (16-bit) parameters X and Y passed on the stack.
    . . .
    . . .

; Assumed that value of parameter X is now in CX and Y is in DX.
        PUSH DX         ; Put value Y onto the stack.
        PUSH CX         ; Put value X onto the stack.
        CALL XYZ        ; Call subroutine required.
        . . .           ;⎫
        . . .           ;⎬ Program continuation after return.
        . . .           ;⎭

; Procedure with name XYZ accessed by short CALL (only IP is
; changed, there is no affect on CS)

XYZ  PROC      NEAR
        PUSH BP         ; Save BP in case used elsewhere.
        MOV BP,SP       ; Set BP to point to stack area.
        MOV AX,[BP + 4] ; Get parameter X from stack, put in AX.
        MOV BX,[BP + 6] ; Get parameter Y from stack, put in BX.
        . . .           ;⎫
        . . .           ;⎬ Actions of procedure.
        . . .           ;⎭
        POP BP          ; Restore BP entry value.
        RET 4           ; Return getting correct return address and
                        ; removing 4 parameter bytes from stack.

XYZ  ENDP
```

sets. Most are concerned with organization of data into complicated structures. In commercial applications, companies keep business records in magnetic storage systems; such records are sequences of code numbers representing alphabetic and numeric characters. When information is required from the records data blocks, holding many records, are loaded into the main memory from back-up store and are searched for the information required. This search process requires an examination of a large quantity of data to find a particular item; availability of suitable addressing modes is particularly important. Indexed addressing often assists in the creation of efficient search mechanisms.

Common record searches are for occurrence of specific sequences in records; a typical case is a sophisticated word processor which checks spelling. This must search a dictionary to see if all the words used in the text being checked match words with correct spelling in the dictionary. Advanced data structures reduce the initial search process by determining a small section of the dictionary relevant to a particular text word. The final part of the search is to compare the text word with each word in the small section until a match occurs or the list end is reached. This is a very slow process in general but can be accelerated if suitable addressing modes and instructions are available.

14.3.4 System operation

Software requirements and their influence on instruction sets have been described in terms of required program actions and implementation of high level languages. Operating system software is another important requirement of many modern systems; its production is assisted by suitable features in the instruction set. Such requirements are more complex than those that have been considered but are met by some processors.

14.4   Summary

Processor system architecture is influenced by the requirements of programmers, and the hardware designer must have some knowledge of their requirements. While programmers do not make full use of large instruction sets, the actual set available will affect the development of programs for a processor system. Software design is also influenced by the addressing modes implemented by a CPU and restrictions on their use.

14.5   Problems

1 For one processor determine all the methods used to obtain all source and destination operands for each arithmetic instruction in the instruction set.

2 Arrays of data are common features of high level languages. A particular language stores integers as 32-bit values in contiguous memory locations. The language allows two dimensional arrays of integers with elements of the form VAR(i,j); i is an integer from 0 to m and j is 0 to n.

   Using the instruction set and addressing modes of one 8-bit CPU, show how such an array would be stored in memory. Also write a section of assembly language program showing how the address of the first byte of element VAR(i, j) would be determined. Restrict i and j to 8-bit values to reduce the amount of code required.

Part 6
Processor Systems, Applications and Alternatives

15 Systems and applications

The previous sections have described the components of processor systems and their inter-connection. General purpose microprocessors were emphasized because of their avail-ability and low cost. Further, most essential concepts and techniques required to use common processor systems can be studied using microprocessors. These properties make microprocessor based systems suitable for laboratory exercises; other systems tend to be too expensive and too complex for student use.

A wide range of engineering design tasks are involved in the development and use of pro-cessor systems. Engineers employed by a processor manufacturer may be concerned with detailed design of components, for example arithmetic circuits or control logic. At the other extreme, engineers using processors as components of control systems may purchase com-plete systems and make relatively minor adaptations.

The combination of a wide range of design tasks and many applications makes it impos-sible to give any general design methods. Instead processor systems have been arbitrarily classified into groups by approximate size and speed. Typical examples are introduced, with an indication of some applications. It is not considered necessary to give examples of pro-cessors functioning as calculators and as business administration systems. The large range and number of general purpose computers in use today demonstrates that processor systems are ideal for such functions.

15.1 Small systems

A processor system is a sequential logic circuit; that is, once programmed it steps through a fixed sequence of states. It is more flexible than a sequential circuit designed for a specific task because the sequence followed is defined by a program which may be changed. There are many situations where a small processor system may be used instead of a purpose designed sequential circuit. However, for high speed systems direct design of sequential circuit is often essential; fast operation may imply insufficient time to execute a sequence of instructions. Dedicated sequential circuits may also be more appropriate when a high level of performance validation is necessary; it is easier to ensure that hardware operates correctly than to guarantee software behaviour.

The boundary between sequential logic systems and small processor systems is not dis-tinct. When a sequential system requires many states, some form of programmed system simplifies design. For many small tasks with a fixed program, microcontrollers are often chosen. These are intermediate between custom designed integrated circuits and standard processor systems. A **microcontroller** is a complete processor system with CPU, ROM, RAM and I–O on one integrated circuit. Such processors are used with a fixed program, so the ROM and RAM are usually separate; they do not occupy the same address space and the system does not have a von Neumann architecture.

In large quantity manufacture, microcontrollers with mask programmed ROM are inexpensive and final product assembly costs are low. The earliest widely used microcon-trollers are the Texas Instruments TMS1000 series found in many products, particularly domestic items such as washing machines, timers, etc. This type of device is restricted to large quantity manufacture, typically over a thousand units, so that initial ROM produc-

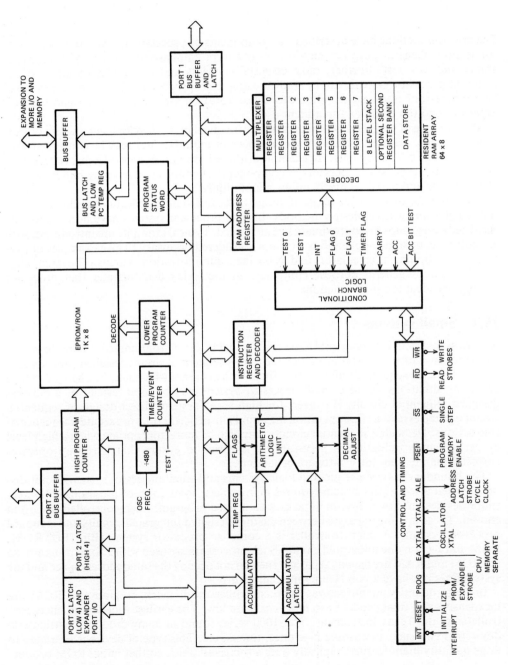

Fig. 15.1   Intel 8048 architecture

tion costs can be distributed over many final products. Applications of microcontrollers increased with the introduction of the Intel 8048 family of devices; Fig. 15.1 shows their basic architecture. This family now contains many devices but was introduced with three members. The 8048 has mask programmed ROM, the 8035 has no ROM but can be connected to external ROMs (or EPROMs) with some loss of I–O capability, and the 8748 has on chip EPROM. In operation the three devices differ marginally in electrical performance only. Consequently prototypes and small quantities can be produced using the 8748 or the 8035 plus EPROM; if errors are discovered, the program may be erased and an amended one written into the EPROM. The 8748 version is more expensive than the basic 8048; hence, when the product is proven to operate correctly, and if sales justify the use of masked ROM, production may be changed to 8048 devices instead of 8748 types.

The 8048 architecture and instruction set are strongly orientated towards control applications, but only provide a few arithmetic operations. Newer designs of microcontroller are more powerful than the 8048; except for limited size data RAM they perform as well as many general purpose systems with separate devices for CPU, ROM, RAM and I–O.

Many small systems are built with separate CPU, ROM, RAM and I–O devices rather than microcontrollers. Choices based on economic factors become somewhat arbitrary once a complete task requires several devices in addition to a microcontroller. In such cases the hardware and software design problems are similar for both types of system. Instruction sets may make a microcontroller the better choice for control applications; a separate general purpose CPU has advantages when a significant amount of calculation is required.

15.2 A microcontroller application

Modern industrial and domestic systems which operate automatically often use processor systems to perform the control functions. Applications range from portable self-contained units to systems as large and complex as the electrical power distribution network for an entire country. Microcontrollers are frequently used as the processor in small automatic control systems.

Figure 15.2 is a schematic representation of one system, a fluid control valve available in

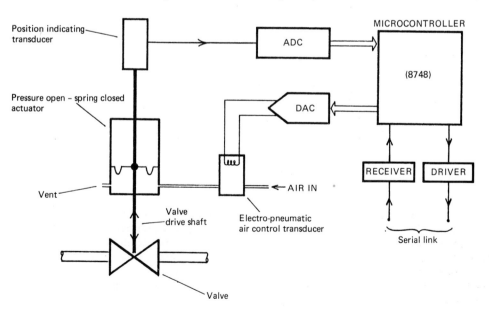

Fig. 15.2 Outline of an automatic system for a control valve

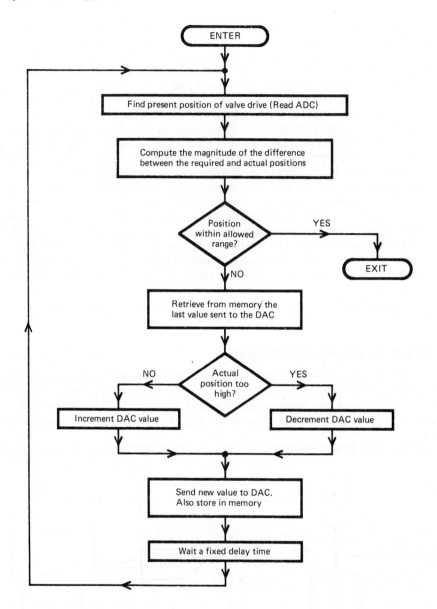

Fig. 15.3 Flow diagram for valve control subroutine

sizes to fit pipelines from 10 mm to over 250 mm diameter. The valve is opened by a compressed air driven actuator and closed by a return spring, and the degree of opening is set by a balance between the air pressure and the spring. Air escapes from the actuator chamber through a fixed vent and is replenished by an electropneumatic transducer which is a constant pressure source. This pressure is set by the current supplied to the transducer coil (resistance about 500 Ω). Currents from 4 mA to 20 mA control the pressure linearly from zero at 4 mA to the maximum value at 20 mA.

Additions of a microcontroller (8748 used) with an ADC, a DAC, and an analogue position transducer connected to the valve actuator produce an automated system. The com-

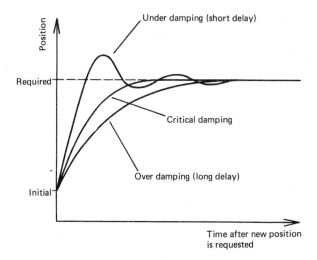

Fig. 15.4 Effects of delay on valve control subroutine

plete valve assembly is able to maintain any degree of opening requested by commands sent to it on a serial communication link. The actual position of the actuator is frequently reported to the command source; any problems in maintaining the position requested are also indicated. Position control is by a closed loop subroutine which compares the measured and requested positions. If the actuator is not within preset limits of the required position, the current to the transducer is adjusted. Figure 15.3 is a **simplified** flow diagram for the control routine; note the delay between a change in transducer current and a check of position. This delay, **damping**, compensates for different response speeds of the mechanical and electronic components. Figure 15.4 shows the effect of delay values on the system response; these are typical responses for control systems with feedback. In extreme cases of under-damping the consequent overshoot could produce continuous oscillation. In this application the control routine is more complex than shown; the extra features and a small degree of overdamping prevent oscillation. A small overshoot may occur under unusual operating conditions.

Fitting the valve with its own processor control system allows a reduction in the complexity of a computer system in overall control of a large plant with many valves. Programs to adjust and maintain valve positions are not executed by the main plant control computer. As the valve's independent processor is dedicated to one task, it can respond rapidly to local events affecting the valve behaviour.

15.3 Moderate size systems

Moderate size is arbitrarily chosen to define systems with memory size from a few kilobytes to several hundred kilobytes operating at moderate speed. These are typically systems with 8-bit and 16-bit MOS microprocessors as the CPU. Such systems are low cost but powerful and widely used; home and personal computers, often called **microcomputers**, are common examples.

Many microcomputers are built to domestic rather than to industrial standards, and consequently they are unsuitable for use in critical applications. However, many high quality **single board computers** are available; most have an MOS microprocessor as the CPU. The boards also have RAM, I-O devices, and sockets for ROM. Some form of standard interface is usually included; this connects the CPU bus system to a well defined universal bus system. (Multibus and VMEbus are typical examples.) Other boards meeting bus specifications are available, and more memory, extra or special purpose I-O devices, etc., may be added to the basic unit. When applications require a moderate size processor system but production quantities do not justify manufacture of a special unit, a system may be rapidly assembled from these boards. The main penalty is cost; to provide flexibility, many features are included and in most applications not all are utilized.

The most obvious examples of moderate size processor systems are the various mass produced home and personal computers. The smaller 8-bit systems tend to use the Z80 or the 6502 as the CPU with the full 64kbytes of memory address space occupied. Designs are often unconventional with each machine having its own unique features. Most larger 16-bit systems use the 8086 or a derivative as the CPU; designs are more conventional and systematic. These machines tend not to have the maximum memory allowed by the address bus width but have facilities for extension. Microcomputer systems normally include hardware and software for the addition of back-up memory, usually floppy disc systems. Low cost machines may use domestic cassette recorders while high specification ones have Winchester hard disc systems.

Single board systems and purpose built microprocessor based systems are widely used in industrial control. With the exception of systems controlling large plants, or applications requiring high speed calculations, most automation systems are based on processors of this size.

15.4   Minicomputers

Small minicomputers differ little in capability from the largest microcomputers, while large ones approach some mainframe computers in power. Early minicomputers were 8-bit machines with less power than modern microcomputers. Current machines are usually 16-bit or 32-bit systems with large main memory, backing store, and multi-user operating systems. The 32-bit machines are often termed *super-minis*; their power exceeds that of many mainframes of less than a decade ago. Classification boundaries are so indistinct that it is difficult to define minicomputers precisely. The name usually implies small physical size, relatively few restrictions on operating environment, and speed at least an order of magnitude above typical microcomputers. The CPU normally consists of bipolar integrated circuits, although some smaller minicomputers use sets of specially developed MOS devices.

Minicomputers are widely used; they are probably used in a greater range of applications than any other type of processor.

15.5   Mainframe computers

Large processor systems, usually called **mainframe computers**, are now extremely complex and sophisticated. They tend to be installed in controlled environments, the largest requiring elaborate cooling systems. Most use ECL circuits for high speed although this results in high power consumption. At the speeds achieved the propagation delays on interconnecting links are significant and all elements of the CPU and main memory must be positioned as closely together as possible. Description of large computer architectures is outside the range of this book, but the basic structure of most is still essentially that of a von Neumann machine. Elaborate memory hierarchies are used and many performance enhancement techniques are adopted. Smaller processors are used to organize work and data for the system so that the CPU and memory are efficiently utilized. Often the main system cannot operate without these auxiliary processors, and consequently such machines are multi-processor systems.

15.6 Application of minicomputers and mainframes

As a consequence of their size, those situations requiring large processor systems are extremely complex, hence they are not easily or briefly described. Figure 15.5 is an attempt to show, in greatly simplified form, a section of a continuous production process plant. Such plants often require several days to start and stop; therefore they are run continuously for long periods, often years. High reliability and performance are required from all components, including the control system. A section of the form shown will probably have its own dedicated control computer, usually a minicomputer, with communication links to a master computer for the whole plant. An alternative is for the master computer to undertake control of this section as one task of many (in a multi-tasking mode). The form of system used will depend on the particular process and on choices in plant design.

Failure in plant control systems may cause damage to the plant or lead to loss of high value materials and product. One protection method involves use of dual computers in place of each individual computer. If any computer in control fails, its dual has up-to-date

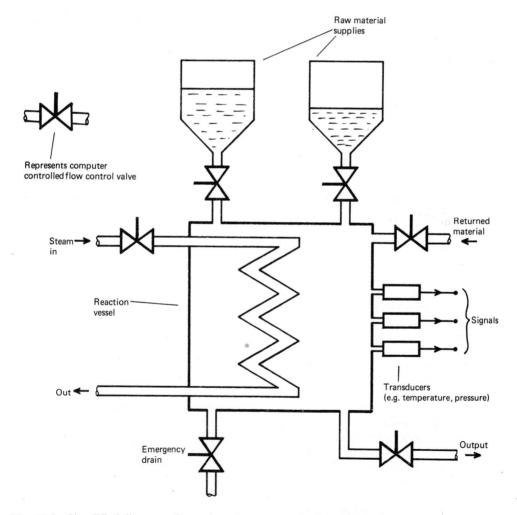

Fig. 15.5 Simplified diagram of a section of an automatically controlled process plant

program conditions and data; failure detection systems transfer control to the back-up system rapidly and automatically. For cases when major hazards may arise if a component fails, for example in aircraft systems, three or more totally independent monitoring and control systems are used and operate simultaneously. If the systems indicate different actions at any point, a majority decision is implemented and warning systems are activated.

In the example system, a reaction unit is fed with two raw materials and with incompletely processed materials returned from a separation unit. Input and output rates are controlled by adjusting valves, and heating is by steam passed through a heat exchanger. The process control computer must arrange for the correct control of raw materials, recirculated material and heating. The unit must be operated within its temperature and pressure limitations with efficient use of materials, energy, and capital resources required to build and maintain the plant. Operation is complicated because the different control devices interact with one another; adjustment of the controls usually requires rapid performance of complex calculations. Further, this reaction unit is only one section of the plant; there will be others each requiring control and the performance of one unit affects all others. All sections must operate under a general requirement that the plant produces the final product safely and economically. Study of the behaviour and control of such complex systems is a major branch of **control engineering**.

Plant control with computers is one application when processors must run in **real-time**. Changes in the controlled system must lead to responses by the processor which occur in times that are short compared with times for changes in the plant. That is, the time to detect any change and initiate the correct control actions must be shorter than the time in which further significant changes can occur. Systems operating in real-time impose constraints on designers and programmers which are not present in simple applications. For example when performing computations to solve a problem in mathematics, the results of a program are acceptable at almost any time after it starts running. For a real-time system a program (or section of program) must be executed within a restricted time. A simple case for the example is when the pressure begins to rise towards the maximum allowed. The control computer must detect this, determine the actions which will stop or reverse the rise, and completely execute such actions in time to prevent the pressure exceeding the set limit.

15.7   System design and development

Design and development of any product is a complex process requiring a disciplined approach. Initial specifications must be developed that are precise and realistic. When a specification requires development of an electronic system to perform some function the first choices concern its general form. These early choices determine whether the system will contain any processor systems, their specifications and the form of software. As already indicated, proportions of hardware and software may be adjusted; frequently one may be traded for the other.

Once a specification has been prepared and the proportions of hardware and software selected, the design and development process still requires many decisions. The basic hardware design must be completed; this includes decisions regarding CPU type (and possibly the number of CPUs), size of memory, types of memory device, and selection of I-O devices. With experience the power of the CPU and the memory size may be estimated; in many cases today's low hardware costs allow inclusion of a degree of overcapacity. Even when the CPU, memory and I-O requirements have been decided, further choices range from designing and constructing the complete system, through intermediate stages, to the purchase of a complete fully tested and operational computer system. The choice is generally economic; costs of developing a new processor system vary with size, but in most cases cannot be justified when only a small number of systems will be built.

In addition to developing hardware, the software to perform the required functions must be prepared. Once hardware and software prototypes are constructed, a rigorous test, modification and development program is necessary. The test and performance verification process is long and expensive, requiring methodical approaches. Usually the final stage in developing a system is some form of proof that it meets specified performance and reliability criteria.

Design of processor systems, or systems incorporating them, is a complex task. The great flexibility of processor systems means that different designers rarely produce identical solutions to a meet a particular specification.

16 Other architectures and future developments

Throughout this text, only common forms of processor system have been described; these tend to have a von Neumann form. There are alternative architectures in use, and many others are being studied in research and development laboratories. However, the history of processor development shows only a few fundamental developments in processor architecture. Most advances have been changes in component technology leading to large increases in size, complexity and speed. That is, most developments have produced physically smaller but logically larger processors running at higher speed.

16.1 Architecture alternatives

The general form of processor systems with von Neumann architecture is powerful and flexible. However, as the example of microcontrollers indicated, there are alternatives and these may have advantages in specific situations.

As processor applications in any area develop, there are usually demands for higher performance; this may be obtained with larger and faster processor systems. There are other methods; further, at any time there is always an upper limit to the capability of systems that can be built. One alternative to increasing the power of a single processor is to divide a task into components; several processors are used with one for each component task. This has already been suggested in principle by the example of control valves with their own processor systems linked to a command source (Section 15.2). In an automated plant the command source would be a computer, and with use of such valves the tasks involved in complete plant control are distributed between several units. The use of dual computers for high overall reliability is another structure incorporating more than one processor.

Multi-processor systems can be powerful but are complex, and there are often problems in their development and use. The range of designs is large; systems may even be developed without deliberate effort. As external devices used with processors become more complex, the elaborate connections between them and the processor require special circuits. Such circuits may be individually designed logic circuits, while others are small processor systems with fixed programs; their use creates a multi-processor system. For simple multiple systems one processor is a master in overall control. At a point when an action by one of the other processors is required, the master transfers any necessary data to it, initiates its operation, and waits for an indication that the task is complete. More complex systems allow the master to continue with another task until the subsidiary processor signals completion of its task.

A current development in MOS microprocessor systems is the use of **co-processors**; these are programmable devices, processors, which perform a limited range of tasks but perform these efficiently. A typical example is the 8087 mathematics co-processor for use with the 8086 CPU. Both processors are connected in parallel to the system buses with a small number of connections directly between the two processors, as shown in Fig. 16.1. The 8087 is designed to perform only mathematical operations; it performs floating point operations, working internally with 80-bit numbers; input and output values are adjusted to 64-bit IEEE format. The combination operates as a standard 8086 system with the 8086 performing the instruction code fetch; however, both processors examine the instruction codes

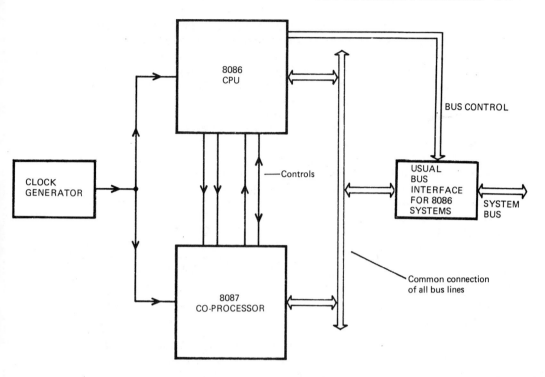

Fig. 16.1 Interconnection of an 8086 CPU and 8087 co-processor

as they are fetched. When the programmer requires operations to be performed by the 8087, special (reserved) codes are included in the instruction sequence. On receipt of any special code, the 8086 fetches any further elements of the instruction code but performs no action using it. The 8087 ignores normal 8086 codes fetched but takes the special code as one of its own instructions. Software and hardware controls are provided so that the 8086 can be forced to wait while the 8087 completes an instruction; other more complex modes of operation may be implemented.

A simple system of one processor waiting for another to perform a task is little more than expansion of the CPU to form a larger one with an increased instruction set. A more sophisticated development is to allow two, or more, CPUs to run simultaneously; each CPU performs a different component task of the complete program. (To some extent 8086/8087 systems may be programmed so that both processors run simultaneously.) This concept of dividing a program into separate tasks was introduced for program preparation and for multi-tasking systems. However, this was for systems in which each task is executed separately in strict sequence, just as instructions in a program are executed in sequence. Step-by-step sequential processor action is often referred to as the *bottleneck* in systems with von Neumann architecture. Multi-processor systems allowing simultaneous (**concurrent** or **parallel**) operation are one approach to improving performance by removing the bottleneck.

A high degree of parallel processing is achieved by a number of multiple CPU systems available. Various architectures have been developed; typical forms are **associative** and **array processors**. A relatively simple multi-processor might consist of two equal size areas of memory with a separate small processor connected between each corresponding pair of locations in the two memory areas. If the small processors all obtain their instruction codes from the same source, they will execute identical programs simultaneously. However, each processor will read from, or write to, the unique memory locations with which it is associated. Thus the same process will be performed on all the elements of arrays of data simultaneously; a conventional processor system has to manipulate each element in turn. Designs of multi-processor systems are frequently complex, and programming methods for efficient operation are still being developed.

Multi-processor systems with simultaneous operation of processors are used to improve performance. Such techniques change the total system architecture, although the component processors often have a conventional form. An alternative approach is to develop processors with architectures devised for particular applications. Although conventional processors are flexible and may be applied to many different tasks, they suffer from the faults of most general purpose devices. They can perform many tasks moderately well but do not perform any single task as well as a special purpose unit designed solely for that task. In areas where a large number of processor systems will be required, processors with architectures orientated towards a particular type of task are available. One area is signal processing, particularly in applications for telecommunication systems. Several special purpose processor systems have been produced for signal processing; examples include the Texas Instruments TMS310 and Intel 2920. These are two very different processor designs; both have features which are unusual when compared with those of common processors.

16.2 Communications

Multi-processor systems range from simple systems with two CPUs communicating by a single serial link to large numbers of processors linked together and sharing common sections of memory. When one processor has only limited ability to cause another to react, the processors are **loosely coupled**. An example is when one CPU transmits data to another on a serial link and the receiving CPU only responds if its program causes it to look at the link. Other systems may be arranged so that a receiving processor must always respond rapidly when data is sent to it; these are **tightly coupled** systems. An extreme case is when several CPUs all share the same main memory; a memory write by any processor makes an immediate change seen by all others.

Large investments are being made in research and development concerned with communication methods for all types of digital system. Tightly coupled systems are best regarded as multi-processor systems; that is, their development is one aspect processor system development. Major developments are also being made in long distance communications between all forms of digital system.

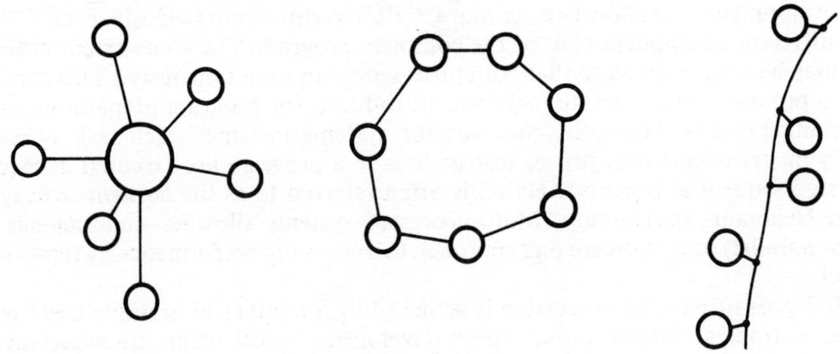

(a) Star   (b) Ring   (c) Bus

Fig. 16.2 Common layouts for processor interconnection networks

Many situations require the transfer of information easily and quickly from any one processor system in a group to any other. This has led to the development of loosely coupled systems of many processors in a limited size area, typically one large building. The connection systems are known as **local area networks, LANs**. Figure 16.2 outlines some of the more common network layouts. Figure 16.2a, a star system, is typical of the form that arises in a haphazard manner as additions are made to a centralized system. The central machine becomes a switching unit connecting processors together; its behaviour is similar to that of a telephone exchange. Such systems are not ideal for processor interconnection because there is a tendency for the central switch to become overloaded under conditions of heavy use. This often causes communication system failure rather than the reduced performance which occurs with overload on alternative forms of network. The other systems in Fig. 16.2 illustrate two common networks currently used. One is a ring and the other is a bus system; typical examples are the Cambridge Ring and Ethernet respectively.

Both Cambridge Ring and Ethernet operate by formatting the data into **packets** containing codes showing source, destination, and packet status as well as the data. Specific packet formats are shown in Fig. 16.3; they are clearly different. The Cambridge Ring uses an empty slot technique with packets continuously circulating round the ring. Every packet is examined at each node and then transmitted either unchanged or with the status information changed. To transmit data a unit detects an empty packet, replaces it with a data packet, and then restores the empty packet when data has passed once round the ring. Additional rules ensure that all units share the ring equally.

Ethernet is a Carrier Sense Multiple Access/Collision Detect (CSMA/CD) system. To transmit data, a unit must examine the bus; if no other unit is using the bus it transmits, otherwise it waits a variable random time and then tries again. Because two units could begin transmission at the same time, units must read and check their own output. If there is corruption, a collision is assumed and the unit transmits again after a random wait. Performance of the two systems differs; the Ring has advantages in control and instrumentation where individual data items tend to be small but where there are many of them. Ethernet offers advantages in commercial environments when data is in large blocks but where transfers are infrequent.

One LAN problem is that even with defined standards, some manufacturers are developing systems to their own specifications. LANs should allow easy interconnection of a wide

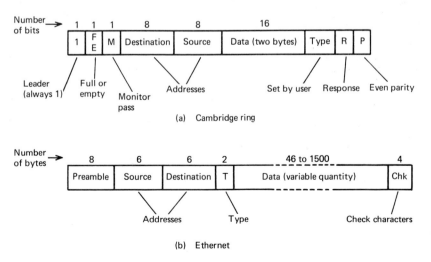

Fig. 16.3 Data packet formats for LANs

range of systems from many suppliers, but failure to apply standards greatly reduces their effectiveness.

16.3   Future developments

Almost all past predictions of long term developments of processor systems have proved to be wrong; no such predictions are attempted here. In the short term many research developments have still to be implemented in production systems. Silicon integrated circuit design in both MOS and bipolar technology has not yet reached fundamental limits of speed and size. Larger scale circuits operating at higher speed will continue to be produced for some time. For example 1M-bit DRAMs are now available, and 4M-bit devices are being designed. Should the technological problems of manufacturing integrated circuits in gallium arsenide be solved, speeds well above those of silicon ECL devices will be possible.

Higher densities can be achieved for magnetic surface recording, although great increases in seek access times appear unlikely. Frequent claims are being made of the successful operation of optical and magneto-optical bulk storage systems. If these can be successfully produced in quantity, two orders of magnitude increase in storage capacity should be easily achieved.

Processor architectures are also advancing, although changes in performance are gradual. There are many areas of research; these include multi-processor architectures, reduced instruction set computers (RISCs), and memory organization and access.

Perhaps the greatest opportunities for advances are in software. For many years processor system performance was limited by availability, cost, and reliability of hardware. With the exception of projects requiring extremely large processors, these limits no longer apply; restrictions are more often the time and cost of developing software. Changes in software concepts and preparation methods are rapid. The greatest problems are the absence of standards and non-adherence to standards when they exist.

16.4   Comments

Processor systems were introduced as a flexible approach providing sequential logic systems that are easily adapted to any task, almost regardless of its complexity. Hence the primary objective of this book has been examination of the architecture, design, and application of processor systems. Emphasis has been placed on conventional systems of a single CPU connected by a bus structure to ROM, RAM, and I–O units; these are common and illustrate most basic principles.

This final chapter has attempted to indicate some areas of development and also alternatives to conventional systems. However, simple processor systems are versatile and will continue to be used for some time. They remain economical methods of performing a wide range of tasks.

Appendix A

References and Further Reading

This is a personal selection of more detailed or alternative treatments of the topics that have been introduced; it is not a comprehensive literature review. Only a few original papers have been referenced in the main text. The sources of the papers by von Neumann (1946) and by Wilkes (1951) are difficult to obtain so more accessible versions or alternatives are suggested.

Most of the more advanced treatments of specific topics contain further references in their specialist area. Publications with details of specific processors are not listed; manufacturers provide a large amount of documentation concerning their systems although the quality varies from excellent to obscure.

References

Hamming R.W. *Error detecting and error correcting codes*. Bell System Tech. Jnl. **29** p 147–160. 1950

von Neumann J. *Collected Works*, Vol. **V** p 34–79 (ed. A.H. Taub). Pergammon 1963 (Reprint of Burks A.W., Goldstine H.H., and von Neumann J. *Preliminary Discussion of the Logical Design of an Electronic Computing Instrument*. Institute for Advanced Study Report, 1946)

Wilkes M.V. *The Best Way to Design an Automatic Calculating Machine*. Report of the Manchester University Computer Inaugural Conference. p 16–18. 1951

Wilkes M.V. and Stringer J.B. *Micro-programming and the Design of the Control Circuits in an Electronic Digital Computer*. Proc. Camb. Phil. Soc. **49** p 230–238. 1953

General texts concerning processor systems

Byewater R.E.H. *Hardware–Software Design of Digital Systems*. Prentice-Hall 1981
Cripps M. *An Introduction to Computer Hardware*. Arnold 1977
Lewin D. *Theory and Design of Digital Computer Systems*. (2nd Edition). Halsted 1980
Ogdin C.A. *Microcomputer Design*. Prentice-Hall 1978

Logic design

Floyd T.L. *Digital Fundamentals*. (2nd Edition). Merrill 1982
Gibson J.R. *Electronic Logic Circuits*. (2nd Edition). Arnold 1983
Lewin D. *Design of Logic Systems*. Van Nostrand Reinhold 1985
Mowle F.J. *A Systematic Approach to Digital Logic Design*. Addison–Wesley 1976
Tokheim R.L. *Theory and Problems of Digital Principles*. McGraw–Hill 1980

CPU and ALU topics

Banerji D.K. and Raymond J. *Elements of Microprogramming*. Prentice-Hall 1982

Boulaye G.G. *Microprogramming*. MacMillan 1975
Flores I. *The Logic of Computer Arithmetic*. Prentice–Hall 1963
Gosling J.B. *Design of Arithmetic Units for Digital Computers*. MacMillan 1980
Husson S.S. *Microprogramming: Principles and Practices*. Prentice–Hall 1970
Hwang K. *Computer Arithmetic: Principles, Architecture and Design*. Wiley 1979
Wong D.G. *Digital Systems Design*. Arnold 1985

Semiconductor devices (including memory devices)

Cardon A. and Fransen L.J.L. *Dynamic Semiconductor RAM Structures*. Pergammon
    1984
Glaser A.B. and Subak–Sharpe G.E. *Integrated Circuit Engineering*. Addison–Wesley
    1977
Hodges D.A. and Jackson H.G. *Analysis and Design of Digital Integrated Circuits*.
    McGraw–Hill 1983
Mead C. and Conway L. *Introduction to VLSI Systems*. Addison–Wesley 1980
Prince B. and Due–Gundersen G. *Semiconductor Memories*. Wiley 1983

Other memory topics

IBM Journal of Research and Development. **18** p 479–562 1974
Jorgensen F. *The Complete Handbook on Magnetic Recording*. TAB Books 1980
Pohm A.V. and Agrawal O.P. *High-speed Memory Systems*. Reston 1983

Data transmission

Lathi B.P. *Modern Digital and Analog Communication Systems*. Holt, Reinhart and
    Winston 1983
Peterson W.W. and Weldon E.J. *Error Correcting Codes*. (2nd Edition) Wiley 1972
Shu Lin and Costello D.J. *Error Control Coding: Fundementals and Applications*.
    Prentice–Hall 1983

Analogue interfaces

Doeblin E.O. *Measurement Systems: Applications and Design*. (3rd Edition).
    McGraw–Hill 1983
Garrett P.H. *Analog I/O Design*. Reston 1981
Schmid H. *Electronic Analog/Digital Conversions*. Van Nostrand Reinhold 1970

Software topics

Aho A.V. and Ullman J.D. *Principles of Compiler Design*. Addison–Wesley 1977
Deitel H.M. *An Introduction to Operating Systems*. Addison–Wesley 1984
Dahl O., Dijkstra E. and Hoare C. *Structured Programming*. Academic Press 1972
Lister A.M. *Fundementals of Operating Systems* (2nd Edition). Macmillan 1979
Pressman R.S. *Software Engineering: A Practitioners Approach*. McGraw–Hill 1982

Applications and control

Barney G.C. *Intelligent Instrumentation*. Prentice–Hall 1985
Dorf R.C. *Modern Control Systems*. (3rd Edition). Addison–Wesley 1980
Healey M. *Principles of Automatic Control*. (3rd Edition). Hodder and Stoughton 1975

Kochhar A.K. and Burns N.D. *Microprocessors and their Manufacturing Applications*. Arnold 1983

Architectures, networks, etc.

Dallas I.N. and Spratt E.B. (eds) *Ring Technology Local Area Networks*. North–Holland 1984
Gee K.C.E. *Introduction to Local Area Computer Networks*. MacMillan 1983
Hockney R.W. and Jesshope C.R. *Parallel Computers: Architecture, Programming and Algorithms*. Adam Higher 1981
Tanenbaum A.S. *Computer Networks*. Prentice–Hall 1981

Appendix B

Conversion Tables

Many different codes are used to represent alphabetic characters, symbols, etc., in digital systems. One of the most common is the American Standard Code for Information Interchange, **ASCII**. This is the 7-bit code listed in Table B.1 with both hexadecimal and decimal values given. The various characters indicated as NUL (null), SOH (start of heading), BEL (bell), BS (backspace), etc., are control characters required to operate many output devices such as printers. Although the code is basically 7-bit it is often used in 8-bit forms with the extra bit added in the MSB position using some fixed convention. Two common choices are to always make the MSB zero (reset) or to select the MSB so that the 8-bits have fixed parity, usually even parity.

Although ASCII is probably the most widely used code there are many others. For example Extended Binary Coded Decimal Interchange Code, EBCDIC, is an 8-bit code frequently used within large computer systems.

Decimal equivalents of positive integral powers of two and the range of integers that may be represented by various size binary numbers are given in Table B.2.

Table B.1 ASCII Codes.

Character	ASCII code (hexadecimal)	Decimal equiv.	Character	ASCII code' (hexadecimal)	Decimal equiv.
NUL	00	0	@	40	64
SOH	01	1	A	41	65
STX	02	2	B	42	66
ETX	03	3	C	43	67
EOT	04	4	D	44	68
ENQ	05	5	E	45	69
ACK	06	6	F	46	70
BEL	07	7	G	47	71
BS	08	8	H	48	72
HT	09	9	I	49	73
LF	0A	10	J	4A	74
VT	0B	11	K	4B	75
FF	0C	12	L	4C	76
CR	0D	13	M	4D	77
SO	0E	14	N	4E	78
SI	0F	15	O	4F	79
DLE	10	16	P	50	80
DC1	11	17	Q	51	81
DC2	12	18	R	52	82
DC3	13	19	S	53	83
DC4	14	20	T	54	84
NAK	15	21	U	55	85
SYN	16	22	V	56	86
ETB	17	23	W	57	87
CAN	18	24	X	58	88
EM	19	25	Y	59	89
SUB	1A	26	Z	5A	90
ESC	1B	27	[	5B	91
FS	1C	28	\	5C	92
GS	1D	29	]	5D	93
RS	1E	30	↑	5E	94
US	1F	31	←	5F	95
SP	20	32	`	60	96
!	21	33	a	61	97
''	22	34	b	62	98
#	23	35	c	63	99
$	24	36	d	64	100
%	25	37	e	65	101
&	26	38	f	66	102
'	27	39	g	67	103
(	28	40	h	68	104
)	29	41	i	69	105
*	2A	42	j	6A	106
+	2B	43	k	6B	107
,	2C	44	l	6C	108
−	2D	45	m	6D	109
.	2E	46	n	6E	110
/	2F	47	o	6F	111
0	30	48	p	70	112
1	31	49	q	71	113
2	32	50	r	72	114
3	33	51	s	73	115
4	34	52	t	74	116
5	35	53	u	75	117
6	36	54	v	76	118
7	37	55	w	77	119
8	38	56	x	78	120
9	39	57	y	79	121
:	3A	58	z	7A	122
;	3B	59	{	7B	123
<	3C	60			7C	124
=	3D	61	}	7D	125
>	3E	62	~	7E	126
?	3F	63	DEL	7F	127

Table B.2 Powers of 2 and Ranges of Binary Integers.

n	2^n	Largest n-bit unsigned integer	Range of n-bit signed integers
0	1	—	—
1	2	1	—
2	4	3	± 1
3	8	7	± 3
4	16	15	± 7
5	32	31	± 15
6	64	63	± 31
7	128	127	± 63
8	256	255	± 127
9	512	511	± 255
10	1024	1023	± 511
11	2048	2047	± 1023
12	4096	4095	± 2047
13	8192	8191	± 4095
14	16384	16383	± 8191
15	32768	32767	± 16383
16	65536	65535	± 32767
17	131072	131071	± 65535
18	262144	262143	± 131071
19	524288	524287	± 262143
20	1048576	1048575	± 524287
21	2097152	2097151	± 1048575
22	4194304	4194303	± 2097151
23	8388608	8388607	± 4194303
24	16777216	16777215	± 8388607
25	33554432	33554431	± 16777215
26	67108864	67108863	± 33554431
27	134217728	134217727	± 67108863
28	268435456	268435455	± 134217727
29	536870912	536870911	± 268435455
30	1073741824	1073741823	± 536870911
31	2147483648	2147483647	± 1073741823
32	4294967296	4294967295	± 2147483647

Appendix C

Instruction Sets for Some Common Microprocessors

The instruction sets for 8080/85, 6502, 6800 and 8086/88 microprocessors are briefly outlined in the tables which follow. The manufacturer's complete data should be consulted for detailed descriptions of the instruction sets.

Table C.1 8080 and 8085 instructions. (Reproduced with permission of Intel Corporation).

Data Transfer

Instruction	Description	Encoding		
MOV r1,r2	Move register to register	01DDDSSS		
MOV M,r	Move register to memory	01110SSS		
MOV r,M	Move memory to register	01DDD110		
MVI r,data	Move immediate to register	00DDD110	data	
MVI M,data	Move immediate to memory	00110110	data	
LXI rp,addr	Load register pair immediate	00pp0001	addr low	addr high
LDA addr	Load A direct	00111010	addr low	addr high
STA addr	Store A direct	00110010	addr low	addr high
LHLD addr	Load H and L direct	00101010	addr low	addr high
SHLD addr	Store H and L direct	00100010	addr low	addr high
LDAX B	Load A indirect using (B–C)	00001010		
LDAX D	Load A indirect using (D–E)	00011010		
STAX B	Store A indirect using (B–C)	00000010		
STAX D	Store A indirect using (D–E)	00010010		
XCHG	Exchange H and L with D and E	11101011		

Arithmetic

Instruction	Description	Encoding	
ADD r	Add register	10000SSS	
ADD M	Add memory	10000110	
ADI data	Add immediate	11000110	data
ADC r	Add register with carry	10001SSS	
ADC M	Add memory with carry	10001110	
ACI data	Add immediate with carry	11001110	data
SUB r	Subtract register	10010SSS	
SUB M	Subtract memory	10010110	
SUI data	Subtract immediate	11010110	data

Table C.1 *Continued*

Arithmetic

SBB r	Subtract register with borrow	`10011SSS`
SBB M	Subtract memory with borrow	`10011110`
SBI data	Subtract immediate with borrow	`11011110` `data`
INR r	Increment register	`00DDD100`
INR M	Increment memory	`00110100`
DCR r	Decrement register	`00DDD101`
DCR M	Decrement memory	`00110101`
INX rp	Increment register pair	`00pp0011`
DCX rp	Decrement register pair	`00pp1011`
DAD rp	Add register pair to H–L	`00pp1001`
DAA	Decimal adjust accumulator	`00100111`

Logical

ANA r	And register	`10100SSS`
ANA M	And memory	`10100110`
ANI data	And immediate	`11100110` `data`
XRA r	Exclusive-OR register	`10101SSS`
XRA M	Exclusive-OR memory	`10101110`
XRI data	Exclusive-OR immediate	`11101110` `data`
ORA r	Or register	`10110SSS`
ORA M	Or memory	`10110110`
ORI data	Or immediate	`11110110` `data`
CMP r	Compare register	`10111SSS`
CMP M	Compare memory	`10111110`
CPI data	Compare immediate	`11111110` `data`
RLC	Rotate left	`00000111`

Table C.1 *Continued*

Logical

RRC	Rotate right	00001111
RAL	Rotate left through carry	00010111
RAR	Rotate right through carry	00011111
CMA	Complement accumulator	00101111
CMC	Complement carry	00111111
STC	Set carry	00110111

Branch

JMP addr	Jump always	11000011	addr low	addr high
JNZ addr	Jump on not zero	11000010	addr low	addr high
JZ addr	Jump on zero	11001010	addr low	addr high
JNC addr	Jump on no carry	11010010	addr low	addr high
JC addr	Jump on carry	11011010	addr low	addr high
JPO addr	Jump on parity odd	11100010	addr low	addr high
JPE addr	Jump on parity even	11101010	addr low	addr high
JP addr	Jump on plus	11110010	addr low	addr high
JM addr	Jump on minus	11111010	addr low	addr high
CALL addr	Call subroutine always	11001101	addr low	addr high
CNZ addr	Call on not zero	11000100	addr low	addr high
CZ addr	Call on zero	11001100	addr low	addr high
CNC addr	Call on no carry	11010100	addr low	addr high
CC addr	Call on carry	11011100	addr low	addr high
CPO addr	Call on parity odd	11100100	addr low	addr high
CPE addr	Call on parity even	11101100	addr low	addr high
CP addr	Call on plus	11110100	addr low	addr high
CM addr	Call on minus	11111100	addr low	addr high

Table C.1 *Continued*

Branch

RET	Return always	11001001
RNZ addr	Return on not zero	11000000
RZ addr	Return on zero	11001000
RNC addr	Return on no carry	11010000
RC addr	Return on carry	11011000
RPO addr	Return on parity odd	11100000
RPE addr	Return on parity even	11101000
RP addr	Return on plus	11110000
RM addr	Return on minus	11111000
RST n	Restart n (n = NNN, 0 to 7)	11NNN111
PCHL	Load PC with (H–L)	11101001

Stack, I–O, and control.

PUSH rp	Push register pair	11pp0101	
POP rp	Pop register pair	11pp0001	
XTHL	Exchange stack top and H–L	11100011	
SPHL	Copy H–L to SP	11111001	
IN data	Input from port	11011011	data
OUT data	Output from port	11010011	data
EI	Enable interrupts	11111011	
DI	Disable interrupts	11110011	
HLT	Halt	01110110	
NOP	No operation	00000000	
RIM*	Read interrupt mask	00100000	
SIM*	Set interrupt mask	00110000	

*8085 only

Table C.1 *Continued*

Notation

> data = any 8-bit value
> addr = any 16-bit value
> addr low = the low 8-bits of a 16-bit value
> addr high = the high 8-bits of a 16-bit value

DDD (destination) or SSS (source) is a code replaced by the value for the actual register (r, r1, or r2) used.

Register	DDD or SSS
A	111
B	000
C	001
D	010
E	011
H	100
L	101

pp is a code replaced by the value for the actual register pair used.

Register pair	pp
B–C	00
D–E	01
H–L	10
SP+	11

+ Except for PUSH and POP when pair code 11 represents program status word (PSW) of A and flags.

Table C.2 6502 instructions. (Reproduced with permission of Rockwell International).

ADDRESSING MODES
The R6500 CPU family has 13 addressing modes. In the following discussion, a bracketed expression follows the title of the mode. This expression is the term used in the Instruction Set Op Code Matrix table to identify the addressing mode used by the instruction.

ACCUMULATOR ADDRESSING [Accum] — This form of addressing is represented with a one byte instruction, implying an operation on the accumulator.

IMMEDIATE ADDRESSING [IMM] — The second byte of the instruction contains the operand, with no further memory addressing required.

ABSOLUTE ADDRESSING [Absolute] — In absolute addressing, the second byte of the instruction specifies the eight low order bits of the effective address while the third byte specifies the eight high order bits.

ZERO PAGE ADDRESSING [ZP] — Zero page instructions allow for shorter code and execution times by fetching only the second byte of the instruction and assuming a zero high address byte.

INDEXED ZERO PAGE ADDRESSING [ZP, X or Y] — (X, Y indexing) — This form of addressing is used with the index register and is referred to as "Zero Page, X" or "Zero Page, Y". The effective address is calculated by adding the second byte to the contents of the index register. Since this is a form of "Zero Page" addressing, the content of the second byte references a location in page zero. No carry is added to the high order eight bits of memory and crossing of page boundaries does not occur.

INDEXED ABSOLUTE ADDRESSING [ABS, X or Y] — (X, Y indexing) — This form of addressing is used in conjunction with X and Y index register and is referred to as "Absolute, X" and "Absolute, Y". The effective address is formed by adding the contents of X or Y to the address contained in the second and third bytes of the instruction.

IMPLIED ADDRESSING [Implied] — In the implied addressing mode, the address containing the operand is implicitly stated in the operation code of the instruction.

RELATIVE ADDRESSING [Relative] — Relative addressing is used with branch instructions and establishes a destination for the conditional branch. The second byte of the instruction becomes the operand which is an 'Offset" added to the contents of the lower eight bits of the program counter when the counter is set at the next instruction. The range of the offset is −128 to +127 bytes from the next instruction.

INDEXED INDIRECT ADDRESSING [(IND, X)] — In indexed indirect addressing (referred to as (Indirect, X)), the second byte of the instruction is added to the contents of the X index register, discarding the carry. The result of this addition points to a memory location on page zero whose contents are the low order eight bits of the effective address. The next memory location in page zero contains the high order eight bits of the effective address.

INDIRECT INDEXED ADDRESSING [(IND), Y] — In indirect indexed addressing (referred to as (Indirect), Y), the second byte of the instruction points to a memory location in page zero. The contents of this memory location are added to the contents of the Y index register, the result being the low order eight bits of the effective address. The carry from this addition is added to the contents of the next page zero memory location, the result being the high order eight bits of the effective address.

ABSOLUTE INDIRECT [Indirect] — The second byte of the instruction contains the low order eight bits of a memory location. The high order eight bits of that memory location are contained in the third byte of the instruction. The contents of the fully specified memory location are the low order byte of the effective address. The next memory location contains the high order byte of the effective address which is loaded into the sixteen bits of the program counter. (JMP (IND) only)

Table C.2 Continued

MNE- MONIC	OPERATION	IMM Op	n	#	ABS Op	n	#	ZP Op	n	#	ACC Op	n	#	IMP Op	n	#	(IND,X) Op	n	#	(IND),Y Op	n	#	ZP,X Op	n	#	ABS,X Op	n	#	ABS,Y Op	n	#	REL Op	n	#	IND Op	n	#	ZP,Y Op	n	#	N(7)	V(6)	•(5)	B(4)	D(3)	I(2)	Z(1)	C(0)
ADC	A + M + C → A (4)(1)	69	2	2	6D	4	3	65	3	2							61	6	2	71	5	2	75	4	2	7D	4	3	79	4	3										N	V	.	.	.	.	Z	C
AND	A ∧ M → A (1)	29	2	2	2D	4	3	25	3	2							21	6	2	31	5	2	35	4	2	3D	4	3	39	4	3										N	.	.	.	.	.	Z	.
ASL	C ← [7 ... 0] ← 0				0E	6	3	06	5	2	0A	2	1										16	6	2	1E	7	3													N	.	.	.	.	.	Z	C
BCC	BRANCH ON C = 0(2)																															90	2	2							.	.	.	.	.	.	.	.
BCS	BRANCH ON C = 1(2)																															B0	2	2							.	.	.	.	.	.	.	.
BEQ	BRANCH ON Z = 1(2)																															F0	2	2							.	.	.	.	.	.	.	.
BIT	A ∧ M				2C	4	3	24	3	2																															M_7	M_6	.	.	.	.	Z	.
BMI	BRANCH ON N = 1(2)																															30	2	2							.	.	.	.	.	.	.	.
BNE	BRANCH ON Z = 0(2)																															D0	2	2							.	.	.	.	.	.	.	.
BPL	BRANCH ON N = 0(2)																															10	2	2							.	.	.	.	.	.	.	.
BRK	BREAK													00	7	1																									.	.	.	1	.	.	.	.
BVC	BRANCH ON V = 0(2)																															50	2	2							.	.	.	.	.	.	.	.
BVS	BRANCH ON V = 1(2)																															70	2	2							.	.	.	.	.	.	.	.
CLC	0 → C													18	2	1																									.	.	.	.	.	.	.	0
CLD	0 → D													D8	2	1																									.	.	.	.	0	.	.	.
CLI	0 → I													58	2	1																									.	.	.	.	.	0	.	.
CLV	0 → V													B8	2	1																									.	0	.	.	.	.	.	.
CMP	A − M	C9	2	2	CD	4	3	C5	3	2							C1	6	2	D1	5	2	D5	4	2	DD	4	3	D9	4	3										N	.	.	.	.	.	Z	C
CPX	X − M	E0	2	2	EC	4	3	E4	3	2																															N	.	.	.	.	.	Z	C
CPY	Y − M	C0	2	2	CC	4	3	C4	3	2																															N	.	.	.	.	.	Z	C
DEC	M − 1 → M				CE	6	3	C6	5	2													D6	6	2	DE	7	3													N	.	.	.	.	.	Z	.
DEX	X − 1 → X													CA	2	1																									N	.	.	.	.	.	Z	.
DEY	Y − 1 → Y													88	2	1																									N	.	.	.	.	.	Z	.
EOR	A ⊻ M → A (1)	49	2	2	4D	4	3	45	3	2							41	6	2	51	5	2	55	4	2	5D	4	3	59	4	3										N	.	.	.	.	.	Z	.
INC	M + 1 → M				EE	6	3	E6	5	2													F6	6	2	FF	7	3													N	.	.	.	.	.	Z	.
INX	X + 1 → X													EB	2	1																									N	.	.	.	.	.	Z	.
INY	Y + 1 → Y													C8	2	1																									N	.	.	.	.	.	Z	.
JMP	JUMP TO NEW LOC				4C	3	3																												6C	5	3				.	.	.	.	.	.	.	.
JSR	JUMP SUB				20	6	3																																		.	.	.	.	.	.	.	.
LDA	M → A (1)	A9	2	2	AD	4	3	A5	3	2							A1	6	2	B1	5	2	B5	4	2	BD	4	3	B9	4	3										N	.	.	.	.	.	Z	.
LDX	M → X (1)	A2	2	2	AE	4	3	A6	3	2																			BE	4	3							B6	4	2	N	.	.	.	.	.	Z	.
LDY	M → Y (1)	A0	2	2	AC	4	3	A4	3	2													B4	4	2	BC	4	3													N	.	.	.	.	.	Z	.
LSR	0 → [7 ... 0] → C				4E	6	3	46	5	2	4A	2	1										56	6	2	5E	7	3													0	.	.	.	.	.	Z	C
NOP	NO OPERATION													EA	2	1																									.	.	.	.	.	.	.	.
ORA	A ∨ M → A (1)	09	2	2	0D	4	3	05	3	2							01	6	2	11	5	2	15	4	2	1D	4	3													N	.	.	.	.	.	Z	.

Table C.2 *Continued*

Mnemonic	Operation	Absolute (OP n #)	Zero Page (OP n #)	Accum (OP n #)	Implied (OP n #)	(IND,X) (OP n #)	(IND),Y (OP n #)	Z Page,X/Y (OP n #)	ABS,X (OP n #)	ABS,Y (OP n #)	Status
PHA	A → Ms, S − 1 → S				48 3 1						. . . .
PHP	P → Ms, S − 1 → S				08 3 1						. . . .
PLA	S + 1 → S, Ms → A				68 4 1						N . . . . . Z .
PLP	S + 1 → S, Ms → P				28 4 1						(RESTORED)
ROL	[7 ← 0 ← C]	2E 6 3	26 5 2	2A 2 1				36 6 2	3E 7 3		N . . . . . Z C
ROR	[C → 7 → 0]	6E 6 3	66 5 2	6A 2 1				76 6 2	7E 7 3		N . . . . . Z C
RTI	RTRN INT				40 6 1						(RESTORED)
RTS	RTRN SUB				60 6 1						. . . .
SBC	A − M − C → A (1)	ED 4 3	E5 3 2		E9 2 2 (imm)	E1 6 2	F1 5 2	F5 4 2	FD 4 3	F9 4 3	N V . . . . Z (3) C
SEC	1 → C				38 2 1						 1
SED	1 → D				F8 2 1						. . . . 1 . . .
SEI	1 → I				78 2 1						. . . . . 1 . .
STA	A → M	8D 4 3	85 3 2			81 6 2	91 6 2	95 4 2	9D 5 3	99 5 3	. . . .
STX	X → M	8E 4 3	86 3 2					96 4 2			. . . .
STY	Y → M	8C 4 3	84 3 2					94 4 2			. . . .
TAX	A → X				AA 2 1						N . . . . . Z .
TAY	A → Y				A8 2 1						N . . . . . Z .
TSX	S → X				BA 2 1						N . . . . . Z .
TXA	X → A				8A 2 1						N . . . . . Z .
TXS	X → S				9A 2 1						. . . .
TYA	Y → A				98 2 1						N . . . . . Z .

(1) ADD 1 to "N" IF PAGE BOUNDARY IS CROSSED
(2) ADD 1 TO "N" IF BRANCH OCCURS TO SAME PAGE
    ADD 2 TO "N" IF BRANCH OCCURS TO DIFFERENT PAGE
(3) CARRY NOT = BORROW
(4) IF IN DECIMAL MODE, Z FLAG IS INVALID
    ACCUMULATOR MUST BE CHECKED FOR ZERO RESULT

X	INDEX X	+	ADD
Y	INDEX Y	−	SUBTRACT
A	ACCUMULATOR	<	AND
M	MEMORY PER EFFECTIVE ADDRESS	v	OR
Ms	MEMORY RER STACK POINTER	↛	EXCLUSIVE OR

M_7	MEMORY BIT 7
M_6	MEMORY BIT 6
n	NO. CYCLES
#	NO. BYTES

Table C.3 6800 instructions. (Reproduced with permission of Motorola Incorporated).

ACCUMULATOR AND MEMORY OPERATIONS

OPERATIONS	MNEMONIC	IMMED OP	~	#	DIRECT OP	~	#	INDEX OP	~	#	EXTND OP	~	#	IMPLIED OP	~	#	BOOLEAN/ARITHMETIC OPERATION (All register labels refer to contents)	H (5)	I (4)	N (3)	Z (2)	V (1)	C (0)
Add	ADDA	8B	2	2	9B	3	2	AB	5	2	BB	4	3				A + M → A	↕	•	↕	↕	↕	↕
	ADDB	CB	2	2	DB	3	2	EB	5	2	FB	4	3				B + M → B	↕	•	↕	↕	↕	↕
Add Acmltrs	ABA													1B	2	1	A + B → A	↕	•	↕	↕	↕	↕
Add with Carry	ADCA	89	2	2	99	3	2	A9	5	2	B9	4	3				A + M + C → A	↕	•	↕	↕	↕	↕
	ADCB	C9	2	2	D9	3	2	E9	5	2	F9	4	3				B + M + C → B	↕	•	↕	↕	↕	↕
And	ANDA	84	2	2	94	3	2	A4	5	2	B4	4	3				A • M → A	•	•	↕	↕	R	•
	ANDB	C4	2	2	D4	3	2	E4	5	2	F4	4	3				B • M → B	•	•	↕	↕	R	•
Bit Test	BITA	85	2	2	95	3	2	A5	5	2	B5	4	3				A − M	•	•	↕	↕	R	•
	BITB	C5	2	2	D5	3	2	E5	5	2	F5	4	3				B − M	•	•	↕	↕	R	•
Clear	CLR							6F	7	2	7F	6	3				00 → M	•	•	R	S	R	R
	CLRA													4F	2	1	00 → A	•	•	R	S	R	R
	CLRB													5F	2	1	00 → B	•	•	R	S	R	R
Compare	CMPA	81	2	2	91	3	2	A1	5	2	B1	4	3				A − M	•	•	↕	↕	↕	↕
	CMPB	C1	2	2	D1	3	2	E1	5	2	F1	4	3				B − M	•	•	↕	↕	↕	↕
Compare Acmltrs	CBA													11	2	1	A − B	•	•	↕	↕	↕	↕
Complement, 1's	COM							63	7	2	73	6	3				$\overline{M}$ → M	•	•	↕	↕	R	S
	COMA													43	2	1	$\overline{A}$ → A	•	•	↕	↕	R	S
	COMB													53	2	1	$\overline{B}$ → B	•	•	↕	↕	R	S
Complement, 2's	NEG							60	7	2	70	6	3				00 − M → M	•	•	↕	↕	①	②
(Negate)	NEGA													40	2	1	00 − A → A	•	•	↕	↕	①	②
	NEGB													50	2	1	00 − B → B	•	•	↕	↕	①	②
Decimal Adjust, A	DAA													19	2	1	Converts Binary Add. of BCD Characters into BCD Format	•	•	↕	↕	①	③
Decrement	DEC							6A	7	2	7A	6	3				M − 1 → M	•	•	↕	↕	④	•
	DECA													4A	2	1	A − 1 → A	•	•	↕	↕	④	•
	DECB													5A	2	1	B − 1 → B	•	•	↕	↕	④	•
Exclusive OR	EORA	88	2	2	98	3	2	A8	5	2	B8	4	3				A ⊕ M → A	•	•	↕	↕	R	•
	EORB	C8	2	2	D8	3	2	E8	5	2	F8	4	3				B ⊕ M → B	•	•	↕	↕	R	•
Increment	INC							6C	7	2	7C	6	3				M + 1 → M	•	•	↕	↕	⑤	•
	INCA													4C	2	1	A + 1 → A	•	•	↕	↕	⑤	•
	INCB													5C	2	1	B + 1 → B	•	•	↕	↕	⑤	•
Load Acmltr	LDAA	86	2	2	96	3	2	A6	5	2	B6	4	3				M → A	•	•	↕	↕	R	•
	LDAB	C6	2	2	D6	3	2	E6	5	2	F6	4	3				M → B	•	•	↕	↕	R	•
Or, Inclusive	ORAA	8A	2	2	9A	3	2	AA	5	2	BA	4	3				A + M → A	•	•	↕	↕	R	•
	ORAB	CA	2	2	DA	3	2	EA	5	2	FA	4	3				B + M → B	•	•	↕	↕	R	•
Push Data	PSHA													36	4	1	A → Msp, SP − 1 → SP	•	•	•	•	•	•
	PSHB													37	4	1	B → Msp, SP − 1 → SP	•	•	•	•	•	•
Pull Data	PULA													32	4	1	SP + 1 → SP, Msp → A	•	•	•	•	•	•
	PULB													33	4	1	SP + 1 → SP, Msp → B	•	•	•	•	•	•

Table C.3 *Continued*

Operation	Mnemonic	IMMED OP ~ #	DIRECT OP ~ #	INDEX OP ~ #	EXTEND OP ~ #	IMPLIED OP ~ #	Boolean/Arithmetic Operation	H	I	N	Z	V	C
Rotate Left	ROL			69 7 2	79 6 3		M }	•	•	↕	↕	⑥	↕
	ROLA					49 2 1	A }	•	•	↕	↕	⑥	↕
	ROLB					59 2 1	B }	•	•	↕	↕	⑥	↕
Rotate Right	ROR			66 7 2	76 6 3		M }	•	•	↕	↕	⑥	↕
	RORA					46 2 1	A }	•	•	↕	↕	⑥	↕
	RORB					56 2 1	B }	•	•	↕	↕	⑥	↕
Shift Left, Arithmetic	ASL			68 7 2	78 6 3		M }	•	•	↕	↕	⑥	↕
	ASLA					48 2 1	A }	•	•	↕	↕	⑥	↕
	ASLB					58 2 1	B }	•	•	↕	↕	⑥	↕
Shift Right, Arithmetic	ASR			67 7 2	77 6 3		M }	•	•	↕	↕	⑥	↕
	ASRA					47 2 1	A }	•	•	↕	↕	⑥	↕
	ASRB					57 2 1	B }	•	•	↕	↕	⑥	↕
Shift Right, Logic	LSR			64 7 2	74 6 3		M }	•	•	R	↕	⑥	↕
	LSRA					44 2 1	A }	•	•	R	↕	⑥	↕
	LSRB					54 2 1	B }	•	•	R	↕	⑥	↕
Store Acmltr	STAA		97 4 2	A7 6 2	B7 5 3		A → M	•	•	↕	↕	R	•
	STAB		D7 4 2	E7 6 2	F7 5 3		B → M	•	•	↕	↕	R	•
Subtract	SUBA	80 2 2	90 3 2	A0 5 2	B0 4 3		A − M → A	•	•	↕	↕	↕	↕
	SUBB	C0 2 2	D0 3 2	E0 5 2	F0 4 3		B − M → B	•	•	↕	↕	↕	↕
Subtract Acmltrs	SBA					10 2 1	A − B → A	•	•	↕	↕	↕	↕
Subtr with Carry	SBCA	82 2 2	92 3 2	A2 5 2	B2 4 3		A − M − C → A	•	•	↕	↕	↕	↕
	SBCB	C2 2 2	D2 3 2	E2 5 2	F2 4 3		B − M − C → B	•	•	↕	↕	↕	↕
Transfer Acmltrs	TAB					16 2 1	A → B	•	•	↕	↕	R	•
	TBA					17 2 1	B → A	•	•	↕	↕	R	•
Test, Zero or Minus	TST			6D 7 2	7D 6 3		M − 00	•	•	↕	↕	R	R
	TSTA					4D 2 1	A − 00	•	•	↕	↕	R	R
	TSTB					5D 2 1	B − 00	•	•	↕	↕	R	R

LEGEND:

- OP   Operation Code (Hexadecimal);
- ~   Number of MPU Cycles;
- #   Number of Program Bytes;
- +   Arithmetic Plus;
- −   Arithmetic Minus;
- ·   Boolean AND;
- M$_{SP}$ Contents of memory location pointed to be Stack Pointer;
- +   Boolean Inclusive OR;
- ⊕   Boolean Exclusive OR;
- M̄   Complement of M;
- →   Transfer Into;
- 0   Bit = Zero;
- 00   Byte = Zero;

Note — Accumulator addressing mode instructions are included in the column for IMPLIED addressing

CONDITION CODE SYMBOLS:

- H   Half-carry from bit 3;
- I   Interrupt mask
- N   Negative (sign bit)
- Z   Zero (byte)
- V   Overflow, 2's complement
- C   Carry from bit 7
- R   Reset Always
- S   Sat Always
- ↕   Test and set if true, cleared otherwise
- •   Not Affected

CONDITION CODE REGISTER NOTES:

(Bit set if test is true and cleared otherwise)

1 (Bit V)   Test: Result = 10000000?
2 (Bit C)   Test: Result = 00000000?
3 (Bit C)   Test: Decimal value of most significant BCD
            Character greater than nine?
            (Not cleared if previously set.)
4 (Bit V)   Test: Operand = 10000000 prior to execution?
5 (Bit V)   Test: Operand = 0111111 prior to execution?
6 (Bit V)   Test: Set equal to result of N⊕C after shift

Table C.3 *Continued*

INDEX REGISTER AND STACK POINTER INSTRUCTIONS

POINTER OPERATIONS	MNEMONIC	IMMED OP	~	#	DIRECT OP	~	#	INDEX OP	~	#	EXTND OP	~	#	IMPLIED OP	~	#	BOOLEAN/ARITHMETIC OPERATION	COND. CODE REG. 5 H	4 I	3 N	2 Z	1 V	0 C
Compare Index Reg	CPX	8C	3	3	9C	4	2	AC	6	2	BC	5	3				$X_H - M, X_L - (M + 1)$	•	•	①	↕	②	•
Decrement Index Reg	DEX													09	4	1	$X - 1 \rightarrow X$	•	•	•	↕	•	•
Decrement Stack Pntr	DES													34	4	1	$SP - 1 \rightarrow SP$	•	•	•	•	•	•
Increment Index Reg	INX													08	4	1	$X + 1 \rightarrow X$	•	•	•	↕	•	•
Increment Stack Pntr	INS													31	4	1	$SP + 1 \rightarrow SP$	•	•	•	•	•	•
Load Index Reg	LDX	CE	3	3	DE	4	2	EE	6	2	FE	5	3				$M \rightarrow X_H, (M + 1) \rightarrow X_L$	•	•	③	↕	R	•
Load Stack Pntr	LDS	8E	3	3	9E	4	2	AE	6	2	BE	5	3				$M \rightarrow SP_H, (M + 1) \rightarrow SP_L$	•	•	③	↕	R	•
Store Index Reg	STX				DF	5	2	EF	7	2	FF	6	3				$X_H \rightarrow M, X_L \rightarrow (M + 1)$	•	•	③	↕	R	•
Store Stack Pntr	STS				9F	5	2	AF	7	2	BF	6	3				$SP_H \rightarrow M, SP_L \rightarrow (M + 1)$	•	•	③	↕	R	•
Indx Reg → Stack Pntr	TXS													35	4	1	$X - 1 \rightarrow SP$	•	•	•	•	•	•
Stack Pntr → Indx Reg	TSX													30	4	1	$SP + 1 \rightarrow X$	•	•	•	•	•	•

① (Bit N) Test: Sign bit of most significant (MS) byte of result = 1?

② (Bit V) Test: 2's complement overflow from subtraction of ms bytes?

③ (Bit N) Test: Result less than zero? (Bit 15 = 1)

Table C.3 *Continued*

JUMP AND BRANCH INSTRUCTIONS

OPERATIONS	MNEMONIC	RELATIVE OP	~	#	INDEX OP	~	#	EXTND OP	~	#	IMPLIED OP	~	#	BRANCH TEST	H (5)	I (4)	N (3)	Z (2)	V (1)	C (0)
Branch Always	BRA	20	4	2										None	•	•	•	•	•	•
Branch If Carry Clear	BCC	24	4	2										C = 0	•	•	•	•	•	•
Branch If Carry Set	BCS	25	4	2										C = 1	•	•	•	•	•	•
Branch If = Zero	BEQ	27	4	2										Z = 1	•	•	•	•	•	•
Branch If ≥ Zero	BGE	2C	4	2										$N \oplus V = 0$	•	•	•	•	•	•
Branch If > Zero	BGT	2E	4	2										$Z + (N \oplus V) = 0$	•	•	•	•	•	•
Branch If Higher	BHI	22	4	2										$C + Z = 0$	•	•	•	•	•	•
Branch If ≤ Zero	BLE	2F	4	2										$Z + (N \oplus V) = 1$	•	•	•	•	•	•
Branch If Lower Or Same	BLS	23	4	2										$C + Z = 1$	•	•	•	•	•	•
Branch if < Zero	BLT	2D	4	2										$N \oplus V = 1$	•	•	•	•	•	•
Branch If Minus	BMI	2B	4	2										N = 1	•	•	•	•	•	•
Branch If Not Equal Zero	BNE	26	4	2										Z = 0	•	•	•	•	•	•
Branch If Overflow Clear	BVC	28	4	2										V = 0	•	•	•	•	•	•
Branch If Overflow Set	BVS	29	4	2										V = 1	•	•	•	•	•	•
Branch If Plus	BPL	2A	4	2										N = 0	•	•	•	•	•	•
Branch To Subroutine	BSR	8D	8	2										See Special Operations	•	•	•	•	•	•
Jump	JMP				6E	4	2	7E	3	3					•	•	•	•	•	•
Jump To Subroutine	JSR				AD	8	2	8D	9	3					•	•	•	•	•	•
No Operation	NOP										01	2	1	Advances Prog. Cntr. Only	•	•	•	•	•	•
Return From Interrupt	RTI										3B	10	1	See Special Operations	•	•	①	•	•	•
Return From Subroutine	RTS										39	5	1		•	•	•	•	•	•
Software Interrupt	SWI										3F	12	1	See Special Operations	•	•	•	•	•	•
Wait for Interrupt*	WAI										3E	19	1		•	②	•	•	•	•

CCR: 5 H, 4 I, 3 N, 2 Z, 1 V, 0 C

*WAI puts Address Bus, R/W, and Data Bus in the three-state mode while VMA is held low.

① (All) Load Condition Code Register from Stack. (See Special Operations)
② (Bit 1) Set when interrupt occurs. If previously set, a Non-Maskable Interrupt is required to exit the wait state.

Table C.3 *Continued*

CONDITION CODE REGISTER INSTRUCTIONS

OPERATIONS	MNEMONIC	IMPLIED			BOOLEAN OPERATION	COND. CODE REG.					
		OP	~	#		5 H	4 I	3 N	2 Z	1 V	0 C
Clear Carry	CLC	0C	2	1	0 → C	•	•	•	•	•	R
Clear Interrupt Mask	CLI	0E	2	1	0 → I	•	R	•	•	•	•
Clear Overflow	CLV	0A	2	1	0 → V	•	•	•	•	R	•
Set Carry	SEC	0D	2	1	1 → C	•	•	•	•	•	S
Set Interrupt Mask	SEI	0F	2	1	1 → I	•	S	•	•	•	•
Set Overflow	SEV	0B	2	1	1 → V	•	•	•	•	S	•
Acmltr A → CCR	TAP	06	2	1	A → CCR			①			
CCR → Acmltr A	TPA	07	2	1	CCR → A	•	•	•	•	•	•

R = Reset
S = Set
• = Not affected
① (ALL) Set according to the contents of Accumulator A.

Addressing Modes

Accumulator addressing One byte instructions in which one, or both, accumulators are used for operands. No memory location is involved, this appears in the implied column in the tables.

Immediate addressing The operand is contained in the second byte of the instruction (2 byte instructions) or in the second and third bytes (3 byte instructions).

Direct addressing The low 8-bits of the operand address are contained in the second byte of the instruction. The address high 8-bits are all zero.

Extended addressing The operand address is contained in the second byte (high 8-bits) and third byte (low 8-bits).

Indexed addressing The second byte extended to 16-bits with zeros in the high 8-bits is added to the contents of the index register. This result is the operand address.

Implied addressing Sources and destinations of operands are implied (inherent) by the one byte instruction.

Relative addressing The second byte as 7-bits plus sign is added to the contents of the program counter after both bytes are fetched. (i.e. initial value plus 2). Carry or borrow is propagated to adjust the high byte. This result left in the program counter.

Table C.4 8086 and 8088 instructions. (Reproduced with permission of Intel Corporation).

DATA TRANSFER
MOV = Move:

Register/memory to/from register

1 0 0 0 1 0 d w	mod reg r/m

Immediate to register/memory

1 1 0 0 0 1 1 w	mod 0 0 0 r/m	data	data if w 1

Immediate to register

1 0 1 1 w reg	data	data if w 1

Memory to accumulator

1 0 1 0 0 0 0 w	addr-low	addr-high

Accumulator to memory

1 0 1 0 0 0 1 w	addr-low	addr-high

Register/memory to segment register

1 0 0 0 1 1 1 0	mod 0 reg r/m

Segment register to register/memory

1 0 0 0 1 1 0 0	mod 0 reg r/m

PUSH = Push:

Register/memory

1 1 1 1 1 1 1 1	mod 1 1 0 r/m

Register

0 1 0 1 0 reg

Segment register

0 0 0 reg 1 1 0

POP = Pop:

Register/memory

1 0 0 0 1 1 1 1	mod 0 0 0 r/m

Register

0 1 0 1 1 reg

Segment register

0 0 0 reg 1 1 1

XCNG = Exchange:

Register/memory with register

1 0 0 0 0 1 1 w	mod reg r/m

Register with accumulator

1 0 0 1 0 reg

IN = Input from:

Fixed port

1 1 1 0 0 1 0 w	port

Variable port

1 1 1 0 1 1 0 w

OUT = Output to:

Fixed port

1 1 1 0 0 1 1 w	port

Variable port

1 1 1 0 1 1 1 w

XLAT = Transiate byte to AL

1 1 0 1 0 1 1 1

LEA = Load EA to register

1 0 0 0 1 1 0 1	mod reg r/m

LDS = Load pointer to DS

1 1 0 0 0 1 0 1	mod reg r/m

LES = Load pointer to ES

1 1 0 0 0 1 0 0	mod reg r/m

Table C.4 *Continued*

DATA TRANSFER

LAHF = Load AH with flags

1 0 0 1 1 1 1 1

SAHF = Store AH into flags

1 0 0 1 1 1 1 0

PUSHF = Push flags

1 0 0 1 1 1 0 0

POPF = Pop flags

1 0 0 1 1 1 0 1

ARITHMETIC
ADD = Add:

Reg/memory with register to either

0 0 0 0 0 0 d w	mod reg r/m

Immediate to register/memory

1 0 0 0 0 0 s w	mod 0 0 0 r/m	data	data if s w 01

Immediate to accumulator

0 0 0 0 0 1 0 w	data	data if w 1

ADC = Add with carry:

Reg./memory with register to either

0 0 0 1 0 0 d w	mod reg r/m

Immediate to register/memory

1 0 0 0 0 0 s w	mod 0 1 0 r/m	data	data if s w 11

Immediate to accumulator

0 0 0 1 0 1 0 w	data	data if w 1

INC = Increment:

Register/memory

1 1 1 1 1 1 1 w	mod 0 0 0 r/m

Register

0 1 0 0 0 reg

AAA = ASCII adjust for add

0 0 1 1 0 1 1 1

DAA = Decimal adjust for add

0 0 1 0 0 1 1 1

SUB = Subtract:

Reg./memory and register to either

0 0 1 0 1 0 d w	mod reg r/m

Immediate from register/memory

1 0 0 0 0 0 s w	mod 1 0 1 r/m	data	data if s w 01

Immediate from accumulator

0 0 1 0 1 1 0 w	data	data if w 1

SBB = Subtract with borrow

Reg./memory and register to either

0 0 0 1 1 0 d w	mod reg r/m

Immediate from register/memory

1 0 0 0 0 0 s w	mod 0 1 1 r/m	data	data if s w 01

Immediate from accumulator

0 0 0 1 1 1 0 w	data	data if w 1

DEC = Decrement

Register/memory

1 1 1 1 1 1 1 w	mod 0 0 1 r/m

Register

0 1 0 0 1 reg

Table C.4 *Continued*

ARITHMETIC

NEG Change sign	1 1 1 1 0 1 1 w	mod 0 1 1 r/m		

CMP Compare:

Register/memory and register	0 0 1 1 1 0 d w	mod reg r/m		
Immediate with register/memory	1 0 0 0 0 0 s w	mod 1 1 1 r/m	data	data if s w 01
Immediate with accumulator	0 0 1 1 1 1 0 w	data	data if w 1	

AAS ASCII adjust for subtract	0 0 1 1 1 1 1 1
DAS Decimal adjust for subtract	0 0 1 0 1 1 1 1

MUL Multiply (unsigned)	1 1 1 1 0 1 1 w	mod 1 0 0 r/m
IMUL Integer multiply (signed)	1 1 1 1 0 1 1 w	mod 1 0 1 r/m
AAM ASCII adjust for multiply	1 1 0 1 0 1 0 0	0 0 0 0 1 0 1 0
DIV Divide (unsigned)	1 1 1 1 0 1 1 w	mod 1 1 0 r/m
IDIV Integer divide (signed)	1 1 1 1 0 1 1 w	mod 1 1 1 r/m
AAD ASCII adjust for divide	1 1 0 1 0 1 0 1	0 0 0 0 1 0 1 0

CBW Convert byte to word	1 0 0 1 1 0 0 0
CWD Convert word to double word	1 0 0 1 1 0 0 1

LOGIC

NOT Invert	1 1 1 1 0 1 1 w	mod 0 1 0 r/m		
SHL/SAL Shift logical arithmetic left	1 1 0 1 0 0 v w	mod 1 0 0 r/m		
SHR Shift logical right	1 1 0 1 0 0 v w	mod 1 0 1 r/m		
SAR Shift arithmetic right	1 1 0 1 0 0 v w	mod 1 1 1 r/m		
ROL Rotate left	1 1 0 1 0 0 v w	mod 0 0 0 r/m		
ROR Rotate right	1 1 0 1 0 0 v w	mod 0 0 1 r/m		
RCL Rotate through carry flag left	1 1 0 1 0 0 v w	mod 0 1 0 r/m		
RCR Rotate through carry right	1 1 0 1 0 0 v w	mod 0 1 1 r/m		

AND = And:

Reg./memory and register to either	0 0 1 0 0 0 d w	mod reg r/m		
Immediate to register/memory	1 0 0 0 0 0 0 w	mod 1 0 0 r/m	data	data if w 1
Immediate to accumulator	0 0 1 0 0 1 0 w	data	data if w 1	

Table C.4 *Continued*

LOGIC
TEST = And function to flags. no result:

Register/memory and register

1 0 0 0 0 1 0 w	mod reg r/m

Immediate data and register/memory

1 1 1 1 0 1 1 w	mod 0 0 0 r/m	data	data if w 1

Immediate data and accumulator

1 0 1 0 1 0 0 w	data	data if w 1

OR = Or:

Reg./memory and register to either

0 0 0 0 1 0 d w	mod reg r/m

Immediate to register/memory

1 0 0 0 0 0 0 w	mod 0 0 1 r/m	data	data if w 1

Immediate to accumulator

0 0 0 0 1 1 0 w	data	data if w 1

XOR = Exclusive or:

Reg./memory and register to either

0 0 1 1 0 0 d w	mod reg r/m

Immediate to register/memory

1 0 0 0 0 0 0 w	mod 1 1 0 r/m	data	data if w 1·

Immediate to accumulator

0 0 1 1 0 1 0 w	data	data if w 1

STRING MANIPULATION

REP = Repeat

1 1 1 1 0 0 1 z

MOVS = Move byte/word

1 0 1 0 0 1 0 w

CMPS = Compare byte/word

1 0 1 0 0 1 1 w

SCAS = Scan byte/word

1 0 1 0 1 1 1 w

LODS = Load byte/wd to AL/AX

1 0 1 0 1 1 0 w

STOS = Stor byte/wd from AL/A

1 0 1 0 1 0 1 w

CONTROL TRANSFER
CALL = Call:

Direct within segment

1 1 1 0 1 0 0 0	disp-low	disp-high

Indirect within segment

1 1 1 1 1 1 1 1	mod 0 1 0 r/m

Direct intersegment

1 0 0 1 1 0 1 0	offset-low	offset-high
	seg-low	seg-high

Indirect intersegment

1 1 1 1 1 1 1 1	mod 0 1 1 r/m

JMP = Unconditional Jump:

Direct within segment

1 1 1 0 1 0 0 1	disp-low	disp-high

Table C.4 *Continued*

CONTROL TRANSFER
JMP = Unconditional Jump:

Direct within segment-short	1 1 1 0 1 0 1 1	disp	

Indirect within segment	1 1 1 1 1 1 1 1	mod 1 0 0 r/m	

Direct intersegment	1 1 1 0 1 0 1 0	offset-low	offset-high
		seg-low	seg-high

Indirect intersegment	1 1 1 1 1 1 1 1	mod 1 0 1 r/m	

RET = Return from CALL:

Within segment	1 1 0 0 0 0 1 1		

Within segment adding immed to SP	1 1 0 0 0 0 1 0	data-low	data-high

Intersegment	1 1 0 0 1 0 1 1		

Intersegment adding immediate to SP	1 1 0 0 1 0 1 0	data-low	data-high

JE/JZ = Jump on equal/zero	0 1 1 1 0 1 0 0	disp
JL/JNGE = Jump on less/not greater or equal	0 1 1 1 1 1 0 0	disp
JLE/JNG = Jump on less or equal/not greater	0 1 1 1 1 1 1 0	disp
JB/JNAE = Jump on below/not above or equal	0 1 1 1 0 0 1 0	disp
JBE/JNA = Jump on below or equal/not above	0 1 1 1 0 1 1 0	disp
JP/JPE = Jump on parity/parity even	0 1 1 1 1 0 1 0	disp
JO = Jump on overflow	0 1 1 1 0 0 0 0	disp
JS = Jump on sign	0 1 1 1 1 0 0 0	disp
JNE/JNZ = Jump on not equal/not zero	0 1 1 1 0 1 0 1	disp
JNL/JGE = Jump on not less/greater or equal	0 1 1 1 1 1 0 1	disp
JNLE/JG = Jump on not less or equal/greater	0 1 1 1 1 1 1 1	disp
JNB/JAE = Jump on not below/above or equal	0 1 1 1 0 0 1 1	disp
JNBE/JA = Jump on not below or equal/above	0 1 1 1 0 1 1 1	disp
JNP/JPO = Jump on not par/par odd	0 1 1 1 1 0 1 1	disp
JNO = Jump on not overflow	0 1 1 1 0 0 0 1	disp
JNS = Jump on not sign	0 1 1 1 1 0 0 1	disp

Table C.4 *Continued*

CONTROL TRANSFER

LOOP = Loop CX times	1 1 1 0 0 0 1 0	disp

LOOPZ/LOOPE = Loop while zero/equal	1 1 1 0 0 0 0 1	disp

LOOPNZ/LOOPNE = Loop while not zero/equal	1 1 1 0 0 0 0 0	disp

JCXZ = Jump on CX zero	1 1 1 0 0 0 1 1	disp

INT   Interrupt

Type specified	1 1 0 0 1 1 0 1	type

Type 3	1 1 0 0 1 1 0 0

INTO Interrupt on overflow	1 1 0 0 1 1 1 0

IRET Interrupt return	1 1 0 0 1 1 1 1

PROCESSOR CONTROL

CLC Clear carry	1 1 1 1 1 0 0 0

CMC Complement carry	1 1 1 1 0 1 0 1

STC Set carry	1 1 1 1 1 0 0 1

CLD Clear direction	1 1 1 1 1 1 0 0

STD Set direction	1 1 1 1 1 1 0 1

CLI Clear interrupt	1 1 1 1 1 0 1 0

STI Set interrupt	1 1 1 1 1 0 1 1

HLT Halt	1 1 1 1 0 1 0 0

WAIT Wait	1 0 0 1 1 0 1 1

ESC Escape (to external device)	1 1 0 1 1 × × ×	mod × × × r/m

LOCK Bus lock prefix	1 1 1 1 0 0 0 0

Footnotes:

AL = 8-bit accumulator
AX = 16-bit accumulator
CX = Count register
DS = Data segment
ES = Extra segment
Above/below refers to unsigned value
Greater = more positive;
Less = less positive (more negative) signed values
if d = 1 then "to" reg; if d = 0 then "from" reg
if w = 1 then word instruction; if w = 0 then byte instruction

if mod = 11 then r/m is treated as a REG field
if mod = 00 then DISP = 0*, disp-low and disp-high are absent
if mod = 01 then DISP = disp-low sign-extended to 16-bits, disp-high is absent
if mod = 10 then DISP = disp-high: disp-low

if r/m = 000 then EA = (BX) + (SI) + DISP
if r/m = 001 then EA = (BX) + (DI) + DISP
if r/m = 010 then EA = (BP) + (SI) + DISP
if r/m = 011 then EA = (BP) + (DI) + DISP
if r/m = 100 then EA = (SI) + DISP
if r/m = 101 then EA = (DI) + DISP
if r/m = 110 then EA = (BP) + DISP*
if r/m = 111 then EA = (BX) + DISP
DISP follows 2nd byte of instruction (before data if required)

*except if mod = 00 and r/m = 110 then EA = disp-high: disp-low.

if s:w = 01 then 16 bits of immediate data form the operand.
if s:w = 11 then an immediate data byte is sign extended to form the 16-bit operand.
if v = 0 then "count" = 1; if v = 1 then "count" in (CL)
x = don't care
z is used for string primitives for comparison with ZF FLAG.

SEGMENT OVERRIDE PREFIX

```
0 0 1  reg  1 1 0
```

REG is assigned according to the following table:

16-Bit (w = 1)		8-Bit (w = 0)		Segment	
000	AX	000	AL	00	ES
001	CX	001	CL	01	CS
010	DX	010	DL	10	SS
011	BX	011	BL	11	DS
100	SP	100	AH		
101	BP	101	CH		
110	SI	110	DH		
111	DI	111	BH		

Instructions which reference the flag register file as a 16-bit object use the symbol FLAGS to represent the file:

FLAGS = X:X:X:X:(OF):(DF):(IF):(TF):(SF):(ZF):X:(AF):X:(PF):X:(CF)

Appendix D

Solution Hints for Selected Problems

Final values of result, partial outlines, or hints are given for selected problems (or selected sections). When the result must taken a single value only this is given. However many solutions contain an element of design or choice of processor and there is not a single correct result. In cases with several solutions only one is suggested.

Chapter 3

2 a) $D8_H$; c) $B9_H$; e) 31_H; g) 00_H; i) FF_H.

3 a) $(CY)=0$, $(Z)=0$; c) $(CY)=1$, $(Z)=0$; e) $(CY)=0$, $(Z)=0$;
   g) (CY) undefined (depends on CPU type), $(Z)=1$;
   i) (CY) undefined (depends on CPU type), $(Z)=0$.

4 Before CALL to $3A05_H$ $(PC)=231E_H$, $(SP)=5100_H$
   After CALL to $3A05_H$ $(PC)=3A05_H$, $(SP)=50FE_H$
   Before CALL to $3D2C_H$ $(PC)=3A56_H$, $(SP)=50FE_H$ assuming that no PUSH instructions are used.
   After CALL to $3D2C_H$ $(PC)=3D2C_H$, $(SP)=50FC_H$
   Before first   RET performed $(PC)=3D5A_H$, $(SP)=50FC_H$
   After first   RET performed $(PC)=3A59_H$, $(SP)=50FE_H$
   Before second RET performed $(PC)=3AFF_H$, $(SP)=50FE_H$
   After second RET performed $(PC)=2321_H$, $(SP)=5100_H$

Chapter 4

1 Figure D.1 is a partial outline of one solution and map.

3 5.33MHz. Including T* 8MHz. Marginally faster with wait state. (4 states at 8MHz $= 0.5\mu$secs; 3 states at 5.33MHz $= 0.56\mu$secs).

Chapter 5

2 It is assumed that latches are used or interrupts are cleared by actions in the service routines. One design uses an 8-bit latched output port with a specific port bit for each interrupt. The interrupt signal and its port bit are inputs to a 2-input AND gate, the output is used as the encoder input. After enabling interrupts send all ones to the port (the interrupt mask). On interrupt each service routine must first write zero to its bit of the port and to all lower priority bits then enable interrupts again. At the end of the routine all ones are sent to the port again.

Chapter 6

1 $+12_D$ values 00001100; 00001100; 00001100; and 10001011 (offset 127_D)
   -104_D values 11101000; 10010111; 10011000; and 00010111 (offset 127_D)
   $+1_D$ values 00000001; 00000001; 00000001; and 10000000 (offset 127_D)

3 a) 0100 0111 0100 1110 0100 0011 1010 0001
   c) 0100 0100 1001 0011 1010 1001 1010 0001

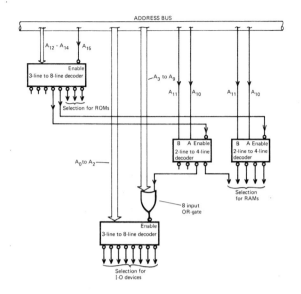

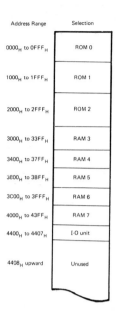

Address Range	Selection
0000_H to $0FFF_H$	ROM 0
1000_H to $1FFF_H$	ROM 1
2000_H to $2FFF_H$	ROM 2
3000_H to $33FF_H$	RAM 3
3400_H to $37FF_H$	RAM 4
3800_H to $3BFF_H$	RAM 5
$3C00_H$ to $3FFF_H$	RAM 6
4000_H to $43FF_H$	RAM 7
4400_H to 4407_H	I-O unit
4408_H upward	Unused

Fig. D.1

4 a) 01010111 with carry $=0$
  c) 01110011 with carry $=1$, out of range.

6 327·056 + 19·782 performed in IEEE format gives
  0100 0011 1010 1101 0110 1011 1010 1010
  This is 346·8411 . . . ; comment!

Chapter 7

1 123nsecs.

3 For addition cases control $=0$ so the input digit values are unchanged by the exclusive-OR gates. The two n-bit numbers are added as simple binary integers with the logic value at the first stage carry-in also added. This first stage carry-in value is $(D \cdot E) \oplus F$ where $D =$ carry/borrow input, $E =$ control for operation with or without carry/borrow, and $F =$ add or subtract control. For addition $F = 0$ so that $(D \cdot E) \oplus F = (D \cdot E) \oplus 0 = D \cdot E$.

  When $E = 0$ then $D \cdot E = 0$ so 0 is added to total (carry/borrow has no effect). When $E = 1$ the first stage carry-in equals D, i.e. the carry/borrow input, which is added to the total as required. The subtaction cases are similar but more complex.

  Example case of $n = 4$, inputs (-3) and (-2) for add with carry when carry $=1$. A inputs 1101 are applied to the adders. B inputs 1110 are applied to the exclusive-OR gates, as $F = 0$ the gate outputs equal the B inputs. The first carry-in is from $D = 1$, $E = 1$, $F = 0$ in $(D \cdot E) \oplus F$, it is $1 \cdot 1 \oplus 0 = 1$. Performing $1101_2 + 1110_2 + 1$ gives $1100_2 = (-4)$ with final carry of 1 (unchanged by the output gate).

4 See any manufacturer's application notes for 74S274.

Chapter 9

2 1031 bits per sector. Round this (not the number per track or side), obviously choose $1024 = 2^{10}$ so $N_{max} \approx 6 \cdot 119$Mbits.

  After formatting 106 bytes per sector, 633456 bytes on disc. The difference $\approx 1 \cdot 052$Mbits, thus formatting reduces storage by about 17% (quite high efficiency).

3	1 0 1 1 1 0 1 1 0 1	Track 8
	0 1 0 1 0 1 1 1 1 0	
	0 1 0 1 1 1 1 1 1 0	
	1 0 1 1 0 1 1 0 1 0	
	1 1 1 0 1 0 1 0 1 1	
	0 1 0 0 1 1 0 0 1 1	
	1 0 1 1 1 1 1 1 1 0	
	1 0 0 1 0 0 1 0 1 1	
	1 1 0 1 0 0 1 0 1 0	Track 0

Chapter 11

1 a) An outline is shown in Fig. D.2 with the bi-directional port at 00_H for both input and output.

3 b) Requires an 8-bit latched output port and 5-bit input port with pull-up resistors on each line (or *vice versa*). One possible program sequence for only one key pressed is:—

                        Send all zeros to output port
                        Loop reading inputs until all 1 (last key released)
                        Set a mask to 01111111 and a counter X to 8

 LOOP: Send the mask to the output port
                        Read inputs, go to ADVANCE if all are 1
                        Save input pattern
                        Wait 5 to 10msecs (de-bounce time)
                        Read inputs again, compare with stored value
                        If different go to LOOP (key-bounce, test again)
                        Determine which key (from output mask and inputs)
                        Exit indicating the key pressed

ADVANCE: Rotate (or shift moving in 1) mask one place right
                        Decrement counter X, if not zero go to LOOP
                        Exit indicating no key pressed

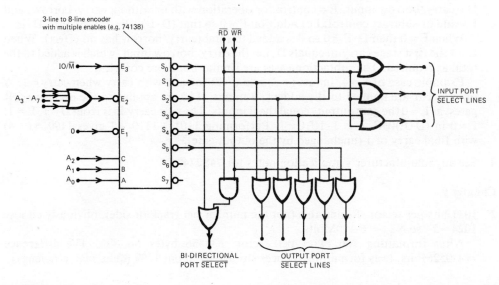

Fig. D.2

Chapter 12

1 Form in Fig. 12.8 gives 7-bit maximum. Frequency 1Mhz (max).

Chapter 14

2 Assume *m* and *n* fixed when compiled and array start at $bbbb_H$. With 4 bytes per element the first $4 \times n$ bytes store all elements VAR(*i*,0), the second all VAR(*i*,1) and so on. Selecting an 8080 with *j* in D and *i* in E form the required address in H–L. Assume a subroutine MUL which multiplies B by C (allowing zeros) leaving the result in B–C with no other changes. Table D.1 is a subroutine for the solution.

Table D.1 8080 subroutine for array address.

; Subroutine for problem 14.2. Computes the address of the first byte of element VAR(*i*,*j*).
; Enter with *j* in D and *i* in E.
;

ADDIJ:	PUSH	PSW	; ⎫
	PUSH	B	; ⎬ Save status except result registers
	PUSH	D	; ⎭
	MVI	B,*m*	; Known fixed value of m
	MOV	C,D	; Put *j* into C
	CALL	MUL	; Now have $m \times j$ in B–C
	MOV	H,B	
	MOV	L,C	; Copied $m \times j$ to H–L
	DAD	H	
	DAD	H	; $4 \times m \times j$ now in H–L (4 byte elements)
	MVI	D,0	; Extend *i* to 16-bits.
	DAD	D	; H–L now holds $4 \times m \times j + i$
	LXI	B,0*bbbb*H	; Array base address to B–C
	DAD	B	; Result now in H–L as required
	POP	D	; ⎫
	POP	B	; ⎬ Restore status
	POP	PSW	; ⎭
	RET		

Index